Special Edition

USING
NETSCAPE
LIVECONNECT

Special Edition

USING
NETSCAPE
LIVECONNECT

Written by Lori Marzilli Leonardo

Special Edition Using Netscape LiveConnect

Credits

PRESIDENT
Roland Elgey

SENIOR VICE PRESIDENT/PUBLISHING
Don Fowley

PUBLISHER
Stacy Hiquet

PUBLISHING MANAGER
Jim Minatel

GENERAL MANAGER
Joe Muldoon

EDITORIAL SERVICES DIRECTOR
Elizabeth Keaffaber

ACQUISITIONS EDITORS
Stephanie Gould
Stephanie J. McComb

PRODUCT DIRECTOR
Jacquelyn Mosley Eley

PRODUCTION EDITOR
Sean Medlock

STRATEGIC MARKETING MANAGER
Barry Pruett

WEB MASTER
Thomas H. Bennett

PRODUCT MARKETING MANAGER
Kristine R. Ankney

ASSISTANT PRODUCT MARKETING MANAGER/ DESIGN
Christy M. Miller

ASSISTANT PRODUCT MARKETING MANAGER/ SALES
Karen Hagen

TECHNICAL EDITOR(S)
Ernie Sanders

MEDIA DEVELOPMENT SPECIALIST
Brandon Penticuff

TECHNICAL SUPPORT SPECIALIST
Nadeem Muhammed

SOFTWARE RELATIONS COORDINATOR
Susan D. Gallagher

EDITORIAL ASSISTANT
Andrea Duvall

BOOK DESIGNER
Ruth Harvey

COVER DESIGNER
Dan Armstrong

PRODUCTION TEAM
Marcia Brizendine
Trey Frank
Daryl Kessler
Laura A. Knox
Kaylene Riemen
Paul Wilson

INDEXER
Robert Long

Composed in *Century Old Style* and *Franklin Gothic* by Que Corporation.

For my parents, Dr. Rocco and Kathryn Marzilli, who brought me up right.

Especially for my son, Raymond (known as RugRat Ray on the Web), for being my most inspirational little person in my life. "The soul is healed by being with children."—Fyodor Dostoevsky

About the Authors

Lori Leonardo lives in Jamestown, Rhode Island with her son Raymond. She is owner of L. Leonardo Consulting, a computer services company that provides Internet consulting and training. She is also an instructor at Brown University Learning Community, where she teaches "Personal Finance: How to Capitalize on the Web" and "For KIDS: Web Ventures—Cyber Out on the Web." She has previously worked on *SE Using the Internet, SE Using Netscape 3.0,* and *Running a Perfect Web Site* for Que. For more information about Lori and her company, visit her Web page at **http://www.lleonardo.com/**. Lori can be reached by e-mail at **lorileo@aol.com** or **llc@lleonardo.com**.

Govind Seshadri (Govind_Seshadri@mgic.com) currently leads Java development at MGIC Investment Corp. in Milwaukee, Wisconsin. His primary areas of interest include design of large-scale Java client/server systems, distributed computing, and network security.

He also has extensive teaching experience, and holds Masters and Bachelors degrees in Computer Science. Govind indicates that being married to Mini, a Java architect and consultant, helps him stay at the leading edge of the Java revolution.

Michael Morgan is founder and president of DSE, Inc., a full-service Web presence provider and sofware development shop. He has given seminars for the IEEE, National Seminars, the University of Hawaii, Purdue University, and Notre Dame. Prior to founding DSE in 1988, Mike was a member of the technical staff at Magnavox Electronic Systems Company in Fort Wayne, Indiana.

In the early '80s Mike was employed by the City of Virginia Beach, where he completed the development of the world's first automated municipal water distribution system. Mike was an Army Signal Corps officer with active duty in the 5th Infantry Division and Reserve duty with the U.S. Rapid Deployment Force.

The author of over twenty technical papers and presentations on various aspects of information technology, he is the co-developer of the Project Unit Costing Method, which allows project managers to construct justifications for information technology projects based on cost savings and cost avoidance. He is also the inventor of GAELIC, the Gallium Arsenide Experimental Lisp Integrated Circuit, an ultra-high-speed processor optimized for artificial intelligence applications, and the co-inventor of MEND, a Multiple Expert iNtelligent Diagnostics system. Mike is the co-manager of the CGI archives of the HTML Writers Guild, and is a member of the Help Team for Matt Wright's Script Archive.

He holds a Master of Science in Systems Management from the Florida institute of Technology, and a Bachelor of Science in Mathematics from Wheaton College, where he concentrated his studies on computer science. He also has taken numerous graduate courses in computer science through the National Technological University. Mike is a member of the IEEE Computer society. Mike can usually be found in his office at DSE, drinking Diet Pepsi and writing Perl and C++. He lives in Virginia Beach with his wife, Jean, and their six children.

Acknowledgments

Putting a book together in such a short amount of time takes an incredible amount of hard work and drive from many, many people.

I would like to thank those writers associated with this book, Mike Morgan and Govind Seshadri. I would also like to thank the editors and staff at Que, who are so efficient and patient with the authors. It is always exciting and rewarding working on projects with Que. A special thanks goes out to Cheryl Willoughby (who brought me into my first project at Que), Stephanie McComb, Jacquie Eley, and Sean Medlock for their special assistance, patience, and guidance. I would like to add a special "thank you" to Mark Cierzniak and Stephanie Gould for first bringing me into this project.

I cannot forget to thank all my family and friends for their patience during all the crazy long hours I spent working on this book. I would also like to thank my brother, Stephen, for my brand new MMX computer he speedily shipped out to me when I was in dire need to finish my book, and my current computer was on its way out. Finally, my most heartfelt thanks go to my son, Raymond, who is the most patient and sweet "pookie" there ever was.

We'd Like to Hear from You!

As part of our continuing effort to produce books of the highest possible quality, Que would like to hear your comments. To stay competitive, we *really* want you, as a computer book reader and user, to let us know what you like or dislike most about this book or other Que products.

You can mail comments, ideas, or suggestions for improving future editions to the address below, or send us a fax at (317) 581-4663. For the online inclined, Macmillan Computer Publishing has a forum on CompuServe (type **GO QUEBOOKS** at any prompt) through which our staff and authors are available for questions and comments. The address of our Internet site is **http://www.mcp.com** (World Wide Web).

In addition to exploring our forum, please feel free to contact me personally to discuss your opinions of this book: I'm **jeley@mail.mcp.com** on the Internet.

Thanks in advance—your comments will help us to continue publishing the best books available on computer topics in today's market.

Jacquelyn Eley
Product Development Specialist
Que Corporation
201 W. 103rd Street
Indianapolis, Indiana 46290
USA

Contents at a Glance

Table of Contents

Introduction

"Books must follow sciences, and not sciences books."

—Sir Francis Bacon

Proposition touching Amendment of Laws

Like the above quote, this book follows a remarkable new technology, Netscape LiveConnect. Welcome to this new plug-in protocol, which enables Navigator plug-ins and Java applets to call each other from within a Web document and can be run simultaneously or in any sequence. For example, a Web document with embedded LiveConnect could enable video and audio files to play at the same time, or the audio file could play first and trigger the video file to play next. Now Web site developers can customize screen buttons to allow users to play or stop video as well as sound.

Using LiveConnect, Web programmers are able to create interaction between HTML elements with Java applets, JavaScript, and plug-ins. This now creates a new and higher level of interchange between applications and information.

LiveConnect is platform-independent and works through a Java interface, so each Web page component can call other different functions. LiveConnect also uses the Java Runtime Interface (JRI). This enables developers to create distributed client/server applications that were once only available to JavaScript programmers. ■

Who Should Read This Book?

This book is meant for those Web site developers and programmers who already have an understanding of plug-in technology. You should also have a general working knowledge of Visual C++ 4.0. The material covered in this book will help you best decide if the LiveConnect plug-in SDK has the capabilities to benefit your Web site.

If you have just started integrating plug-ins in your Web pages, Part II of this book, "Plug-In Developer's Guide," will review what plug-ins can do, as well as explaining this new interconnectivity between HTML, plug-ins, JavaScript, and Java.

If you are new to programming plug-ins, the author recommends *Netscape Plug-Ins Developer's Kit* by Mike Morgan (Que, 1996).

If you are new to HTML, then *Special Edition Using HTML* by Mark Brown and John Jung is recommended reading as well (Que, 1996).

Special Edition Using Netscape LiveConnect explains the interaction of these key technologies, Navigator plug-ins, Java applets, and JavaScript and how they all work together to allow developers to add special features and functions to their Web sites.

What This Book Is About

This book describes the LiveConnect methods possible to create a Web design with a higher level of interaction. Some of these capabilities are:

- Navigator plug-ins can be loaded on a Web page and can then interact with JavaScripts running on the same document.
- Java applets loaded on a Web page can also interact with JavaScripts running on the same document.

■ Java programmers and plug-ins can now make these functions available to
JavaScript programmers.

This communication between Java, JavaScript, and plug-ins is not as complicated
as it may first appear. The main goal of this book is to help you become familiar
with this merged Java and JavaScript environment, as well as how the Java
Runtime Interface (JRI) is implemented, thus allowing Navigator plug-ins to interact with the Navigator Java environment.

What This Book Is *Not* About

This book assumes you have a solid understanding of the World Wide Web. It does
not provide information on setting up or connecting to the Internet. Most importantly, this book is neither a guide for setting up and developing a Web site nor a
guide for developing an intranet.

How This Book Is Organized

The sample plug-ins and templates included with the LiveConnect Plug-in SDK do
provide some instruction. However, as most programmers know, it is very little
instruction indeed. This book compiles the best "instruction" available today on
using LiveConnect.

The first chapter, "What Is LiveConnect?," covers how to enable LiveConnect,
LiveConnect objects, and dynamic (live) content.

Chapter 2, "LiveConnect Components," explains how to get started and how the
SDK is organized, as well as showcasing LiveConnect demos and on-line resources.

Chapter 3, "Overview of Plug-In API," Chapter 4, "Creating Plug-Ins," Chapter 5,
"Programming Plug-Ins," and Chapter 6, "Developing Content for Plug-Ins," focus
on issues relating to all aspects of developing plug-ins, including LiveConnect examples.

Chapter 7, "The Java Runtime Interface," explains more about Java support for
native methods, Java classes, and runtime providers. Chapter 8, "Calling Java
Methods from Plug-Ins," and Chapter 9, "Calling the Plug-In from Java Methods,"

focus on accessing fields and methods, defining and using a plug-in class, and implementing native methods.

This book concludes with Chapter 10, "JavaScript to Java Communication," Chapter 11, "Java to JavaScript Communication," and Chapter 12, "Netscape Packages." These chapters cover using LiveConnect technology to integrate Java, JavaScript, and plug-ins.

Finally, the Glossary explains terms covered in this book.

Conventions Used in This Book

Each chapter contains bulleted lists, numbered sequenced lists, and italicized text. Bulleted lists combine related information that is explained in each list. Numbered lists need to be followed in that particular order. They are steps that should be followed in sequence. Key words or terms are italicized to mark new or important technical terms and definitions.

Code listings are also contained in this book. Each code listing describes a technique and is not necessarily a complete set of code program instructions.

When you need to type in commands or text, this information appears in bold font. Placeholders are used for substituting file names and elements and appear in bold italics.

Notice the following command syntax example:

```
<A NAME="L">LORI</A>
<A NAME="R">RAYMOND</A>
```

This book also contains figures, including line art, diagrams, and actual screen shots.

Tables are also found in many of the chapters. These tables list terms and explanations, as well as many features and functions explained in this book.

What Technical Assumptions Does This Book Make?

The LiveConnect Plug-in SDK can be downloaded for the three major operating systems: Windows, Macintosh, and UNIX systems. Examples, instructions, and figures are based on a Windows environment. Differences in how the SDK is used between these operating systems are explained as well. It is assumed that you use one of the three operating systems mentioned above. You should easily be able to adapt any standard configuration to your own system platform.

I hope this Introduction has inspired you to think about how LiveConnect can be utilized effectively for your own developing needs. Regardless of how you decide to use this new technology, turn the page to learn about the Netscape LiveConnect plug-in.

Understanding LiveConnect

What Is LiveConnect?

LiveConnect, new with Navigator 3.0, integrates applets written in the platform-independent language Java (from Sun Microsystems) with Netscape's JavaScript and with your plug-ins. Note that LiveConnect doesn't allow your plug-in to communicate directly with a script written in JavaScript. All communications go through Java. This design isn't a problem, however, as you will learn later in this book. ■

How to Enable LiveConnect

It couldn't be simpler. LiveConnect is enabled when both Java and JavaScript are also enabled.

The Java Console Window

In Netscape Navigator, the Java Console window provides a way for you to view the direct output of an applet as it is running.

LiveConnect and Objects

Plug-ins are software objects that are called by Navigator, and in turn they can call Navigator.

Dynamic (Live) Content

Multimedia publishers are currently developing products that are a mix of online and CD-ROM content, called hybrid technology.

Enabling LiveConnect

LiveConnect is a combination of plug-ins, Java, and JavaScript connectivity. You use LiveConnect to create plug-ins and/or Java applets that can be controlled and implemented by Java and JavaScript. This new SDK technology, LiveConnect, enables you to call Java methods from plug-ins, call Java methods from JavaScript, call JavaScript from Java methods, and implement native methods in plug-ins from Java.

LiveConnect is enabled by default in Navigator 3.01 and later. To confirm that it is enabled, choose Preferences from the Edit menu, then choose Network Preferences. Click the Languages tab. (See Figure 1.1.)

- Make sure Enable Java is checked.
- Make sure Enable JavaScript is checked.

To disable either Java or JavaScript, uncheck the checkboxes.

FIG. 1.1
Network Preferences
window—Languages
tab.

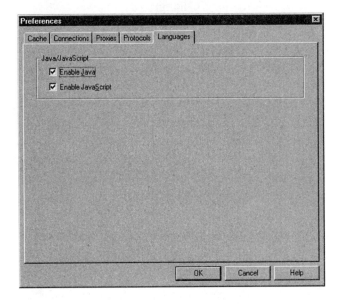

ON THE WEB
You can find out more about LiveConnect from the LiveConnect Developer Information
Web page at **http://home.netscape.com/comprod/products/navigator/
version_3.0/building_blocks/liveconnect/how.html**.

The Java Console Window

Many programmers write their applets so that they print out messages while
they're executing. Usually, this information helps the programmer see whether or
not an applet is encountering problems. In Netscape Navigator, the Java Console
window provides a way for you to view the direct output of an applet as it is running. Just select Show Java Console Window from the Options menu. The Java
Console window pops up, as shown in Figure 1.2.

FIG. 1.2
The Java Console
window.

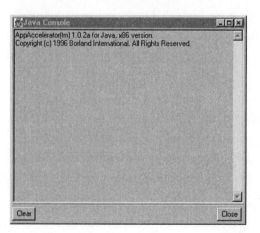

Later, if you write your own applets, this window is your way of keeping tabs on
your applet during the development process. For instance, you can see the code
that you're generating when you're developing an applet. You can then copy code
from the Java Console window and paste it into another document that might uti-
lize the code as well.

▶ **See** Chapter 10, "JavaScript to Java Communication," on "Controlling Applets."

LiveConnect and Objects

Before we go any further, let's talk about functions, objects, methods, and properties. A *function* is just a piece of code that does something; it might play a sound, calculate an equation, or send a piece of e-mail. An *object* is a collection of data and functions that have been grouped together. The object's functions are called *methods*, and its data are called its *properties*. The JavaScript programs you write will have properties and methods, and they'll interact with objects provided by Navigator and its plug-ins (as well as any other Java applets you may supply to your users).

 TIP   A simple guideline: an object's properties are things it knows, and its methods are things it can do.

Individual JavaScript elements are objects; for example, *string literals* are string objects, and they have methods that you can use to do things like change their case. JavaScript also provides a set of useful objects to represent the Navigator browser, the currently displayed page, and other elements of the browsing session.

You access objects by specifying their name. For example, the active document object is named document. To use document's properties or methods, you add a period and the name of the method or property you want. For example, document.title is the title property of the document object, and "Navigator".length would call the length member of the string object named "Navigator."

Plug-ins are a code resource loaded by Netscape Navigator at runtime. These resources have various names—under Windows and OS/2 Warp they are known as Dynamic Link Libraries. On a Macintosh, they are code resources. UNIX programmers call these resources *shared objects*. No matter what they called by developers on the various platforms, plug-ins are software objects that are called by Navigator, and in turn they can call Navigator.

To keep the plug-in methods straight, Netscape uses the convention that the plug-in methods (which are called by Navigator) have names starting with "NPP_". Navigator offers programmers methods that they can call from their plug-ins— these methods all have names that start with "NPN_". As a plug-in programmer, you write the NPP methods. NPN methods are provided for you by Netscape.

Plug-ins consist of two cooperating objects. One object, the plug-in object, has methods that you, as the plug-in programmer, write. Navigator calls these methods to get information from the plug-in or to give it information. The other object, the Netscape peer object, is written by Netscape and lives "inside" Navigator. You call the peer object to get information from Navigator or to ask Navigator to take certain actions. Methods of the plug-in object start with "NPP_" and methods of the NPN object, of course, start with "NPN_".

Start by looking at an example plug-in, build it, and test it out. The Simple example is a good one to start with because it works on all platforms. It demonstrates what's involved in developing a cross-platform plug-in that does both the traditional plug-in functionality and is LiveConnect-enabled (i.e., can be controlled by Java and JavaScript).

The important thing to keep in mind is that Java provides the central point of integration for these technologies. Plug-ins access features of the Navigator through the standard Plug-in API, and by calling into Java. Java can access new features provided by plug-ins by calling native methods they provide that export these features. JavaScript can control plug-ins by invoking the Java native operations that are exported by the plug-in.

 To see how the various NPP methods interact, in Chapter 3, "Overview of Plug-In API," we load and build the plug-in at **www.quecorp.com/liveconnect/** known as zero. Although zero is designed for a Windows environment, it's a simple plug-in and can be easily ported to OS/2 Warp, the Macintosh, and the X-Window System.

Zero is a simple plug-in. It answers the various calls from Navigator and returns. The significance is that each NPP method is instrumented with a call to the Windows method ::MessageBox(), so we can see when Navigator calls each routine.

You can call zero as a full-page plug-in. Start by building a zero "document." Any text file will do, provided its file extension is .zer—the file extent recognized by zero. You use Navigator to open the file, and see the following chain of calls:

- NPP_Initialize()—as the plug-in loads.
- NPP_New()—when the first instance is loaded.
- NPP_SetWindow()—as Navigator passes in the information about the parent window.

- `NPP_NewStream()`—as Navigator starts the data streaming in from the file.
- `NPP_SetWindow()`—which can be called at any time, as the dimensions of the window change.

You can call `zero` as an embedded plug-in as well. You use Navigator to open `single.html`, shown in Listing 1.1. Experiment with various options and see how the plug-in is called. You can find this listing in the source/Chap3/single.html directory at **www.quecorp.com/liveconnect/**.

Listing 1.1   single.html—A Single Instance of the Plug-In

```
<HTML>
<HEAD>
<TITLE>Single</TITLE>
</HEAD>
<BODY>
Here is the plug-in:
<EMBED TYPE="application/x-npZero" HEIGHT=100 WIDTH=100>
</BODY>
</HTML>
```

Notice that this HTML calls the plug-in by using the TYPE attribute of the EMBED tag because the `zero` plug-in doesn't use any of the contents of the source stream.

You can start a second copy of `zero`. The HTML file `double.html`, shown in Listing 1.2, has two calls to the plug-in. This listing can be found in the source/Chap3/double.html directory at **www.quecorp.com/liveconnect/**.

Listing 1.2   double.html—Two Instances of the Plug-In

```
<HTML>
<HEAD>
<TITLE>Single</TITLE>
</HEAD>
<BODY>
Here is the plug-in:
<EMBED TYPE="application/x-npZero" HEIGHT=100 WIDTH=100><BR>
Here is another instance:
<EMBED TYPE="application/x-npZero" HEIGHT=50 WIDTH=50><BR>
</BODY>
</HTML>
```

▶ **See** Chapter 3, "Overview of Plug-In API," on "NPP Methods."

Java and JavaScript

Java is a programming language created by Sun Microsystems, and it has created a lot more excitement than other programming languages usually generate. Programmers are excited about Java because the language supports many useful features, such as an object-oriented structure, intuitive multithreading, and built-in network support. The language also avoids many of the pitfalls of C++. Where C++ forces the programmer to keep track of the memory that he uses, a Java programmer doesn't need to worry about using memory reserved for the system or not freeing up memory appropriately.

Java programmers don't need to worry about how memory is utilized because of how a Java program is run. Java is a semi-compiled language. When you program in a compiled language like C++, the compiler takes your source code and creates a file that is ready for the system to execute. A Java compiler doesn't work this way. Instead, it creates a file that contains bytecodes. This file is then handed to an interpreter on your computer. That interpreter executes the program. The interpreter keeps track of how memory is used, and can let the programmer know if something has gone wrong. This is different from an errant C++ program, which simply stops, sometimes after crashing the system. Because of this, it is much harder to debug C++ programs than programs written in Java.

Java was designed to be an object-oriented language similar to C++ to make it familiar to a large number of programmers. As you'll see later in the book, the syntax of Java is very similar to C++. Because Java is an object-oriented language, this book assumes that you are familiar with basic object-oriented concepts, such as classes and inheritance.

N O T E In Java, the basic object-oriented programming element is the *class*. A class is a collection of related data members and functions, known as *methods*, that operate on that data. Everything in Java exists within a class—there are no global variables or global functions. ▪

In developing Java, Sun chose to leave out several C++ language features. Specifically, Java does not support multiple inheritance, operator overloading, or extensive automatic coercion. Java also takes steps to make pointer operations much safer. Java's pointer model does not allow memory overwrites and data corruption.

In fact, Java does not allow pointer arithmetic at all. It supports true arrays with bounds checking. You cannot change an integer to a pointer via a cast operator. In short, Java eliminates many of the confusing, often misused aspects of C++ and creates a smaller, easier-to-understand language.

JavaScript allows you to embed commands in an HTML page; when a Navigator user downloads the page, your JavaScript commands will be evaluated. These commands can be triggered when the user clicks page items, manipulates gadgets and fields in an HTML form, or moves through the page history list.

N O T E   Java and JavaScript are similar only in name, not in creator, syntax, or pretty much anything else.

Some computer languages are compiled; you run your program through a compiler, which performs a one-time translation of the human-readable program into a binary that the computer can execute. JavaScript is an interpreted language; the computer must evaluate the program every time it's run. You embed your JavaScript commands within an HTML page, and any browser that supports JavaScript can interpret the commands and act on them.

Don't let all these programming terms frighten you off—JavaScript is powerful and simple. If you've ever programmed in dBase or Visual Basic, you'll find JavaScript easy to pick up.

HTML provides a good deal of flexibility to page authors, but HTML by itself is static; once written, HTML documents can't interact with the user other than by presenting hyperlinks. Creative use of CGI scripts (which run on Web servers) has made it possible to create more interesting and effective interactive sites, but some applications really demand client-side scripting.

JavaScript was developed to provide page authors a way to write small scripts that would execute on the users' browsers instead of on the server. For example, an application that collects data from a form and then POSTs it to the server can validate the data for completeness and correctness before sending it to the server. This can greatly improve the performance of the browsing session, since users don't have to send data to the server until it has been verified as correct. The following are some other potential applications for JavaScript:

- JavaScripts can verify forms for completeness, like a mailing list registration form that checks to make sure the user has entered a name and e-mail address before the form is posted.

- Pages can display content derived from information stored on the user's computer—without sending that data to the server. For example, a bank can embed JavaScript commands in their pages that look up account data from a Quicken file and display it as part of the bank's page.

- Because JavaScripts can modify settings for applets written in Java, page authors can control the size, appearance, and behavior of Navigator plug-ins, as well as other Java applets. A page that contains an embedded Director animation might use a JavaScript to set the Director plug-in's window size and position before triggering the animation.

JavaScript provides a rich set of built-in functions and commands. Your JavaScripts can display HTML in the browser, do math calculations (like figuring the sales tax or shipping for an order form), play sounds, open new URLs, and even click buttons in forms.

Code to perform these actions can be embedded in a page and executed when the page is loaded; you can also write methods that contain code that's triggered by events you specify. For example, you can write a JavaScript method that is called when the user clicks the Submit button of a form, or one that is activated when the user clicks a hyperlink on the active page.

JavaScript can also set the attributes, or properties, of Java applets running in the browser. This makes it easy for you to change the behavior of plug-ins or other objects without having to delve into their innards. For example, your JavaScript code could automatically start playing an embedded QuickTime or .AVI file when the user clicks a button.

The LiveConnect environment is a merger of the Java environment with JavaScript. Java programmers would use a public indentifier when defining a class. Now that LiveConnect enables JavaScript to be linked to a Java environment, all public classes can be controlled by the JavaScript script, which allows JavaScript scripts to access anything that a Java applet can access.

LiveConnect Plug-Ins with Java

LiveConnect doesn't give a JavaScript programmer direct access to the plug-in, or vice versa. If you're comfortable with C++ and object technology, you can write a proxy class in Java that sits between your plug-in and JavaScript, giving a JavaScript programmer access to your plug-in.

To get started with Java, you need a Java development environment. The JDK from Sun is available at **www.quecorp.com/liveconnect/**. To use LiveConnect with Java, you also need the java_30 file, which comes with Navigator version 3.0 and later.

To get started in Java, try writing a Java "Hello, world!" program. (See Listing 1.3.) For more examples of Java programming, please read Chapter 10, "JavaScript to Java Communication," and read the sidebar in that chapter titled "A Java Primer." To go further with Java, read on to the next section on "Accessing Java Directly" or check out *Special Edition Using Java* (Que, 1996). Then read on in this chapter to learn about the Netscape-specific packages that you need to use to connect Java to JavaScript and to your plug-ins.

Listing 1.3   hello.java—The Java "Hello, world!" Program

```
import java.applet.*;
import java.awt.*;
public class hello extends Applet
{
  public void init()
  {
  }
  public void paint (Graphics g)
  {
    g.drawString("Hello", 10, 50);
  }
}
```

ON THE WEB

You can download the latest version of Sun's Java Developers Kit (JDK), with Netscape modifications, as part of the Netscape Plug-ins SDK, at **http://home.netscape.com/ eng/mozilla/3.0/handbook/plugins/index.html**.

You also can use commercial packages such as Symantec's Cafe or Natural Intelligence's Roaster, but you need the classes from Netscape's version of the kit. You also need Netscape's special version of javah (also part of the kit).

▶ For more information and examples of LiveConnect communication between Java and JavaScript, **see** Chapter 10, "JavaScript to Java Communication," and Chapter 11, "Java to JavaScript Communication."

LiveConnect Plug-Ins with JavaScript

When you add plug-ins to an HTML page, JavaScript puts them into an array named embeds. For example, if the following is the first <EMBED> tag on your page, JavaScript shows the associated plug-in in document.embeds[0]:

```
<EMBED SRC="http://www.somemachine.com/myFile.tst HEIGHT=100
WIDTH=100>
```

From JavaScript, you can access document.embeds.length to find out how many plug-ins are on the page.

> **N O T E** Because full-page plug-ins are, by definition, on a page with no JavaScript (and no HTML!), it only makes sense to talk about controlling embedded plug-ins. ■

To make a plug-in visible from inside Java, your Java class must use netscape.plugin.Plugin. Netscape provides a file java_30 with Netscape version 3.0 and later. This file contains three Java packages, java, sun, and netscape:

- java
- sun
- netscape.applet
- netscape.net
- netscape.javascript
- netscape.plugin

The java and sun packages are replacements to packages of the same name in the Sun 1.1 Java Development Kit (JDK). They include security enhancements necessary for LiveConnect. Netscape and Sun are working together to ensure that these new packages are included in a future release of the Sun JDK.

`netscape.applet` is Netscape's replacement to `sun.applet`. Similarly, `netscape.net` replaces `sun.net`.

`netscape.javascript` implements `JSObject` and `JSException`, and will be further discussed in this book.

`netscape.plugin` implements the `Plugin` class. As a Java programmer, you use methods on the `Plugin` class to communicate with the plug-in.

N O T E   To use the Netscape-supplied packages with the JDK compiler, add the path of the `java_30` and `classes.zip` to the compiler's `classpath`. You can either specify a `CLASSPATH` environment variable or use the `-classpath` command line option when you run javac. ▨

 As a plug-in programmer, you have a C++ development environment such as Microsoft Visual C++ handy. Don't waste time running javac from the command line. Put your plug-in's Java proxy class in the makefile, and automatically call javac each time your plug-in is rebuilt. If you use Visual C++, just add the javac command line (with the `-classpath` option) to the Custom Build settings.

▶ To learn more about programming plug-ins and utilizing LiveConnect, **see** Chapter 5, "Programming Plug-Ins."

▶ For more information on Netscape Packages, **see** Chapter 12.

Dynamic (Live) Content

Multimedia publishers are currently developing products that are a mix of online and CD-ROM content, called hybrid technology. Chapter 6, "Developing Content for Plug-Ins," contemplates this technology and what it means for those who are new to developing and publishing content.

This is the information age, so it comes as no surprise that there are great advantages to combining retrieval software with up-to-date real-time online information. Large volumes of offline information (CD-ROMs) can be combined with online access (the Web) to supply the user with quicker search and retrieval methods while having the advantages of great graphics, video, and sound.

Design Issues

Chapter 5, "Programming Plug-Ins," introduces the mechanics of building a Navigator plug-in. But just as there is an enormous difference between a C "Hello, world!" program and a useful program that does real work, so too is there far more to a successful plug-in than the Chapter 5 demo.

Real plug-ins generally fall into three categories: those that display a specific data type, those that display a document, and those that give the user the ability to interact with the data (including LiveConnect plug-ins, which interact with JavaScript and Java programs).

Chapter 5 reviews the tools available to the plug-in programmer, and Chapter 3, "Overview of Plug-In API," showcases the most sophisticated plug-in—the interactive plug-in.

Navigator and the plug-in work together as a cooperating set of objects. Take advantage of native multitasking by using threads and processes to move asynchronous work out of the user's view. Use separate processes to "Webify" conventional applications quickly.

You can write a plug-in that helps debug itself. You make the plug-in "smarter" at compile time by using the same techniques that the authors of Microsoft Foundation Classes used.

Merging Java and JavaScript Environments

You now know that the LiveConnect environment is a merger of two other environments: Java and JavaScript. Java programmers would use a public indentifier when defining a class. Now that LiveConnect enables JavaScript to be linked to a Java environment, all public classes can be controlled by the JavaScript script, which allows JavaScript scripts to access anything that a Java applet can access.

Getting Java from a Plug-In

The plug-in talks to Java through Netscape's Java Runtime Interface. Figure 1.3 illustrates the JRI.

FIG. 1.3
The plug-in connects
to the Java Runtime
Interface, which
handles communica-
tions with Java.

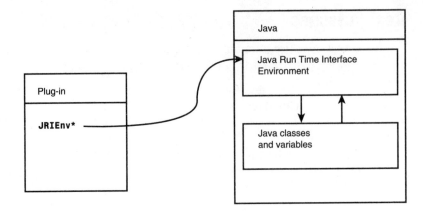

Netscape has defined the Java Runtime Interface to allow native code (such as a plug-in) to call Java methods.

ON THE WEB

The full specification of the Java Runtime Interface is available online as part of the Netscape Plug-in SDK (**http://home.netscape.com/eng/mozilla/3.0/handbook/ plugins/index.html**).

Netscape also supplies a new version of javah, named the JRI (Java Runtime Interface) version, which writes a C/C++ header file from a Java class. To control the count class previously described from your plug-in, start by typing (or including in the makefile) the following:

```
javah -jri -classpath pathTojava_30Andclasses.zip count
```

The result of running javah is a header file for class count. Recall that count has one public data member, i. javah produces in-line accessor functions

```
jint i(JRIEnv* env);
```

and

```
void i(JRI* env, jint);
```

to get and set this data member.

Note that javah has transformed the Java int into a variable of type jint. Table 1.1 shows the JRI definitions of the Java primitive types. Netscape's version of javah transforms Java variables into C/C++ variables with a new Java-specific type.

Table 1.1   JRI Definitions of Java Primitive Types

Java Type	C/C++ Type	Size
boolean	jbool	1 byte
byte	jbyte	1 byte
char	jchar	2 bytes
short	jshort	2 bytes
int	jint	4 bytes
long	jlong	8 bytes
float	jfloat	4 bytes
double	jdouble	8 bytes

These sizes are defined through a series of #ifdefs in the file jri_md.h, which is included in the header file jri.h. Make sure that your compiler sets up the proper preprocessor symbols for your target machine, so your code gets the right size types.

CAUTION

Make sure that you use the JRI types described in Table 1.1 when talking to Java methods. If you use the compiler's types (in other words, int), you run the risk of a size mismatch when you move to a new compiler or a new platform.

CAUTION

javah doesn't do a very good job of protecting the privacy of data members in Java classes. You will be able to access private members from inside your plug-in. Avoid this temptation, and use accessor methods and other public methods exclusively.

By restricting yourself to public methods, your plug-in is less likely to need maintenance when the implementation of the Java class changes.

To call the increment() method of the Java class count, just write the following:

```
count->increment(env);
```

Here, env is the result of the function `NPN_GetJavaEnv()`. `NPN_GetJavaEnv()` has the following specification:

```
JavaEnv* NPN_GetJavaEnv(void);
```

Typically you call `NPN_GetJavaEnv()` once, in `NPP_Initialize()`.

TIP Netscape starts the Java Runtime Interpreter when you first call `NPN_GetJavaEnv()`. This first call can impose a delay on your plug-in. If you're sure that your plug-in needs to call Java, call `NPN_GetJavaEnv()` in `NPP_Initialize()` and get it out of the way. The user expects to wait a few seconds when he or she accesses the plug-in content, anyway.

TIP The pointer to the Java environment is thread-specific. If you call it in `NPP_Initialize()`, you can use it in any instance, but if you spawn a new thread, you need to call `NPN_GetJavaEnv()` for this thread, and reserve the new `JavaEnv` pointer for use in this thread only.

Recall that most object-oriented languages, including both C++ and Java, support overloaded methods. That is, two more methods can have the same name, as long as they take different parameters. (Sets of parameters are called *signatures*.) In C++, the compiler performs *name mangling* to make sure that the internal names are unique. Netscape's javah appends an index to all but the first occurrence of a name. If you have three functions named foo, javah produces foo, foo_1, and foo_2. To find out which name to call for which signature, just check the header file output by javah. Without the use of an index on all but one of the names, the function name "foo" would be ambiguous. For this reason, the index is sometimes known as a "disambiguating index."

TIP If you have overloaded methods, first declare the one you plan to use most frequently from your plug-in. In this way, the declared version of the method will not have an index.

Similarly, if you have a Java-implemented version of a method and a native (such as C or C++) version of the same method, put the declaration of the native method first. In this way, you don't have to worry about index names when you write the native implementation.

TIP Because javah uses the underscore followed by a number to disambiguate overloaded methods, it performs name-mangling on Java methods with an underscore in their name. Save yourself a headache—don't use underscores in Java method names.

▶ **See** Chapter 8, "Calling Java Methods from Plug-Ins," and Chapter 9, "Calling the Plug-In from Java Methods."

Netscape API and JRI

Netscape Plug-ins interact with Navigator through the Application Programming Interface (API). There are two types of functions that form the Plug-in API. The first type is plug-in methods and the second is Netscape methods. As you may recall from earlier in this chapter, plug-in methods are the functions that you actually create in your plug-in and are called by Netscape, while Netscape methods are functions started by Netscape that your plug-in may call.

API functions actually operate the same on all platforms, although a few functions, such as NPN_MemFlush, operate on specific platforms. You will learn more about NPN_MemFlush further along in Chapter 5.

All API functions as well as definitions of all types and structures used in the API are found in the file npapi.h. See Chapter 3, "Overview of Plug-In API," and Chapter 4, "Creating Plug-Ins," for more about API definition types and structures.

It is the Java Runtime Interface (JRI) that allows Netscape Navigator plug-ins to define Java classes and to call native C functions. The JRI, along with Netscape Navigator application programming interface (API), is what allows plug-ins to be accessed in a Java environment.

From Here...

In this chapter you learned how easy it is to enable LiveConnect. In Navigator, you use the Java Console window as an easy way to view the direct output of an applet as it is running. With LiveConnect, plug-ins are software objects that are called by Navigator, and in turn they can call the Navigator. Multimedia publishers are currently developing products that are a mix of online and CD-ROM content called hybrid technology, which you will read further about later in this book.

- The next chapter, "LiveConnect Components," looks at how the SDK is organized and where to download the protocol.
- Chapter 3, "Overview of Plug-In API," looks at the organization of the Application Programming Interface, along with plug-in and Netscape methods.
- Chapter 4, "Creating Plug-Ins," looks at creating plug-ins for Windows and Macintosh platforms.
- Chapter 5, "Programming Plug-Ins," looks at plug-ins and HTML, as well as Simple and CharFlipper LiveConnect plug-ins.
- Chapter 6, "Developing Content for Plug-Ins," looks at LiveCache and CD-ROM developing.

CHAPTER 2

LiveConnect Components

You now know that Netscape Navigator's new LiveConnect protocol allows Web developers to script, link, and control live objects such as plug-ins, Java applets, and HTML elements. LiveConnect links together these objects to allow Java and JavaScript to control their functions. You will learn how Netscape's LiveConnect SDK Plug-in is broken down and organized into directories further along in this chapter. ■

How to Begin Using LiveConnect

You can use LiveConnect to enable separate multimedia files to play simultaneously or sequentially.

Downloading LiveConnect

You choose the download that is compatible with your system platform.

How the SDK Is Organized

The SDK is downloaded and organized into a directory structure based on your operating system platform.

Example Plug-Ins and Templates

Included plug-in examples and templates offer a full implementation of the major methods, including LiveConnect.

How LiveConnect Works with JavaScript

When a function is defined in a JavaScript program, the plug-in will look for and carry out the defined function.

Using LiveConnect

Using LiveConnect can enable separate audio and video files to play at the same time, or can enable the audio file to begin first while cueing the video file to start. Java Applets, plug-ins, and JavaScript-embedded HTML pages can now call any other Applet, plug-in, or embedded JavaScript to run in sequence or at the same time. See Figure 2.1 to see how LiveConnect works.

FIG. 2.1
How LiveConnect
works.

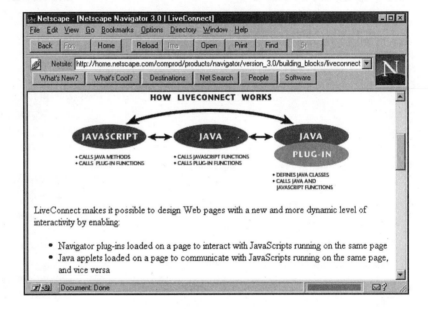

Some of the ways LiveConnect allows developers to design Web pages with a higher level of interactivity:

- JavaScript-embedded pages can interact and run Netscape Navigator plug-ins, all at the same time.
- JavaScript-embedded pages can interact and run Java Applets, all at the same time.
- Java and plug-in programmers can now give JavaScript programmers control over Java and plug-in functions.
- Live applications can be created using buttons, images, and forms that can now interact with any different type objects.

LiveConnect SDK Plug-In

You can use LiveConnect SDK Plug-in to enable separate multimedia files to play simultaneously or sequentially. Included are plug-in examples and templates that offer a full implementation of the major methods, including LiveConnect.

Getting Started   You can download the LiveConnect/Plug-in SDK at **http:// home.netscape.com/comprod/development_partners/plugin_api/ index.html**.

You should choose the download that is compatible with your system platform. Your choices are Macintosh, OS/2 Warp, Windows 95, or UNIX.

ON THE WEB

For online help with developing your own plug-in, check out LiveConnect/Plug-in Developer's Guide, at **http://home.netscape.com/eng/mozilla/3.0/handbook/ plugins/index.html**.

How the SDK Is Organized   Once you download the SDK plug-in, the following directory structure ("platform" refers to your operating system platform) is downloaded to your hard drive:

```
sdk
sdk/bin
sdk/bin/Platform
sdk/bin/Platform/javah
sdk/include/
sdk/common/
sdk/doc/
sdk/classes/
sdk/examples/
sdk/examples/Framework/
sdk/examples/SomeExample/
sdk/examples/SomeExample/src
sdk/examples/SomeExample/test
sdk/examples/SomeExample/win (Windows version only)
sdk/examples/SomeExample/mac (Macintosh version only)
sdk/examples/SomeExample/unix (Unix system only)
```

Example Plug-Ins and Templates   The LiveConnect Plug-in includes three plug-in examples explained in the following sections, as well as templates that offer a full implementation of the major methods, including LiveConnect.

Simple   The sample applications included with the Windows version of the Netscape Plug-in Software Development Kit (SDK) are a tour de force of plug-in programming. They include calls to Java code and allow the user to play AVI movies. Unfortunately, so much is going on in these sample applications that the new plug-in programmer can be overwhelmed.

Traditionally, the first program a C or C++ programmer writes in a new environment is one to put up the words, "Hello, world!". Such a simple program serves to check out the compiler and development environment, because the code itself is trivial. This chapter shows you how to build a "Hello, world!" plug-in—a plug-in that just shows these words to the user.

After "Hello, world!" is working, you can use this plug-in as a foundation for showing more of the calls a plug-in and Navigator can exchange.

Despite its name, the "Simple Plug-In" that Netscape supplies with the Plug-in Software Development Kit (SDK) is far from simple. It includes a full implementation of the major methods, including LiveConnect. LiveConnect (described in more detail in Part III, "Live-Connecting Plug-Ins with Java," and Part IV, "LiveConnect Communication in JavaScript") is Netscape's integration technology that allows your plug-in to communicate with Java and JavaScript.

When compiling the Plug-in, Netscape uses Microsoft's Visual C++ on Windows, and Metroworks' Code Warrior on the Macintosh. You can simplify the installation process if you use the same environment they do. To run the Simple plug-in, follow these steps:

1. In Visual C++'s Developer Studio, you choose File, Open Workspace and open Simple32.mdp in the Examples\Simple\Windows subdirectory of the Plugins SDK directory. After the project opens, you choose Build, Build **NPSimp32.dll**. The project should compile and link with no errors or warnings.

2. You need to copy the Java class file Simple.class to your Navigator plug-ins directory.

3. You also copy the NPSimp32.dll file, which you just built, to the plug-ins directory, and then restart Navigator. Make sure that you are using a version of Navigator that is at least v3.0b5, or you won't be able to see all the features of this plug-in working.

N O T E When Navigator restarts, it examines the files in the plug-ins directory and registers plug-ins based on their MIME media type. Chapter 4, "Creating Plug-Ins," describes this process in more detail. ■

4. After Navigator is up, you use File, Open File to open Examples\Simple\Testing\SimpleExample.html. You probably will want to bookmark this page while you learn about plug-ins.

▶ For detailed information on Simple, **see** Chapter 5, "Programming Plug-Ins."

CharFlipper   The CharFlipper plug-in is considerably more complex than the Simple plug-in you have just looked at.

When running CharFlipper, you will see that it is one of Netscape's principal stream-reading example plug-ins.

The speed of the CharFlipper plug-in reading from its stream is far faster than a human can keep up with. In Chapter 5, a timer is used to slow down the demonstration.

To get an idea of what CharFlipper does, start by compiling and running the plug-in. This chapter uses the Windows version of the plug-in, but Netscape supplies a version for the Mac also.

In Visual C++'s Developer Studio, you choose File, Open Workspace and open CharFlipper.mdp in the Examples\CharFlipper\Windows subdirectory of the Plug-ins SDK directory. After the project opens, you choose Build, Build **NPFlip.dll**.

This project has a few problems. It should compile without errors, but six warnings are issued. These warnings don't affect the running of the plug-in, but they are troublesome. If you choose to build one of your plug-ins around CharFlipper, start by fixing these warnings (see Chapter 5).

You copy the Java class file TimeMediaPlugin.class to the Navigator plug-ins directory.

You also copy the NPFlip.dll file, which you just built, to the plug-ins directory and restart Navigator. Make sure that you are using a version of Navigator that is at least 3.0b5, or you won't be able to see all the features of this plug-in working.

Part
I

Ch
2

When Navigator restarts, it examines the files in the plug-ins directory and registers plug-ins based on their MIME media type. Chapter 4 describes this process in more detail.

After Navigator is up, use File, Open File to open Examples\CharFlipper\Testing\CharFlipperExample.html. You probably will want to bookmark this page while you learn about plug-ins.

As soon as it opens, CharFlipper goes to work. Figure 2.2 shows the CharFlipper.html user interface.

FIG. 2.2

CharFlipper reads from a stream and writes to the window. It's also listening to JavaScript, waiting for a user to press a button.

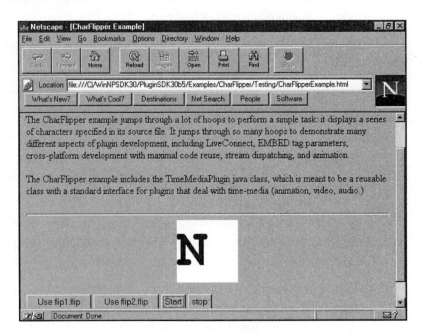

CharFlipper begins to display its data right way. You can use the controls to stop and restart the display or to change the plug-in from one data file to another.

▶ For detailed information on CharFlipper, **see** Chapter 5.

NPAvi   The "NPAvi" plug-in is easily the most complex plug-in in this book. It includes full LiveConnect integration and exercises nearly all of the NPP methods. This plug-in also uses Microsoft Foundation Classes (MFC) to put up a custom pop-up menu. NPAvi has some of the same capabilities as Netscape's LiveVideo plug-in—one of the major features that distinguishes Navigator 3.0 from Navigator 2.0.

There are sample plug-ins described in Chapter 5 that were intended purely for illustrative purposes. In contrast, NPAvi could be released as a commercial product, and few users would question it.

NPAvi displays a video (in AVI format) inside the Navigator window. (It's intended for use as an embedded plug-in.)

For an idea of how NPAvi looks, start by compiling and then running the plug-in. Because this plug-in uses a Windows-specific AVI engine, Netscape provides a version only for Windows. Figure 2.3 shows the npAVI.html user interface.

FIG. 2.3
NPAvi reads from a stream and writes to the window. It's also listening to JavaScript, waiting for a user to press a button.

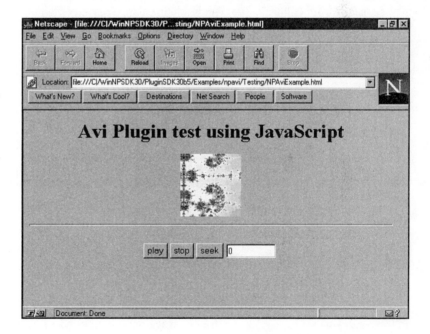

▶ For more information on NPAvi, **see** Chapter 3, "Overview of Plug-In API."

LivePict, PPViewText, and Templates

- LivePict plug-in displays Macintosh PICT images only.
- PPViewText plug-in displays text using Metroworks' PowerPlant (Macintosh only).

- WinTemplate is an empty Windows example and project file that you can start from.
- MacTemplate is an empty Mac example and project file that you can start from.
- UnixTemplate is an empty UNIX example and makefile that you can start from.

LiveConnect with JavaScript

When a function is defined in a JavaScript program, the plug-in will look for and carry out the defined function. All plug-in types have methods and properties along with callbacks that can be defined and carried out. The following is an example of an Embed tag that now can include the Name parameter.

```
<EMBED NAME="VideoName" SRC="videoname.avi">
function StartTheVideo() {
    document.VideoName.play();
}
// Called when advancing the video
function AviFrameCallback(frame_number) {
}
```

N O T E LiveConnect should be enabled in Netscape 3.0 or later. To verify that this is enabled, select Network Preferences from the Options menu and then select the Language tab. Enable Java and Enable JavaScript should both be checked. ■

JavaScript Calls to Java Methods

The Navigator's Java Console displays Java messages. When LiveConnect is enabled, you can directly access Java methods. When you use the java.lang.System class variables out or err, the message appears in the Console.

The following Java code example displays the message "Welcome to the World of LiveConnect!" in the Java Console (see Figure 2.4):

```
public void init() {
    System.out.println("Welcome to the World of LiveConnect!" );
```

FIG. 2.4

The Java Console window.

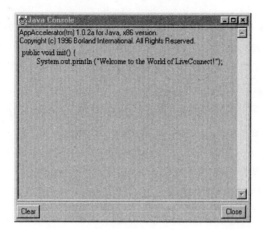

Part
I
Ch
2

Java packages and classes are properties of the *Packages* object in JavaScript. To reference Java objects in JavaScript you use Java syntax, with the name of the *Packages* object:

```
[Packages.] packageName.className.methodName
```

Using the same syntax that you use in Java, you can access fields and methods in a class. For instance, the following JavaScript code prints a message to the Java Console:

```
var System = java.lang.System
System.err.println("This is what JavaScript to Java Communication is
➥all about")
```

LiveConnect with Plug-Ins and Java Applets

There is now a simpler way to get messages into a plug-in. The current techniques hook platform-native controls such as menus and pushbuttons into your plug-in. This approach has the advantage of looking familiar to the user. It also gives you a great deal of control over the appearance of your plug-in. (For example, a pop-up menu that appears in response to the user right-clicking the mouse may offer a dozen or more menu items, yet it doesn't clutter the screen when not in use.)

Sometimes, however, you will be happy to have a little HTML form with some buttons that tell the plug-in to "Start" or "Stop." Netscape provides all this flexibility and more through the technology that we now know as LiveConnect.

There's a distinction between interacting and controlling within a plug-in. Here's an example: If your plug-in downloads a drawing from the Web, and then allows you to annotate it and post it back to the Web, you need to use native controls. For example, you probably want a pop-up menu (perhaps triggered by the right mouse button) that allows you to zoom, save, and revert. These kinds of platform-dependent native controls would be necessary for each plug-in to have this kind of user control and interaction.

However, if your plug-in is simpler, such as a video player, and you want to allow the HTML author to add buttons to the page like "Start" and "Stop," LiveConnect may be faster and easier to implement. You can do more complex tasks with LiveConnect. Many plug-ins will want to use both native controls and LiveConnect. It's up to you to decide how to best design your plug-in.

The LiveConnect environment is a merger of two other environments, Java and JavaScript. Java programmers would use a public indentifier when defining a class. Now that LiveConnect enables JavaScript to be linked to a Java environment, all public classes can be controlled by the JavaScript script, which allows JavaScript scripts to access anything that a Java applet can access.

You don't need to know about how a Java applet is constructed to use JavaScript to control an applet, since all applets' public variables, methods, and properties can be accessed by JavaScript.

Each applet in a document is accessed in JavaScript by document.appletName, where appletName is the value of the NAME attribute of the APPLET tag. The following is an example of how HTML starts an applet called "myApplet":

```
<APPLET CODE=Mytest.class NAME=MyApplet WIDTH=80 HEIGHT=50>
<PARAM NAME=label VALUE=Mytest>
<PARAM NAME=debug VALUE=86>
</APPLET>
```

There are two ways that you can access this applet in JavaScript:

```
document.MyApplet
document.applets["MyApplet"]
```

To also access this applet through an applets array, notice the following example of an applet that is the fourth one in an HTML document:

```
document.applets[3]
```

It's just as simple to control a plug-in in a document accessed in JavaScript as an element in the embeds array. For instance, the following HTML includes an AVI plug-in:

```
<EMBED SRC=plugavi.avi WIDTH=280 HEIGHT=150>
```

This HTML defines the first plug-in in a document, while the following code starts it:

```
document.embeds[0]
```

ON THE WEB

If it's Java Applets you seek, then check out the Gamelan site at **http://www.gamelan.com/**. This site acts as a registry of applets. It contains links to hundreds of applets, all categorized by subject.

The Java Development Team also maintains their own listing of applets, which can be found at **http://www.javasoft.com/Applets**.

LiveConnect and LiveAudio

LiveAudio is LiveConnect-enabled. You use JavaScript to control embedded LiveAudio elements.

Using LiveConnect, LiveAudio, and JavaScript, you can do the following:

- Create alternative sound control interfaces for the user to access.
- Defer loading a sound file until the user clicks the "play" button control.
- Create buttons that make clicking noises when you turn them on and off.
- Create interfaced audio interactions with users by having an object give the user instructions visually or using audio, describing what it does when the users accesses it.

LiveAudio uses the following JavaScript methods for controlling LiveAudio. These methods can be used only if you embed a LiveAudio console on your Web page. Anywhere on the page is fine.

JavaScript Methods for Controlling LiveAudio:

- play({loop[TRUE, FALSE or an INT]}, '{url_to_sound}')
- pause( )
- stop( )
- StopAll( )
- start_time({number of seconds})
- end_time({number of seconds})
- setvol({percentage number - without "%" sign})
- fade_to({volume percent you wish to fade to - without the "%" sign})
- fade_from_to({volume percent start fade}, {volume percent end fade})
- start_at_beginning( )
- stop_at_end( )

The following JavaScript state indication methods give you current information about the plug-in. They do not actually control the LiveAudio plug-in.

- IsReady
- IsPlaying
- IsPaused
- GetVolume

The best way of showing how JavaScript is used to control a LiveAudio plug-in is by having JavaScript play a sound.

Listing 2.1 is an example of the HTML code necessary to play sound with the LiveAudio plug-in. This method is the simplest when playing a sound.

Listing 2.1 HTML Code Using the *Documents.embeds* Array

```
<HTML>
<BODY>
<EMBED SRC="sound1.wav"
    HIDDEN=TRUE>
<A HREF="javascript:document.embeds[0].play(false)">
Let's hear this sound!</A>
</BODY>
</HTML>
```

The preceding method can cause problems if you're using Navigator 2.0, which will cause an error. The documents.embeds array is a feature of Navigator 3.0. Instead, you can use the NAME and MASTERSOUND attributes to identify the <EMBED> tag (see Listing 2.2).

Listing 2.2   HTML Code Using the *NAME* and *MASTERSOUND* Attributes

```
<HTML>
<BODY>
<EMBED SRC="sound1.wav"
    HIDDEN=TRUE
    NAME="firstsound"
    MASTERSOUND>
<A HREF="javascript:document.firstsound.play(false)">
Let's hear this sound!</A>
</BODY>
</HTML>
```

Part
I
Ch
2

The above listing is a better way to describe your plug-in to JavaScript. It's easier for developers to use the NAME and MASTERSOUND attributes, especially if you're embedding many sounds in an HTML document. Whenever a NAME attribute is used, a MASTERSOUND tag must be referred to as well when accessing LiveAudio.

You can also defer starting a sound until the user actually clicks the "play" button (see Listing 2.3).

Listing 2.3   Defer Sound Until User Clicks the "Play" Button

```
<HTML>
<HEAD>
<SCRIPT LANGUAGE=JavaScript>
<!-- Hide JavaScript from older browsers
function playDeferredSound() {
    document.firstsound.play(false, 'http://newsound/sound1.wav');
}
// -->
</SCRIPT>
</HEAD>
```

continues

Listing 2.3   Continued

```
<BODY>
<EMBED
    SRC="stub1.wav"
    HIDDEN=TRUE
    NAME="firstsound"
    MASTERSOUND>
<A HREF="javascript:playDeferredSound()">Load and play the sound</A>
</BODY>
</HTML>
```

The stub file (stub1.wav) will load immediately. The play methods will only load the sound when the user clicks the "play" control button on the console.

ON THE WEB

For a description of how to create a stub file, see the EmeraldNet LiveAudio information at **http://emerald.net/liveaudio/**.

You can also create alternate console interfaces for audio and user interaction. Listing 2.4 is an example of what a Web developer can do with LiveConnect and LiveAudio.

Listing 2.4   Alternate Console Interfaces for Audio and User Interaction

```
<HTML>
<HEAD>
<SCRIPT LANGUAGE=JavaScript>
<!-- Hide JavaScript from older browsers
function playSound() {
    document.firstSound.play(false);
}
function pauseSound() {
    document.firstSound.pause();
}
function stopSound() {
    document.firstSound.stop();
}
function volup() {
    currentVolume = document.firstSound.GetVolume();
```

```
      newVolume = ( currentVolume + 10 ) ;
      if ( document.firstSound.GetVolume() == 100 ) {
         alert("Volume is already at maximum");
      }
      if ( newVolume < 90 ) {
         document.firstSound.setvol(newVolume) ;
      }
      else
      {
         if ( ( newVolume <= 100 ) && ( newVolume > 90 ) ) {
            document.firstSound.setvol(100) ;
         }
      }
   }
   function voldown() {
      currentVolume = document.firstSound.GetVolume();
      newVolume = ( currentVolume - 10 ) ;
      if ( document.firstSound.GetVolume() == 0 ) {
         alert("Volume is already at minimum");
      }
      if ( newVolume > 10 ) {
         document.firstSound.setvol(newVolume) ;
      }
      else
      {
         if ( ( newVolume >= 0 ) && ( newVolume < 10 ) ) {
            document.firstSound.setvol(0) ;
         }
      }
   }
   // -->
   </SCRIPT>
   </HEAD>
   <BODY>
   <EMBED
      SRC="sound1.wav"
      HIDDEN=TRUE
      AUTOSTART=FALSE
      NAME="firstSound"
      MASTERSOUND>
   <P><A HREF="javascript:playSound()">Play the sound now!</A></P>
   <P><A HREF="javascript:pauseSound()">Pause the sound now!</A></P>
   <P><A HREF="javascript:stopSound()">Stop the sound now!</A></P>
   <P><A HREF="javascript:volup()">Increase the Volume!</A></P>
   <P><A HREF="javascript:voldown()">Decrease the Volume!</A></P>
   </BODY>
   </HTML>
```

ON THE WEB

You can find out more about LiveAudio at **http://home.netscape.com/comprod/ products/navigator/version_3.0/building_blocks/examples/lc_example/ lc-showcase.html**.

Java Runtime Interface (JRI)

The Java Runtime Interface (JRI) is the standard interface to Java. JRI enables native methods to operate against any Java platform supporting JRI.

JRI prevents Java classes from affecting native methods when upgrading Java classes. Runtime providers can enhance their runtime, while not changing their clients.

Java runtime clients can either be native methods which are called from Java operations or applications implementing functions. Applications that run applets, like Netscape Navigator, in performing their functions use Java runtime.

The Java Runtime Interface is the device that implements the Java runtime. This does not exclude the existing interfaces that are internal to a runtime, like a compiler.

It is the Java Runtime Interface (JRI) that allows Netscape Navigator plug-ins to define Java classes and to call native C functions. The JRI, along with Netscape Navigator application programming interface (API), is what allows plug-ins to be accessed in a Java environment.

Netscape 4.0, as well as Version 3.0, Includes Borland's Java JIT Compiler

Netscape enhanced its Java support when they struck a deal with Borland International Inc. to include the Borland JIT compiler, AppAccelerator, for Windows 95.

Although the Java programming language produces dynamic live Web pages, users and developers have complained of its slow compile time. AppAccelerator translates Java bytecodes into machine code (Intel in this case), allowing programs to execute 5-10 times faster. The JIT compiler will entice more developers to create Java programs and, given its fast compile time, will enable users to quickly use Java applets without further time delays.

▶ The Java Runtime Interface is discussed further in Chapter 7.

ON THE WEB

For more information on the Java Runtime Interface, take a look at the Netscape site located at **http://home.netscape.com/eng/jri/**.

LiveConnect Demos

LiveConnect is a technology that was a first for Navigator 3.0. Since then, Netscape has put up a site on the Web that has many companies jumping on the LiveConnect bandwagon to showcase. Some of these LiveConnect demos are the following:

- WebMotion by Astound

  WebMotion enables LiveConnect developers to create Java animations without programming. Astound supplies many examples of interactive LiveConnect animation.

- Tumbleweed by Envoy

  The Tumbleweed Envoy plug-in enables users to view Envoy plug-ins from right within Navigator. Interactive applications can be embedded into a Web page and can offer direct user interface.

ON THE WEB

These LiveConnect demos, and many more, can be found at **http:// home.netscape.com/comprod/products/navigator/version_3.0/building_blocks/ examples/lc_example/lc-showcase.html**.

LiveConnect Resources

For more information about plug-ins, take a look at the Plug-in Developer's Guide located at **http://home.netscape.com/eng/mozilla/3.0/handbook/plugins/ index.html**.

From this handbook, you can access documentation on calling Java methods from plug-ins at **http://home.netscape.com/eng/mozilla/3.0/handbook/plugins/ wr2.htm**, as well as documentation on calling plug-in native methods from Java at **http://home.netscape.com/eng/mozilla/3.0/handbook/plugins/wr3.htm**.

From Here...

In this chapter you learned how to begin using LiveConnect. You can use LiveConnect to enable separate multimedia files to play simultaneously or sequentially. When downloading LiveConnect, you choose the download that is compatible with your system platform. The SDK is downloaded and organized into a directory structure based on your operating system platform. Included plug-in examples and templates offer a full implementation of the major methods, including LiveConnect.

When a function is defined in a JavaScript program, the plug-in will look for and carry out the defined function. The current techniques hook platform-native controls such as menus and pushbuttons into your plug-in. LiveAudio is LiveConnect-enabled. You use JavaScript to control embedded LiveAudio elements. The Java Runtime Interface allows native methods to work against any Java platform supporting the JRI.

- The next chapter, "Overview of Plug-In API," looks at the organization of the Application Programming Interface, along with Plug-in and Netscape Methods.

- Chapter 4, "Creating Plug-Ins," looks at creating plug-ins for Windows and Macintosh platforms.

- Chapter 5, "Programming Plug-Ins," looks at plug-ins and HTML, as well as Simple and CharFlipper LiveConnect plug-ins.

- Chapter 6, "Developing Content for Plug-Ins," looks at LiveCache and CD-ROM developing.

P A R T

II

Plug-In Developer's Guide

CHAPTER 3

Overview of Plug-In API

Plug-ins are native to a specific platform and are called dynamic code modules, in which plug-in API enables platform-dependent code to integrate with the Navigator by supporting new data types.

Plug-ins are meant to be integral to platform-native inter-application architectures like OLE and OpenDoc and platform-independent programming languages like Java. Netscape plug-ins are created especially to expand Netscape Navigator and are considered very simple in structure, while Java applets are intrinsically cross-platform. In addition, a relatively new language is necessary to develop Java applets, while Netscape plug-ins can be written in C or C++ using already existing development tools. ■

Netscape API Organization
Netscape plug-ins communicate with Navigator via an Application Programming Interface (API).

The Run-Time Model
Plug-ins are a code resource loaded by Netscape Navigator at run-time.

Accessing the Data
One of the most important tasks of the plug-in is to access the Web data.

Starting the Plug-In
Navigator tells the plug-in how it was called by setting the mode parameter in the NPP_New() call.

Designing for Debug
Use construction techniques that minimize defects in the code, and make it more likely that such defects are caught early.

The NPAvi Plug-In
The NPAvi plug-in is easily the most complex plug-in in this book and includes full LiveConnect integration.

Overview

Plug-ins are capable of registering one or many different MIME types. Hyperlinks or hotspots can be added to link new URLs. Data can be procured and posted to URLs also. Plug-ins enable drawing right into the Navigator window, as well as receiving keyboard and mouse events.

Plug-ins can be either embedded or full-page in their operation. A plug-in that is embedded is only a part of an HTML document. Macromedia Shockwave plug-ins and RealAudio plug-ins are usually embedded on a page.

A full-page plug-in is not part of an HTML page and is loaded by the Navigator when the user opens a file of a MIME type when accessing the URL from within the Navigator. The loaded plug-in entirely encompasses the whole Navigator page. Adobe Acrobat is a common full-page plug-in used for document viewing. Many plug-ins, especially graphic viewers, can be embedded and/or full-page when in operation.

Organization

Netscape plug-ins interact with the Navigator through the Application Programming Interface (API). There are two types of functions that form the Plug-in API: plug-in methods and Netscape methods. Plug-in methods are the functions that you actually create in your plug-in and are called by Netscape. Netscape methods are functions started by Netscape that your plug-in may call. As you will see further along in this chapter, the names of all plug-in functions start with "NPP_", while all Netscape functions start with "NPN_".

API functions actually operate the same on all platforms, although there are a few functions, such as NPN_MemFlush, that operate on specific platforms. You will learn more about NPN_MemFlush later in the chapter.

All API functions, as well as definitions of all types and structures used in the API, are found in the file npapi.h. See Chapter 4, "Creating Plug-Ins," for more about API definition types and structures.

The Run-Time Model

Plug-ins are a code resource loaded by Netscape Navigator at run-time. These resources have various names—under Windows and OS/2 Warp they are known as Dynamic Link Libraries. On a Macintosh, they are code resources. UNIX programmers call these resources shared objects. No matter what they're called by developers on the various platforms, plug-ins are software objects that are called by Navigator, and in turn they can call Navigator.

To keep the plug-in methods straight, Netscape uses the convention that the plug-in methods (which are called by Navigator) have names starting with "NPP_". Navigator offers programmers methods that they can call from their plug-ins—these methods all have names that start with "NPN_". As a plug-in programmer, you write the NPP methods. NPN methods are provided for you by Netscape.

Part
II
Ch
3

NPP Methods

 To see how the various NPP methods interact, load and build the plug-in at **www. quecorp.com/liveconnect/** known as zero. Although zero is designed for a Windows environment, it's a simple plug-in and can be easily ported to OS/2 Warp, the Macintosh, and the X-Window System.

Zero is a simple plug-in. It answers the various calls from Navigator and returns. The significance is that each NPP method is instrumented with a call to the Windows method ::MessageBox(), so we can see when Navigator calls each routine.

Calling *zero* as a Full-Page Plug-In   Start by building a zero "document." Any text file will do, provided its file extension is .zer—the file extent recognized by zero. Use Navigator to open the file, and note the following chain of calls:

- NPP_Initialize()—as the plug-in loads.
- NPP_New()—when the first instance is loaded.
- NPP_SetWindow()—as Navigator passes in the information about the parent window.
- NPP_NewStream()—as Navigator starts the data streaming in from the file.
- NPP_SetWindow()—which can be called at any time, as the dimensions of the window change.

When the plug-in handles `NPP_Initialize()`, it should take all steps and initialize all memory required by the plug-in (as opposed to an instance of the plug-in). `NPP_New()` is the place to handle instance initialization.

Suppose that your plug-in object has class variables that need to be initialized. Initialize them in `NPP_Initialize()`. You should initialize instance variables in `NPP_New()`.

 When your plug-in is exiting, reverse the guidelines of what to initialize where. Memory allocated in `NPP_New()` should be freed in `NPP_Destroy()`. Memory allocated in `NPP_Initialize()` should be freed in `NPP_Shutdown()`.

After the plug-in is running, use the controls of the Navigator window to resize the window with the plug-in. Note that resizing the window triggers a call to `NPP_SetWindow()`—moving the window generally does not. Make the window small enough that a scroll bar appears. Scrolling the window triggers `NPP_SetWindow()`, too. Try printing the contents of the window and see how `NPP_Print()` is called.

Now choose File, New Web Browser and see that `NPP_New()` is called, but not `NPP_Initialize()`. The plug-in is already loaded, so Navigator just instantiates a new instance of the plug-in object (and its Netscape peer).

Now close one of the two Web Browser windows and observe that `NPP_Destroy()` is called. Recall that `NPP_Destroy()` is used alone on all instances of the plug-in (except the last instance). When you either close the last window or move off of this window to a different Web page, Navigator first calls `NPP_Destroy()` to clean up after the instance, and then calls `NPP_Shutdown()` to clean up after the plug-in.

 Calling *zero* as an Embedded Plug-In   Use Navigator to open `single.html`, shown in Listing 3.1. Experiment with various options and see how the plug-in is called. You can find this listing in the source/Chap3/single.html directory at **www. quecorp.com/liveconnect/**.

Listing 3.1   single.html—A Single Instance of the Plug-In

```
<HTML>
<HEAD>
<TITLE>Single</TITLE>
</HEAD>
```

```
<BODY>
Here is the plug-in:
<EMBED TYPE="application/x-npZero" HEIGHT=100 WIDTH=100>
</BODY>
</HTML>
```

Notice that this HTML calls the plug-in by using the TYPE attribute of the EMBED tag because the zero plug-in doesn't use any of the contents of the source stream.

 Starting a Second Copy of *zero* The HTML file double.html, shown in Listing 3.2, has two calls to the plug-in. This listing can be found in the source/Chap3/ double.html directory at **www.quecorp.com/liveconnect/**.

Listing 3.2   double.html—Two Instances of the Plug-In

```
<HTML>
<HEAD>
<TITLE>Single</TITLE>
</HEAD>
<BODY>
Here is the plug-in:
<EMBED TYPE="application/x-npZero" HEIGHT=100 WIDTH=100><BR>
Here is another instance:
<EMBED TYPE="application/x-npZero" HEIGHT=50 WIDTH=50><BR>
</BODY>
</HTML>
```

When this page loads, NPP_Initialize() is only called once, but NPP_New() is called twice—once for each instance. Notice that during resizing, two calls are made to NPP_SetWindow()—again, one for each instance. Similarly, when the window is closed, NPP_Destroy() is called twice and then NPP_Shutdown() is called once.

 Calling *zero* with No Visible Window When Netscape first announced plug-ins for Navigator, they announced that three types of plug-in would be available: embedded, full-page, and background. There are still traces of the "background" or "hidden" type of plug-in in the SDK source code, but the implementation is simplified. To see how hidden plug-ins work, just load hidden.html, shown in Listing 3.3. You can find this listing in the source/Chap3/hidden.html directory at **www.quecorp.com/liveconnect/**.

Listing 3.3 hidden.html—A Hidden Plug-In

```
<HTML>
<HEAD>
<TITLE>Single</TITLE>
</HEAD>
<BODY>
Here is the plug-in:
<EMBED TYPE="application/x-npZero" HIDDEN>
</BODY>
</HTML>
```

Because the plug-in is hidden, Navigator declines to call `NPP_SetWindow()`.

 T I P If your plug-in does any useful work without a window, call this work when you handle `NPP_New()`. `NPP_SetWindow()` is called only when the HIDDEN attribute either isn't present or is set to false directly in the HTML code.

NPN Methods

NPN methods are methods of the Navigator peer object that can be called by the plug-in. This section addresses the design consequences of calling various NPN methods.

NPN_GetURL( )   Figure 3.1 shows what happens when a plug-in calls `NPN_GetURL()`. When the user opens a page that contains an `<EMBED>` tag, Navigator opens the stream and invokes the plug-in. The plug-in, in turn, opens a new URL and directs the content to a specified target. When the new data streams in, Navigator reads the `Content-type` HTTP header and potentially invokes a plug-in to read the stream.

FIG. 3.1
NPN_GetURL( ) can be used to trigger new plug-ins or new copies of the same plug-in.

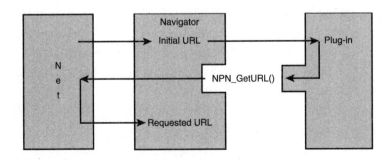

When do you want to run such a sequence? Suppose that you have an existing business application that tracks material being delivered to a warehouse. You access the application, which serves up the data through a CGI or server-side JavaScript program. The first stream of data lists deliveries due today and comes in with its own unregistered MIME media type, application/x-expected_receipts. The plug-in displays the data in its own window, with scroll bars and hot links. When the user passes the cursor over an expected delivery, the status bar shows link information, such as the order ID. If the user selects the link, the plug-in issues NPN_GetURL() to fetch detail information on that delivery. This request goes to a different server script, which returns the data under a different MIME media type, in turn triggering a different plug-in. Figure 3.2 shows the flow of information.

FIG. 3.2
NPN_GetURL() is used here to call for detail information on expected receipts.

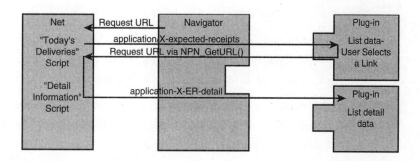

 To give intranet users ready access to an existing application, break this application into client and server portions. Write server scripts, such as CGI or server-side JavaScript programs, to access the server portion of the application. Write plug-ins to display the data on the client machine. Use in-house MIME media types and NPN_GetURL() to integrate the two halves of the application.

NPN_PostURL( )   Many client-server applications need to allow the end user to enter data on the client, which is later processed by the server. In the warehouse business application, for example, a user in the warehouse must inform the system that a particular delivery has arrived. The server then takes this delivery off the "Expected Receipts" list and opens a screen that allows the user to enter the quantity of each item actually received.

HTML forms are often used to post data to the server, but occasionally, this approach is a bit restrictive. In the case of the warehouse application, no one knows how many line items will appear on a given order, so the form can be designed to capture just one line item-quantity pair at a time. This design forces the user to endure network delays after each entry, and makes it difficult to edit the data before sending it to the server for processing. Here's a different design, based on plug-ins:

When the expected receipt arrives, the user opens a "Receive" page, which has a small plug-in waiting to read the Purchase Order number of the expected receipt. After the user enters this number, the plug-in accepts a series of item-number/quantity pairs. The item number is scanned in by a bar code scanner that hooks between the keyboard and the desktop computer (known in the bar code industry as a "wedge"). As each item is entered, it's stored in a data structure in memory on the client computer. It also can be written to the hard drive for added security, in case of a system failure.

If the user enters a line item ID a second time, the second quantity is added to the quantity already stored for this line item. In this way, if the same item comes off the truck on several different pallets, the total quantity is recorded.

When the truck is empty and all the items are counted, the user clicks the Done button, which displays a scrollable list of all items received. The user can review this list, edit it, and print it. Finally, the user selects Send and the list is transferred from the desktop computer to the server by using a series of calls to `NPN_PostURL()`.

This design has the advantage that the data remains on the client as long as it's "local." That is, as long as the warehouse manager has control of the data and can edit it, update it, or print it, he or she has the data on a local computer. When the warehouse manager is ready to announce to the company that the material is now stored in the warehouse, he or she sends this information to the server. The client and the server cooperate to ensure the integrity and validity of the data.

The server, for example, might compare the list of items received with the list of items due in and tell the warehouse manager and the buyer that additional material is still expected on that purchase order (PO). The buyer might allow the PO to remain open, with the remaining items backordered, or she might close the PO, which allows the accounting system to issue a payment for the items that were actually received.

Figure 3.3 illustrates the flow of data through this system.

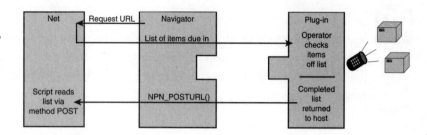

FIG. 3.3
As items are received, the warehouse manager logs them in by using a plug-in.

NPN_UserAgent( ) and NPN_Version( )

Occasionally, you may need to enable certain plug-in features only if they are supported by the browser. By reading the browser's User Agent field, the plug-in can determine information such as the platform (such as 16-bit Windows, 32-bit Windows, or Macintosh) and the version of Navigator.

NPN_Version() returns the major and minor version numbers of both Navigator and the plug-in SDK. Navigator updates the major version number of the SDK every time a new SDK is not backward-compatible with its predecessor. Therefore, if a user attempts to load a version 3 plug-in with a Navigator 2.x, code in the SDK detects the mismatch and forces the plug-in to exit.

 You can use the minor number in the version to check for certain new features or maintenance fixes that, from time to time, may be added to Navigator.

NPN_MemAlloc( ) and Its Kin

When the plug-in needs dynamic memory, you can use built-in routines (malloc() or new) or you can use NPN_MemAlloc(). The advantage of using NPN_MemAlloc() is that the memory is allocated by Navigator. This call has the following two benefits:

- Navigator can free up data structures of its own that are no longer needed, resulting in a smaller memory footprint for the combined Navigator-plug-in application.

- Navigator memory can be preserved by Navigator and made available to later copies of the plug-in.

Often, you know that a call will take memory but you don't know how many bytes the call may require. On the Macintosh, call `NPN_MemFlush()` to request that Navigator free up a block of memory. `NPN_MemFlush()` returns the number of bytes actually freed. Loop through the call until the number of bytes freed is zero (indicating that no more memory can be made available).

CAUTION

Make sure that you use `NPN_MemFree()` to release Navigator memory when you no longer need it. Failure to release memory leads to memory leaks and eventually crashes Navigator.

In C++ dynamic memory is allocated in two steps. The programmer calls `new`, which first allocates the memory and then runs the constructor to initialize the block. You can ensure that all calls to `NPN_MemAlloc()` are balanced with `NPN_MemFree()` by building these calls into `new` and `delete`. The dynamic memory is deallocated by using the second step, which is the operator `Delete()`.

What are `new` and `delete`? They are operators, just like the arithmetic operators + and –. You can override C++'s built-in implementations of `new` and `delete` and write your own for your own classes. For example,

```
TMyClass::operator new(size_t)
{
 NPN_MemAlloc(size_t);
}
TMyClass::operator delete(void* theObject)
{
 NPN_MemFree(theObject);
}
```

Non-class entities (including arrays of objects) are allocated by using the global operator `::operator new()`, and deallocated by using `::operator delete()`. Override these operators if you need to use Navigator memory to store data structures other than objects.

NPN_NewStream( ) `NPN_GetURL()` is used to open a new stream from the server to Navigator. `NPN_NewStream()` is used to open a similar stream from the plug-in to Navigator. The stream can have its own MIME media type and is read in the current window. Navigator reads the content type of the new stream and calls a plug-in or helper application if it cannot handle the media type internally.

`NPN_NewStream()` occupies the same logical position as `Redirect()` occupies in server-side JavaScript, `print "Location...\n\n"` in CGI scripts, and `exec()` in UNIX programming. That is, it replaces the current instance with a new instance. When `NPN_NewStream()` runs, it replaces the current contents of the plug-in window and (potentially) causes a new plug-in to load and be instantiated.

`NPN_NewStream()` is used in connection with `NPN_WriteReady()`, `NPN_Write()`, and `NPN_DestroyStream()`.

NPN_Status( )   One of the lessons learned by the programming community since the mid-1980s is that user interface issues are among the most important issues in program design. In the early days of the Macintosh, memory was tight and Apple provided a toolbox of user-interface routines in ROM. Nearly all Mac programs had the same "look and feel" because they all used the same interface routines. The File Open dialog box is the same on nearly all Macintosh programs.

As time passed Macintoshes with more memory became available, and some programmers tried to improve on the built-in routines. They discovered that Mac users preferred the built-in interface—programs that didn't provide the familiar menu bar and built-in dialogs didn't do well in the marketplace.

The lesson for plug-in developers is clear. Plug-ins are a creature of Netscape Navigator. The plug-ins that do best in the marketplace make the user think that he or she has never left Navigator. The careful plug-in programmer will duplicate the Navigator interface wherever possible.

When a user moves the cursor over a hyperlink in Navigator, for example, the destination appears in the status bar. The plug-in programmer can give the plug-in the same behavior by using `NPN_Status()`, by tracking the mouse-movement messages.

Other NPN Methods   The method `NPN_RequestRead()` is used to request data from a seekable stream. This method is described in greater detail in the "Seekable Streams" section of this chapter.

Navigator also provides four methods that may be used to send data back to the Net through Navigator. `NPN_GetURL()` and `NPN_PostURL()` generate the HTTP transfer methods `GET` and `POST`, respectively. Each method has an associated `...Notify()` method; if you use the `...Notify()` method, your plug-in will be called when Navigator completes the transfer.

If you use the `...Notify()` versions of these methods, Navigator will call your implementation of `NPP_URLNotify()` when the transaction completes.

Moving Existing Applications to the Web

Many plug-ins are built to "Web-enable" existing applications. The warehouse business application referred to previously in this chapter is one example. Often an existing application must be realigned in order to fit into the Web's look and feel. For example, an existing application typically does the following:

- Maps its menu items into the plug-in window because Netscape is already using the menu bar. Sometimes, pop-up menus or other controls are appropriate for this purpose.
- Allows the window to be resized—generally smaller than the full screen the application previously may have enjoyed.
- Is deployed as a shared library or DLL and installed in the Netscape plug-in directory—a rather different approach than is usual with applications.

The ability to link your application to the corporate intranet or World Wide Web can allow your application to take on whole new areas of functionality. Often, much of the cost of developing an application lies in analysis and design—the essence of an application can be "Web-enabled" as a plug-in for a fraction of the cost of developing a full application.

Threads and Processes

Many of the NPN methods do not return a result. Rather, they start Navigator processing and then return almost immediately. As mentioned in the section "Other NPN Methods," versions of the methods are available that call back the plug-in with a notification that the action is complete.

The plug-in programmer can use this same asynchronous behavior in the plug-in. Most operating systems give the programmer a way to start a lightweight process, or thread, that shares the address space with the parent process but follows a separate execution path.

For even more isolation from the other execution path, consider forking a whole new process. (This step is known as *spawning* in some operating systems.) This method frequently is convenient when the core of an existing application can be lifted out of its user interface and called as an asynchronous algorithm.

Accessing the Data

The essence of plug-ins is to take data from the Web and present it to the user, within the context of Netscape Navigator. One of the most important tasks for the plug-in is to access Web data.

Netscape provides three methods for accessing Web data from a URL. The programmer may choose to read and present the data as it comes in from the Net—a process known as *streaming*. Streaming is the preferred method because the user begins to see the data as soon as any of it is available.

An alternate method of accessing the Web data is to allow Navigator to read the entire stream into the cache and then read the data as a whole. This method has two disadvantages.

First, the user must wait until the entire stream is sent before any data is presented. With some file formats, such a design is difficult to avoid. The original JFIF (commonly known as the JPEG image format on the Net) stored some information at the end of the file that was needed to display it. The newer Progressive JPEG files are designed so that the viewer can start work as soon as it has received the first few bytes—a behavior much appreciated by users with a slow modem connection to the Net.

The second disadvantage is that the file may be too large for the cache. In this case Navigator may simply not deliver the file, giving the plug-in a null file name.

The newest and most innovative access method is called seekable streams. An understanding of seekable streams must be based on an understanding of conventional HTTP servers. This topic is taken up in the "Seekable Streams" section of this chapter. The difference between seekable streams and the more conventional kind is that seekable streams are sometimes said to be in pull mode, in contrast with the more conventional push mode.

Part
II

Ch
3

Streaming

When Navigator calls the plug-in's `NPP_NewStream()` method, it passes in a stream mode parameter. The plug-in sets this parameter before it returns. The default setting is `NP_NORMAL`, which means that the contents of the stream will be presented "one byte at a time."

When the stream is delivered in `NP_NORMAL` mode, Navigator delivers the data by using a series of calls to `NPP_Write()`. Navigator tells the plug-in how many bytes are available in the `len` parameter. Under some circumstances the buffer may actually contain more bytes than the `len` parameter advertises. Under these conditions the parameter should process as many bytes as possible, up to the number given in `len`, and should return the number actually processed to Navigator as the return value of the function.

To give Navigator permission to begin writing, the plug-in should respond to the Navigator's call to `NPP_WriteReady()`. Navigator will call `NPP_WriteReady()` to find out how much data the plug-in is ready to accept.

> **N O T E** It's permissible for the plug-in to read fewer bytes in `NPP_Write()` than are actually available, but `NPP_Write()` should be sure to read at least as many bytes as was advertised by `NPP_WriteReady()`, or the number given in the `NPP_Write()` `len` parameter, whichever is smaller. ▓

For efficiency, nearly all of the links between the client and the server buffer their data, so the data probably will arrive in chunks. The plug-in should build these chunks into the data structures associated with this media type and present the data it has as soon as possible.

As File

If the plug-in tells Navigator to save the data as a file (by setting the stream mode to `NP_ASFILE`), Navigator uses its disk caching mechanism as the basis for saving the data to the hard drive. Then it calls the plug-in's `NPP_StreamAsFile()` method and passes a pointer to the file name (referred to as `fname`).

If you want to process the stream as a file in a Navigator 3.0 plug-in, you should set the stream mode to `NP_ASFILEONLY`. This mode is more efficient than `NP_ASFILE` because it reads directly from the file (if the file is local) rather than saving it in the cache. NP_ASFILE remains in the specification to provide backward compatibility with Navigator 2.0.

> **CAUTION**
>
> Make sure that you compare fname with NULL before using it. If an error occurs while Navigator writes the stream to the hard drive, it still may call NPP_StreamAsFile() but sets fname to NULL.

N O T E After the file is in the disk cache, it remains there until the stream or the instance is destroyed. The plug-in can free up disk space by calling NPN_DestroyStream() when it has finished processing the file. ■

Seekable Streams

A Web browser requests an entity from a Web server by using the Hypertext Transport Protocol (HTTP)—the protocol of the Web. With HTTP Version 1.0, the request was all-or-nothing. If the requested entity was a file, the entire file was sent. Over high-speed links this design caused few problems, but with modem-transfer rates sometimes falling below 1,000 bytes per second, the transfer of larger files can take too long for many users' needs.

Newer versions of HTTP support byte-range requests. A client can request just a portion of the file. This design also can be used to allow a client to seek records in a data file on the server, in much the same way that it may read a record from a local hard drive.

If the requested entity is on a server that recognizes the byte-range protocol, the call to NPP_NewStream() will have the Boolean parameter seekable set to true.

N O T E Local disk files are always seekable and afford a good way to test code that depends on seekable streams. ■

It isn't enough that a stream be seekable—the plug-in must explicitly request that the stream be set to mode NP_SEEK. Correspondingly, there is no guarantee of seekablity if the stream is not advertised as "seekable" by the call to

NPP_NewStream(), which should have the Boolean parameter seekable set to true.

When a stream is set up as seekable, the plug-in actively pulls data from the server. (Recall that seekable streams that are set to NP_SEEK mode are in "pull mode".) To request bytes from the stream, the plug-in calls NPN_RequestRead(). Navigator responds by calling NPP_Write() and delivering as much of the data as is available.

Use seekable streams in much the same way as you use fseek() in a conventional application to read records from a hard drive. Suppose that you have a large file on the server stored as a binary tree. Tables 3.1 and 3.2 show the relative times required to fetch an entry from the server. These calculations assume that the file is 10M (megabytes) and that the client connects to the server at 1,700 bytes per second, a typical value for a 14,400 bps (bits per second) modem. Records are assumed to be 100 bytes each. Hard drive access is assumed to take an average of 20 milliseconds. Because the file is organized as a binary tree of records, it takes an average of about eight seeks to find a given record.

Table 3.1 Time to Retrieve a Record from a File, Accessed Through a Non-Seekable Stream

Step	Time
Client sends a GET request for the file	59 milliseconds
Server sends the file to the client	1.7 hours
Client looks up the record from the hard disk	170 milliseconds
Total time	1.7+ hours

Table 3.2   Time to Retrieve a Record from the Server, Using a Seekable Stream

Step	Time
Client sends byte-range requests	502 milliseconds
Server sends the requested records to the client	6.875 seconds
Total Time	7.377 seconds

The advantage of seekable streams becomes stronger as the size of the data file increases. If the file is small or is organized poorly, often it is more efficient to send down the entire file rather than search it over the Net.

The Hollywood Principle

Most formal programming training teaches students to write a complete application. However, applications are often written today as callable routines (although with one entry point—main()). Plug-ins are written as callable libraries with multiple entry points.

Modern object-oriented programs such as Navigator plug-ins are built with the "Hollywood Principle"—"Don't call us, we'll call you." This design can be confusing to programmers trained to follow the flow of control of a program.

Figure 3.4 illustrates classical program design. The program proceeds step by step, as though through a flowchart, from beginning to end.

Modern programs with a graphical user interface have designs more like the one shown in Figure 3.5. The software loops continually, looking for user actions. Depending on the platform, the loop may be part of the application or part of the

Part
II

Ch
3

operating system. When the user takes an action, such as pressing the mouse button, the loop dispatches a message to the underlying software object. (The Macintosh operating system calls these messages "events.") The underlying object handles the message and returns control to the loop. Typical responses to mouse-down messages include popping up a menu, changing the state of a checkbox, or moving the starting point for text entry.

FIG. 3.4

Classical programs proceed through a series of steps and decisions from beginning to end.

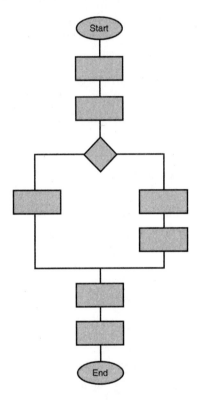

It doesn't matter to the main loop whether the software that handles the message was present when the application was built or was linked in at run-time, as long as the underlying object is there to handle the message when it's called. Therefore, when a plug-in is loaded, it makes itself available to handle messages that occur in the parts of the screen for which it is responsible. If the plug-in instance is deleted later, messages to that part of the screen are directed to the software object that replaces it. Java also uses similar event handling. Figure 3.6 illustrates how a plug-in that loads at run-time handles messages.

FIG. 3.5
Modern programs consist of a loop that issues messages (also known as events) to the program.

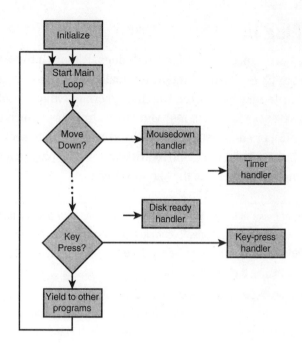

FIG. 3.6
A software object doesn't need to be linked into the application statically in order to be available to handle messages from the main loop.

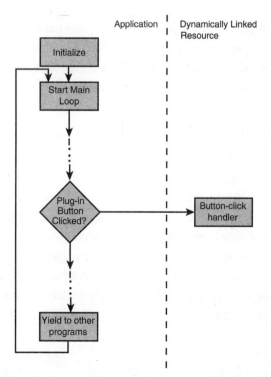

Part

II

Ch

3

Starting the Plug-In

Plug-ins may be full-page, embedded, or hidden. Although these three options are often known as plug-in "types," they are actually three ways of calling a plug-in. The same plug-in may be called through a hyperlink (which results in a full-page plug-in), an <EMBED> tag with HEIGHT and WIDTH attributes (which results in an embedded plug-in), or an <EMBED> tag with the HIDDEN attribute set to true (resulting in a hidden or background plug-in). Navigator tells the plug-in how it was called by setting the mode parameter in the NPP_New() call.

Consider each of these three calling modes when designing your plug-in, and try to do something appropriate for each one. If your plug-in is designed to play an audio stream, for example, and the user calls it as an embedded plug-in, consider displaying a logo in the window and playing the sound anyway.

Similarly, if a video display plug-in is called as a background plug-in, consider popping up a model dialog that tells the user when the plug-in was called incorrectly, perhaps by adding a message that the attributes of HEIGHT and WIDTH in the <EMBED> tag for the URL must be set.

Also note that the HTML coder may place additional parameters and values in an <EMBED> tag. These parameters are passed to the plug-in through the argc, argn, and argv parameters in much the same way as parameters are passed to C and C++ applications when invoked from a command line.

Handling Interaction

For type and document viewers, after the plug-in reads the contents of the stream and draws them into the window, its job is often done. More sophisticated plug-ins may display controls in the window. Scroll bars are a simple example. Pushbuttons, sliders, check boxes, radio buttons, and text fields may all be part of more sophisticated plug-ins. The plug-in programmer can interact with the user by using the mechanisms of the native operating system. Messages or events can be mapped to the parts of the window that serve as controls, allowing the plug-in to change the contents of the window, change an internal state, or communicate back to Netscape and to the network.

TIP Remember that plug-in windows tend to be small—especially for embedded plug-ins. Take care that your plug-in doesn't present so many controls that the user is over- whelmed. Rather, consider offering several plug-ins that communicate with one other. If these plug-ins can run on different machines, you can use the Net for communications. If they all run on a single desktop computer, you can use NPN_NewStream() in one plug- in to generate data for another.

If the plug-in requires many controls at the same time, consider setting up the plug-in as a full-page plug-in to ensure that you have room for all the controls.

Printing

One principal difference between full-page plug-ins and embedded plug-ins is in the way they handle printing. The page is the unit of printing, so Netscape allows full-page plug-ins to control their own printing if necessary.

When the user chooses File, Print while displaying an HTML page with one or more embedded plug-ins, Navigator puts up the printing dialog. It then calls NPP_Print(), which contains the size of the print rectangle and the plug-in, then responds by drawing into the print rectangle.

If the plug-in is full-page, NPP_Print() is called before the print dialog displays, which gives the plug-in an opportunity to modify the print dialog and preset vari- ous controls. If NPP_Print() handles the printing, it should set the parameter pluginPrinted (a component of NPFullPrint, which, in turn, is a component of NPPrint) to true before returning. Otherwise, Navigator itself presents the print dialog and then calls the plug-in to print its contents.

TIP If your full-page plug-in handles its printing, remember the parameters for the dialog box and restore them the next time the user asks to print the same document.

Destroying the Instance

Recall from the beginning of this chapter that Navigator calls NPP_Destroy() when it leaves or closes the window associated with a plug-in instance. It occasionally may be attractive to associate information with the instance. If the user returns to the same URL, Navigator can provide this stored information back to the plug-in.

Part
II

Ch
3

Information about printing defaults, for example, can be associated with a document URL. A plug-in that presents time-based data, such as audio or video, may retain information about the point in the file at which the presentation stopped. When the plug-in is later invoked on the same URL, Navigator restores the time index or frame number so that the plug-in can resume. This design can be attractive, particularly when using seekable streams.

To associate information with a plug-in instance, use `NPN_MemAlloc()` to set up a block of memory, and then store the data in that block. Pass a handle to the block of memory in the `save` parameter of `NPP_Destroy()`.

> **CAUTION**
>
> `NPN_MemAlloc()` returns a pointer to Navigator memory. This memory is not persistent—if the user exits Navigator, information in these blocks is lost. Do not use the `NPP_Destroy()` `save` parameter to store information essential for the plug-in. Rather, use native functions to save the data to the hard drive.

N O T E If you saved data about a specific URL with this plug-in by using the `save` parameter of `NPP_Destroy()` and that data is still available the next time the user visits that URL, the plug-in finds it in the saved parameter of `NPP_New()`.

Designing for Debug

Usually, plug-ins tend to be smaller than complete applications because much of their user interface is already provided by Navigator. Research reported by Steve McConnell in Code Complete (Microsoft Press, 1993) shows that up to 80 percent of the total development time on small programs (around 2,000 lines of code) is taken by the actual construction of the program: detailed design, coding, debugging, and unit testing.

To reduce costs and increase quality in plug-ins, use construction techniques that minimize defects in the code and make it more likely that such defects are caught early.

Get the Compiler to Flag Defects

You can force some defects to be caught by the compiler. A common mistake in C and C++, for example, is to use the assignment operator, =, when you intend to use a comparison operator, ==. The following code is legal C++, but probably is not what the programmer intended:

```
if (myVariable = NULL)
{
  // take some action
}
```

The variable MyVariable is set to NULL. The assignment succeeds, so the if statement takes the "true" path. If the programmer reverses the order of the two elements of the comparison, as in the following example, the compiler will complain because you cannot assign a variable to a constant:

```
if (NULL = MyVariable)
{
  // take some action
}
```

Part
II

Ch
3

TIP Use the C++ const capability to tell the compiler that variables are really constants. For example, the following line of code claims that kFieldLength will not be modified at run-time:

```
const short kFieldLength = 13;
```

If the programmer writes any code that attempts to change the value of kFieldLength, the compiler reports an error.

Many programmers use the convention that an initial lowercase 'k' on a variable's name means that it's a constant. The compiler doesn't care about this naming convention, but its use can help keep you (or the maintenance programmer who comes after you) from becoming confused.

TIP Put const variables first in comparisons so that the compiler will complain if you accidentally forget the second equals sign in the comparison operator.

Use Lint and Warnings

Many examples of code are likely to be defective but nonetheless "legal" C and C++. Most development systems include a program named lint, which sometimes is built into the compiler as a high warning level. If you have lint, use it. If you don't, set the warning level to its highest setting. Set a goal of writing code that generates no warnings. Failing this, make sure that you understand each warning and are confident that it doesn't constitute a defect.

Use the *ASSERT* Macro

Most C/C++ development environments include a macro named ASSERT. This macro takes an expression as a parameter. If the expression is true, the flow of control passes through the macro. If the expression is false, execution stops and the user is told that an ASSERT has failed.

Most environments set up ASSERT so that it's active only when the DEBUG flag is set. In Visual C++, for example, ASSERTs are compiled in when you build the Debug version of the program, but not when you build the Release version.

 TIP Document your assumptions with the ASSERT macro. If you pass a pointer to a function and the pointer should never be NULL, write the following:

```
TMyClass::TMyMethod(TSomeClass* aPointer)
{
 ASSERT(NULL != aPointer);
 .
 .
 .
}
```

During testing, if a chain of circumstances ever conspires to cause aPointer to be NULL, you see the message immediately.

Work with the MFC *ASSERT*s

If you use the Microsoft Foundation Classes, you have undoubtedly run into ASSERT failures coming up from MFC. MFC is loaded with asserts that document the developers' assumptions.

When you receive an ASSERT warning from MFC, note the file name and line number. MFC is a large, complex library, but Microsoft supplies the source code, so you can learn what the ASSERT is complaining about.

If you have Microsoft's Books OnLine, which come with Visual C++, you can search for ASSERT to see a list of each MFC assert and what it means. Use this list and also the MFC source code to understand why your code is triggering the ASSERT.

> **CAUTION**
>
> MFC runs slightly different initialization code depending on whether it's called from an application or a DLL. Consequently, you may see an ASSERT warning when you call a routine from a plug-in, but not when you make the same call from an application.
>
> If you have this problem, write a test harness for your plug-in and follow the failing code in the debugger to see how your code got into the problem. Then go back and change your code so that it doesn't trigger the ASSERT.

Part
II

Ch
3

The NPAvi Plug-In

The "NPAvi" plug-in is easily the most complex plug-in in this book. It includes full LiveConnect integration and exercises nearly all of the NPP methods. This plug-in also uses Microsoft Foundation Classes (MFC) to put up a custom pop-up menu. NPAvi has some of the same capabilities as Netscape's LiveVideo plug-in—one of the major features that distinguishes Navigator 3.0 from Navigator 2.0.

The sample plug-ins described in Chapter 5, "Programming Plug-Ins," were intended purely for illustrative purposes. In contrast, NPAvi could be released as a commercial product and few users would question it.

In this section you will learn:

- How to build NPAvi
- How Netscape's special version of javah builds stub interface classes
- How to use Microsoft Foundation Classes to implement user controls
- About adding resources (from .rc files) to your plug-in
- How to use "dummy commands" to help communications between Java and the plug-in

NPAvi in Action

NPAvi displays a video (in AVI format) inside the Navigator window. (It's intended for use as an embedded plug-in.)

For an idea of how NPAvi looks, start by compiling and then running the plug-in. Because this plug-in uses a Windows-specific AVI engine, Netscape provides a version only for Windows.

Installing the Sun JDK   Chapter 5 describes plug-ins in which the Java classes already have been hooked into the plug-in. This transformation is an essential step in using LiveConnect, Netscape's client-side integration technology. This chapter is a good resource for those of you who are still learning about plug-in functionality.

In the NPAvi project you, as the programmer, are expected to build your own header and interface files from the Java `.class` files. You need the Java compiler, javac, and Netscape's special version of the Java utility javah.

ON THE WEB

Install the Java Developers Kit (JDK) that comes from JavaSoft. You can find the Kit at
http://www.javasoft.com/.

The readme file supplied by Netscape suggests that you install the JDK into a directory named C:\java. Instead, install it in C:\jdk. That way, you can use the makefile's default definition of JDK_ROOT, saving a step (and an opportunity to make a mistake) when building the plug-in with nmake.

Compiling the Plug-In   Unlike the Netscape sample plug-ins in Chapter 5, "Programming Plug-Ins," NPAvi is built from a makefile. Use Microsoft Developer Studio to open Examples\npavi\Source\makefile. Note the message in the file header: you must either set SDK_ROOT and JDK_ROOT in the environment or in your command line. (SDK_ROOT is the directory that contains bin\win32\javah.exe; JDK_ROOT contains bin\javac.exe.) The fastest way to build NPAvi is to specify these directories in the command line. For example, you can type the following:

```
nmake -f makefile JDK_ROOT-\jdk
```

TIP If you leave SDK_ROOT and JDK_ROOT undefined, the makefile has definitions it uses. It defines SDK_ROOT as ..\..\.., which is perfect if you are building in, say, C:\PluginSDK30b5\Examples\npavi\Source\.

If you leave JDK_ROOT undefined, the makefile sets it to c:\jdk\.

TIP If you turn on DEBUG, javah builds type-safe functions rather than macros. Opt for safety, even when you're not building a debug version. Leave DEBUG=1 in the command line all the time.

Building `all` If you previously used any member of the make family (including nmake) you probably know that, by default, make makes the first target it finds in the file. In the Netscape-supplied makefile, that target is specified in the following line:

```
all : java .\objs\$(TARGET).dll
```

Here, $(TARGET) was previously specified by the following:

```
TARGET = npavi32
```

Building `java` The target java includes dirs, $(CLASSES), $(ZIP), $(GEN), and $(STUBS). The target dirs calls the MS-DOS command mkdir for each of the three subdirectories: _gen, _stubs, and objs. These directories are used to hold the results of the builds of the remaining targets.

The target CLASSES resolves to the two targets .\AviPlayer.class and .\AviObserver.class. Toward the bottom of the file is a set of implicit rules. One of these rules, shown on the following lines, says that to make a file of type .class from a file of type .java, run the Java compiler (javac) on the .java file, using the switches given in JAVA_CLASSES:

```
java.class:
 $(JAVAC) $(JAVA_CLASSES) $<
```

These switches resolve to -classpath ..\..\..\classes\moz3_0.zip.

 TIP You can change JAVA_CLASSES if you need to keep your Netscape classes someplace else. Remember, however, that Netscape has a reputation for bringing out a new release of Navigator every few months. You may find it easier to leave the makefile alone and just install the file of the SDK in their default locations.

> **CAUTION**
>
> The file moz3_0.zip is used by Netscape as a convenient package for their Java classes. Under no circumstances should you use WinZip, PKUNZIP, or similar tools to unzip moz3_0.zip.

The target ZIP resolves to three files:

- ._gen\java_lang_Object.h
- ._gen\netscape_plugin_Plugin.h
- ._stubs\netscape_plugin_Plugin.c

These three files are rebuilt with explicit rules every time moz3_0.zip changes. They are built by using a special Java Runtime Interface (JRI) version of the utility javah. The JRI version is produced by Netscape—it builds .h and .c files based on the contents of Java source files.

N O T E   Note that the -jri switch must be on for the Netscape-enhanced version of javah to work correctly. ▓

The real work of javah is to produce header files (which go in the _gen directory) and stub C files (which go in the stub directory). The make targets GEN and STUBS resolve to the header and stub files for the two Java classes AviObserver and AviPlayer. When you build your plug-in, use this makefile as a starting point and change GEN and STUBS to name your own Java classes. The "Implicit Rules" section of the makefile contains rules for transforming .class files to .h and .c files, using javah.

Building .\objs\$(TARGET).dll   The final target associated with all is .\objs\$(TARGET).dll. (By substituting your project name into TARGET, you can easily customize this makefile to generate your own plug-in.) This target depends (via an explicit rule) on $(TARGET).def, $(OBJS), and $(RES). The .def file, of course, is written by hand and identifies the three entry points required of every plug-in:

- ▨ NP_GetEntryPoints
- ▨ NP_Initialize
- ▨ NP_Shutdown

Except for changing the name of the library, you seldom need to edit your plug-in's .def file.

OBJS, of course, lists the object files, which are generated (via implicit rule) from the C++ source files of your plug-in.

Note that NPAvi includes a resource file, npAVI32.res. The final implicit rule in the makefile describes how to run the resource compiler to transform a .rc file into the .res file.

Moving the Files into Position   After you've built the plug-in using nmake, your Source directory will contain the files AviObserver.class and AviPlayer.class, and the objs subdirectory contains npavi32.dll.

Copy the two Java class files and the .dll file to the Navigator plug-ins directory.

You must now restart Navigator. Make sure that you're using a version of Navigator that is at least at v3.0b5, or you won't see all the features of this plug-in working.

Running the Plug-In   When Navigator restarts, it examines the files in the plug-ins directory and registers plug-ins based on their MIME media type.

After Navigator is up, use File, Open File to open Examples\npAVI\Testing \npAVIExample.html. You probably want to bookmark this page while you learn about plug-ins.

As soon as it opens, NPAvi downloads its stream and displays the first frame of the movie. Figure 3.7 shows the npAVIExample.html user interface. The plug-in is now waiting for commands that you enter through the buttons via JavaScript.

NPAvi displays its first frame immediately and then pauses the movie. You can use the controls to stop and resume the movie or to seek directly to a specific frame. (The default movie, "seahorse.avi," has 199 frames.)

FIG. 3.7
NPAvi reads from a
stream and writes
to the window. It's
also listening to
JavaScript, waiting
for a user to press
a button.

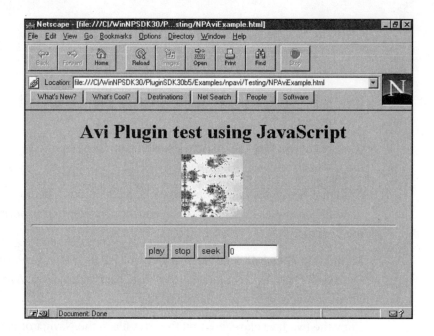

Use Navigator's View, Document Source to see how the buttons are hooked up.
The start and stop buttons call `document.avi.play(false)` and
`document.avi.stop(false)`, respectively. The seek button picks up the value of the
frame field through JavaScript:

```
onclick="document.avi.seek(false, parseInt(form.editSeek.value))"
```

Putting NPAvi into a Project   In its default configuration, you can't use Microsoft
Developer Studio's ClassView to open that function because Netscape has not built
NPAvi into a project.

You can take advantage of ClassView by choosing File, New, Project Workspace.
Select "Makefile" from the list of possible project types and give the project a new
name and path.

Microsoft Developer Studio offers to take you to the Project Settings dialog box,
where you can specify the path to the makefile. (See Figure 3.8.) Answer "Yes" to
this offer.

FIG. 3.8

When you build a
new project from a
makefile, Microsoft
Developer Studio
offers to hook up the
makefile for you.

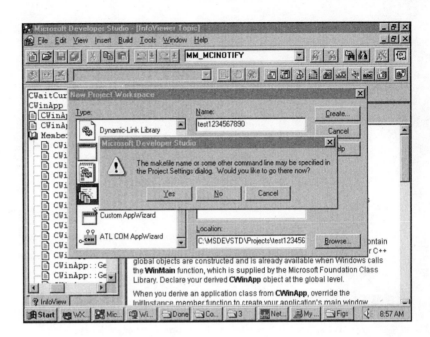

If you want to use this project to build the plug-in, as well as the way to examine classes, fill in the command line field in the Project Settings dialog with your real nmake command line, including DEBUG=1, if you're using it. Make sure that you specify the path of the makefile relative to the project directory. (If you're copying the files into the project directory and have set up the SDK and JDK following the recommended values, use nmake -f makefile DEBUG=1.) Figure 3.9 shows this dialog box.

If you just want to examine the NPAvi files, use Insert, Files into Project... to make the NPAvi .cpp and .rc files in the Examples\npavi\Source directory a part of the new project. To use npAPI as a starting point for your plug-in, copy the npAPI files to the new project directory, and then add them into the project. In this way, all changes you make become part of the new project and you won't inadvertently change NPAvi.

Part
II

Ch
3

FIG. 3.9
By building a project around the makefile, you get the benefits of Microsoft Developer Studio without the complexity of a custom build.

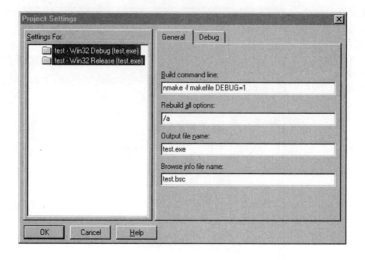

Flow of Control

NPAvi is a sophisticated plug-in that uses nearly all the NPP methods. Open npshell.cpp to begin the process of tracing this plug-in's flow of control.

 If you're new to plug-ins, read Chapter 5. Simple is far smaller than NPAvi, so some of its interaction is easier to follow. Then move on to CharFlipper. When you understand these plug-ins, come back here to NPAvi, the most sophisticated of the bunch.

Follow Navigator As you saw when you ran Simple and CharFlipper, a plug-in has two interfaces—one to Navigator and another to the user. Because the plug-in can't do anything with the user until most of its Navigator functions are called, this section starts by tracing the flow of control between Navigator and NPAvi. Follow along on Figure 3.10.

How NPAvi is Called Unlike Simple (but like CharFlipper) NPAvi reads a stream—in this case, an AVI movie. Because this stream is a local file, there is no server to translate the file extension into a MIME type. Rather, Navigator looks at the file extensions registered by each plug-in and determines that files with suffix .avi get handled by NPAvi.

FIG. 3.10

Navigator makes a series of calls to the plug-in to get things started.

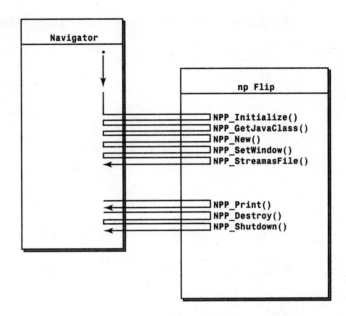

> **CAUTION**
>
> Because the file extension `.avi` and the MIME media types `video/msvideo` and `video/x-msvideo` are so common, you already may have a plug-in configured to handle these types. In Navigator, select Help, About Plug-ins to display the list of configured plug-ins. Figure 3.11 shows the table that describes NPAvi.
>
> If NPAVI32 isn't listed as handling Video for Windows, temporarily remove the conflicting plug-in from the plug-ins subdirectory (the one named "plugins"), restart Navigator, and check Help, About Plug-ins again.

NPP_Initialize() When Navigator sees the <EMBED> tag, it looks up the plug-in that registered to handle files with suffix ".avi". Navigator finds npAVI32 and loads this library into its address space. Then it exchanges entry points. `NPP_Initialize()` is the first method it calls for which you, the programmer, are responsible.

FIG. 3.11

Be sure that about:plugins shows NPAvi handling the Video for Windows types.

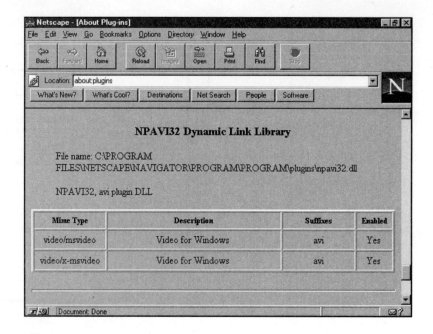

If you build NPAvi into a project as previously described, you can use Microsoft Developer Studio's ClassView to open this function. (It's in the Globals folder because it isn't part of any class.)

You will see that NPP_Initialize() is less than trivial: It simply returns NPERROR_NO_ERROR.

NPP_GetJavaClass()   NPP_GetJavaClass() follows a classic design: NPAvi gets a pointer to the Java runtime environment through NPN_GetJavaEnv(). Then it calls the use... function for each of the Java classes: netscape.plugin.Plugin, AviObserver, and AviPlayer. The function returns the reference from use_AviPlayer(). Here's the implementation of NPP_GetJavaClass().

```
jref NPP_GetJavaClass(void)
{
 JRIEnv* env = NPN_GetJavaEnv();
 use_netscape_plugin_Plugin(env);
 use_AviObserver(env);
 return use_AviPlayer(env);
}
```

The use... functions like `use_netscape_plugin_Plugin()` and `use_AviObserver()` are written by javah.

NPP_New()   Now Navigator is ready to make the plug-in instance. Open `NPP_New()` with ClassWizard. Note that the new instance parses out the `autostart` and `loop` parameters from `argv`. Then it builds a `CPluginWindow`, which is used as the basis for instance data.

```
// NPP_New
//
// create a new plugin instance
// handle any instance specific code initialization here
//
NPError NP_LOADDS
NPP_New(NPMIMEType pluginType,
    NPP instance,
    uint16 mode,
    int16 argc,
    char* argn[],
    char* argv[],
    NPSavedData* saved)
{
 BOOL bAutoStart, bLoop;
 // CPluginWindow is the main plugin object. Keep state information
 // about the specific instance to be created
 CPluginWindow* pluginData;
 // trap a NULL ptr
 if (instance == NULL)
  return NPERR_INVALID_INSTANCE_ERROR;
 // extract the pseudo command line arguments which were passed as
 // attributes in the embed tag of the document
 // for this example the plugin takes a true/false value for both
 // autostart and loop to determine the plugin style characteristics
 bAutoStart = FALSE;
 bLoop = FALSE;
 for (int idx =0; idx<argc; idx++) {
  if (!strcmpi(argn[idx],"autostart")) {
   if (!strcmpi(argv[idx],"true")) {
    bAutoStart = TRUE;
   }
  }
  if (!strcmpi(argn[idx],"loop")) {
   if (!strcmpi(argv[idx],"true")) {
    bLoop = TRUE;
   }
  }
```

continues

Part
II

Ch

3

```
    }
    // create a data pointer to pass around with the instance
    pluginData = new CPluginWindow (bAutoStart, bLoop, mode, instance);
    // save my data pointer in the instance pdata pointer
    instance->pdata = pluginData;
    // this will be passed back to me in all calls so that I
    // can extract it later
    return NPERR_NO_ERROR;
}
```

Because you encapsulated NPAvi in a project, you can read the definition of CPluginWindow by using ClassView. Double-click the class name at the top of the ClassView pane. (You can view the implementation by expanding that branch of the tree and double-clicking the member name.) Figure 3.12 shows CPluginWindow as viewed through ClassView.

FIG. 3.12
Use ClassView to examine the classes of NPAvi.

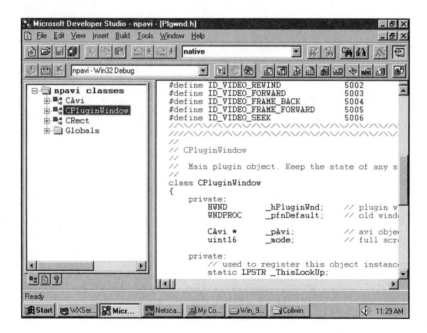

NPP_SetWindow() NPP_SetWindow() quickly gets through to CPluginWindow::SetWindow(). It lets the work be done by this class member and then calls InvalidateRect() and UpdateWindow() so that the plug-in gets a new WM_PAINT message and redraws the window's contents. Here's the implementation of NPP_SetWindow(), from npshell.cpp:

```
// NPP_SetWindow
//
// Associates a platform specific window handle with a plug-in instance.
//   Called multiple times while, e.g., scrolling. Can be called for
//   three reasons:
//
//      1. A new window has been created
//      2. A window has been moved or resized
//      3. A window has been destroyed
//
// There is also the degenerate case; that it was called spuriously, and
// the window handle and or coords may have or have not changed, or
// the window handle and or coords may be ZERO. State information
// must be maintained by the plug-in to correctly handle the degenerate
// case.
//
NPError NP_LOADDS
NPP_SetWindow(NPP instance, NPWindow* window)
{
 // strange...
 if (!window)
  return NPERR_GENERIC_ERROR;
 // strange...
 if (!instance)
  return NPERR_INVALID_INSTANCE_ERROR;
 // get back the plugin instance object
 CPluginWindow * pluginData = (CPluginWindow *)instance->pdata;
 if (pluginData) {
  if (!window->window) {
   // watch out this case.
   // window went away
   //delete pluginData; (?????)
   return NPERR_NO_ERROR;
  }
  if (!pluginData->GetWndProc()) {
   //\\// First time in //\\//
   // grab the handle so we can control the messages flow
   pluginData->SetWindow((HWND)window->window);
  }
  // resize or moved window (or newly created)
  InvalidateRect(*pluginData, NULL, TRUE);
  UpdateWindow(*pluginData);
  return NPERR_NO_ERROR;
 }
 // return an error if no object defined
 return NPERR_GENERIC_ERROR;
}
```

Part

II

Ch

3

`CPluginWindow::SetWindow()` is quite short: it simply subclasses the Netscape-supplied window with our own `CPluginWindow::PluginWndProc`:

```
// SetWindow
//
// store the window handle and subclass the window proc
// Associate "this" with the window handle so we can redirect window
// messages to the proper instance
//
void
CPluginWindow::SetWindow(HWND hWnd)
{
 hPluginWnd = hWnd;
 // subclass
 pfnDefault = (WNDPROC)::SetWindowLong(hWnd,
                    GWL_WNDPROC,
                    (LONG)CPluginWindow::
                    PluginWndProc);
 // register "this" with the window structure
 ::SetProp(hWnd, CPluginWindow::ThisLookUp, (HANDLE)this);
}
```

Figure 3.13 illustrates how the components of `NPP_SetWindow()` communicate.

FIG. 3.13
As a result of calling
NPP_SetWindow(),
CPluginWindow:
:PluginWndProc is
installed as the new
WindowProc for the
plug-in's window.

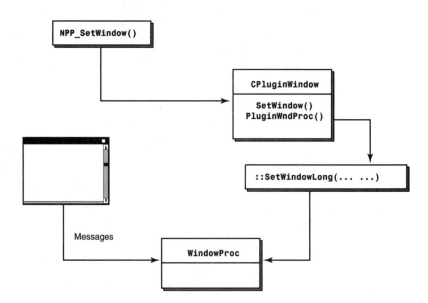

`CPluginWindow::PluginWndProc()` is defined in plgwnd.cpp, as follows:

```
// PluginWndProc
//
// static member function of CPluginWindow
// this is the window proc used to subclass the plugin window the
// navigator created and passed in NPP_SetWindow (npshell.c)
//
LRESULT CALLBACK
CPluginWindow::PluginWndProc(HWND hWnd,
              UINT Msg,
              WPARAM WParam,
              LPARAM lParam)
{
 // pull out the instance object receiving the message
 CPluginWindow* pluginObj =
  (CPluginWindow*)GetProp(hWnd,
              CPluginWindow::ThisLookUp);
 // message switch
 switch (Msg) {
 case WM_LBUTTONDOWN:
  {
  POINT p;
  p.x = LOWORD(lParam);
  p.y = HIWORD(lParam);
  pluginObj->OnLButtonDown(WParam, &p);
  break;
  }
 case WM_RBUTTONDOWN:
  {
  POINT p;
  p.x = LOWORD(lParam);
  p.y = HIWORD(lParam);
  pluginObj->OnRButtonDown(WParam, &p);
  break;
  }
 case WM_PAINT:
  {
  PAINTSTRUCT PaintStruct;
  ::BeginPaint(hWnd, &PaintStruct);
  pluginObj->OnPaint();
  ::EndPaint(hWnd, &PaintStruct);
  break;
  }
 case WM_PALETTECHANGED:
  pluginObj->OnPaletteChanged((HWND)WParam);
 break;
 // the following two messages are used from the CAvi class
 // MM_MCINOTIFY informs about a stop event
 case MM_MCINOTIFY:
  pluginObj->GetAviStream().OnStop();
```

Part
II

Ch
3

```
      break;
      // WM_TIMER is used to update the position status
      case WM_TIMER:
       pluginObj->GetAviStream().OnPositionChange();
      break;
      // menu handling
      // pass to CPluginWindow instance? (too much work...)
      //
      // WARNING
      // those ids are also used from the native functions (avijava.cpp)
      // when the flag isAsync is set to TRUE (see avijava.cpp
      // and AviPlayer.java)
      case WM_COMMAND:
       if (!HIWORD(WParam)) {
        switch LOWORD(WParam) {
         case ID_VIDEO_PLAY:
          pluginObj->OnLButtonDown(0, 0);
          return 0;
         case ID_VIDEO_STOP:
          pluginObj->GetAviStream().Stop();
          return 0;
         case ID_VIDEO_REWIND:
          pluginObj->GetAviStream().Rewind();
          return 0;
         case ID_VIDEO_FORWARD:
          pluginObj->GetAviStream().Forward();
          return 0;
         case ID_VIDEO_FRAME_BACK:
          pluginObj->GetAviStream().FrameBack();
          return 0;
         case ID_VIDEO_FRAME_FORWARD:
          pluginObj->GetAviStream().FrameForward();
          return 0;
         // this is hidden to the menu but it's used from
         // the java class in asynchronous mode (see AviPlayer.java
         // and avijava.cpp)
         case ID_VIDEO_SEEK:
          pluginObj->GetAviStream().Seek(lParam);
          return 0;
         }
        }
        default:
        return CallWindowProc(pluginObj->GetWndProc(), hWnd, Msg, WParam,
        ➥lParam);
       };
       return 0;
      }
```

Notice that CPluginWindow::PluginWndProc() includes handlers for WM_LBUTTONDOWN, WM_RBUTTONDOWN, and WM_COMMAND, and also the now-expected

WM_PAINT. When the user clicks the left mouse button,
CPluginWindow::OnLButtonDown() gets called—this method toggles the run state of
the AVI movie.

When the user right-clicks the mouse, the plug-in calls the Windows global function ::CreatePopupMenu() and reads strings from the string table in the resource
file to populate the menu.

Here's the implementation of OnRButtonDown():

```
// OnRButtonDown
//
// bring up a menu with avi commands
//
void
CPluginWindow::OnRButtonDown(UINT uFlags, LPPOINT pPoint)
{
 UINT uState;
 char szMenuString[128];

 // Create the popup.
 HMENU hPopup = ::CreatePopupMenu();
 if(hPopup == 0) {
  return;
 }
 if(_pAvi->isPlaying())
  uState = MF_GRAYED;
 else
  uState = MF_ENABLED;
 //"Play..."
 ::LoadString(g_hDllInstance, MENU_PLAY, szMenuString, 128);
 ::AppendMenu(hPopup, uState, ID_VIDEO_PLAY, szMenuString);
 //"Pause..."
 ::LoadString(g_hDllInstance, MENU_PAUSE, szMenuString, 128);
 ::AppendMenu(hPopup, !uState, ID_VIDEO_STOP, szMenuString);
 // Separator
 ::AppendMenu(hPopup, MF_SEPARATOR, 0, 0);
 uState = MF_ENABLED;
 //"Rewind (Start of movie)..."
 ::LoadString(g_hDllInstance, MENU_REWIND, szMenuString, 128);
 ::AppendMenu(hPopup, uState, ID_VIDEO_REWIND, szMenuString);
 //"Forward (End of movie)..."
 ::LoadString(g_hDllInstance, MENU_FORWARD, szMenuString, 128);
 ::AppendMenu(hPopup, uState, ID_VIDEO_FORWARD, szMenuString);
 // Separator
 ::AppendMenu(hPopup, MF_SEPARATOR, 0, 0);
 //"Frame Back..."
 ::LoadString(g_hDllInstance, MENU_FRAME_BACK, szMenuString, 128);
 ::AppendMenu(hPopup, uState, ID_VIDEO_FRAME_BACK, szMenuString);
```

```
//"Frame Forward..."
::LoadString(g_hDllInstance, MENU_FRAME_FORWARD, szMenuString, 128);
::AppendMenu(hPopup, uState, ID_VIDEO_FRAME_FORWARD, szMenuString);
::ClientToScreen(_hPluginWnd, pPoint);
::TrackPopupMenu(hPopup,
        TPM_LEFTALIGN ¦ TPM_RIGHTBUTTON,
        pPoint->x,
        pPoint->y,
        0,
        hPluginWnd,
        NULL);
}
```

T I P To add new commands to the menu, just add a string for the menu item in the string table and add the string to the menu in CPluginWindow::OnRButtonDown(). Then add the handler for the new command in the WM_COMMAND section of CPluginWindow::PluginWndProc.

NPP_NewStream( ), NPP_StreamAsFile( )   Movies (AVI and also other formats) take too much bandwidth to play in realtime. NPAvi specifies *stype=NP_ASFILE so that the entire movie is downloaded to the cache. Here's the implementation of NPP_NewStream():

```
// NPP_NewStream
//
// Notifies the plugin of a new data stream.
// The data type of the stream (a MIME name) is provided.
// The stream object indicates whether it is seekable.
// The plugin specifies how it wants to handle the stream.
//
// In this case, I set the streamtype to be NPAsFile. This tells the
// Navigator the plugin doesn't handle streaming and can only deal with
// the object as a complete disk file. It will still call the write
// functions but it will also pass the filename of the cached file in
// a later NPE_StreamAsFile call when it is done transferring the file.
//
// If a plugin handles the data in a streaming manner, it should set
// streamtype to NPNormal (e.g. *streamtype = NPNormal)...the NPE_
// StreamAsFile function will never be called in this case
//
NPError NP_LOADDS
NPP_NewStream(NPP instance,
        NPMIMEType type,
        NPStream *stream,
        NPBool seekable,
        uint16 *stype)
```

```
{
 if(!instance)
  return NPERR_INVALID_INSTANCE_ERROR;
 // save the plugin instance object in the stream instance
 stream->pdata = instance->pdata;
 *stype = NP_ASFILE;
 return NPERR_NO_ERROR;
}
```

Then `NPP_StreamAsFile()` is called so that the player can play the movie from the hard drive. Here's how this function is implemented:

```
// NPP_StreamAsFile
//
// The stream is done transferring and here is a pointer to the file
// in the cache. This function is only called if the streamtype was
// set to NPAsFile.
//
void NP_LOADDS
NPP_StreamAsFile(NPP instance, NPStream *stream, const char* fname)
{
 if(fname == NULL |¦ fname[0] == NULL)
  return;
 // get back the plugin instance object
 CPluginWindow * pluginData = (CPluginWindow *)instance->pdata;
 // get the avi object controller
 CAvi& aviPlayer = pluginData->GetAviStream();
 // open the avi driver with the specified name
 aviPlayer.Open(*pluginData, fname);
 aviPlayer.Update();
 // The AVI window Update() paint doesn't work in Win95.
 // It works fine in NT and Win3.1, but Win95 is doing something
 // hostile. So, I have a hack here that steps the frame forward
 // to paint the window; barf ...
 // figure out whether to hack for Win 95
 DWORD dwVer = GetVersion();
 int iVer = (LOBYTE(LOWORD(dwVer))*100)+HIBYTE(LOWORD(dwVer));
 if(iVer > 394) {
  // Win 95
  aviPlayer.FrameForward();
 }
}
```

`NPP_StreamAsFile()` gets the `aviPlayer` object (`_pAvi`) built into `CPluginWindow`, directs it to open on the Netscape-supplied filename, and calls the player's `Update` method. These Java-based methods are described in following sections of this chapter.

NPP_Print( ) `NPP_Print()` is hooked up, drawing a rectangle onto the print window's device context. Here's the implementation of `NPP_Print()`:

```
// NPP_Print
//
// Printing the plugin (to be continued...)
//
void NP_LOADDS
NPP_Print(NPP instance, NPPrint* printInfo)
{
 if(printInfo == NULL)  // trap invalid parm
  return;
 if (instance != NULL) {
  CPluginWindow* pluginData = (CPluginWindow*) instance->pdata;
  pluginData->Print(printInfo);
 }
}
The work is done in CPluginWindow::Print(), shown here:
// Print
//
void
CPluginWindow::Print(NPPrint* printInfo) const
{
 if (printInfo->mode == NP_FULL) {
  //
  // *Developers*: If your plugin would like to take over
  // printing completely when it is in full-screen mode,
  // set printInfo->pluginPrinted to TRUE and print your
  // plugin as you see fit. If your plugin wants Netscape
  // to handle printing in this case, set printInfo->pluginPrinted
  // to FALSE (the default) and do nothing. If you do want
  // to handle printing yourself, printOne is true if the
  // print button (as opposed to the print menu) was clicked.
  // On the Macintosh, platformPrint is a THPrint; on Windows,
  // platformPrint is a structure (defined in npapi.h) containing
  // the printer name, port, etc.
  //
  void* platformPrint = printInfo->print.fullPrint.platformPrint;
  NPBool printOne = printInfo->print.fullPrint.printOne;
  printInfo->print.fullPrint.pluginPrinted = FALSE; // Do the default
 }
 else {
  // If not fullscreen, we must be embedded
  //
  // *Developers*: If your plugin is embedded, or is full-screen
  // but you returned false in pluginPrinted above, NPP_Print
  // will be called with mode == NP_EMBED. The NPWindow
```

```
    // in the printInfo gives the location and dimensions of
    // the embedded plugin on the printed page. On the Macintosh,
    // platformPrint is the printer port; on Windows, platformPrint
    // is the handle to the printing device context.
    //
    NPWindow* printWindow = &(printInfo->print.embedPrint.window);
    void* platformPrint = printInfo->print.embedPrint.platformPrint;
    HPEN hPen, hPenOld;
#ifdef WIN32
    /* Initialize the pen's "brush" */
    LOGBRUSH lb;
    lb.lbStyle = BS_SOLID;
    lb.lbColor = RGB(128, 128, 128);
    lb.lbHatch = 0;
    hPen = ::ExtCreatePen(PS_COSMETIC ¦ PS_SOLID, 1, &lb, 0, NULL);
#else
    COLORREF cref = RGB(128, 128, 128);
    hPen = ::CreatePen(PS_SOLID, 32, cref);
#endif
    HDC hDC = (HDC)(DWORD)platformPrint;
    hPenOld = (HPEN)::SelectObject(hDC, hPen);
    BOOL result = ::Rectangle(hDC,
                  (int)(printWindow->x),
                  (int)(printWindow->y),
                  (int)(printWindow->x + printWindow->width),
                  (int)(printWindow->y + printWindow->height));
    ::SelectObject(hDC, hPenOld);
    ::DeleteObject(hPen);
  }
}
```

Part
II

Ch
3

Although this Print() function doesn't attempt to print the contents of the plug-in window, it at least prints a rectangle as a place-holder on the page with an embedded plug-in. You can use this routine as a starting point for the implementation of NPP_Print() in your plug-in, and then replace the call to ::Rectangle() with something more meaningful for your plug-in's content.

LiveConnect Details

The real work of NPAvi is done through the Java classes. Much of this work, in turn, is implemented back in the plug-in through native methods Figure 3.14 shows the interaction between JavaScript, Java, and the plug-in.

FIG. 3.14
Although the plug-in and JavaScript cannot talk directly, the Java peer object is quick and easy to set up.

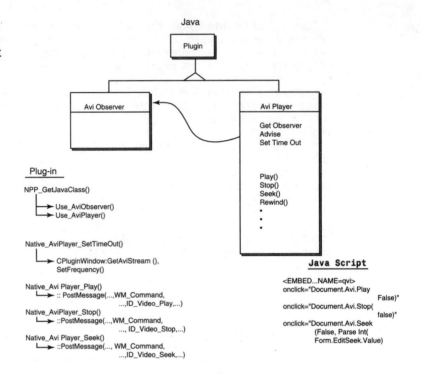

Examining the Java Code   Open the file AviPlayer.java. (You have to use File, Open; .java files are not part of the project.) Note that class AviPlayer includes a private member, AviObserver. This section looks at the implementation of both classes.

 Make sure that you turn on the browser information to make it easier to trace from one class and method to the next.

Java Class AviPlayer   Most of the methods in class AviPlayer are native. Follow the thread of control out of class AviPlayer and back to AviPlayer.c, in the _stubs directory. Pick one function, such as SetTimeOut(). SetTimeOut() is specified as native in AviPlayer.java, so it appears in the stub file AviPlayer.c. Here's the native declaration, in AviPlayer.java:

```
public class AviPlayer extends Plugin {
    .
    .
    .
    // set the timeout for the position checking timer
    public native void setTimeOut(int timeout);
    .
    .
    .
}
```

Note, also, that by specifying DEBUG you get the typesafe C function
AviPlayer_setTimeOut() rather than the macro. AviPlayer_setTimeOut() relies on
use_AviPlayer_setTimeOut() being called as part of use_AviPlayer. (Recall that
use_AviPlayer() was called by NPP_GetJavaClass().)

The programmer's implementations for native methods such as SetTimeOut() are
in the file avijava.cpp. There, you learn that native_AviPlayer_setTimeOut() calls
CAvi::SetFrequency(), which, in turn, calls the Window API ::SetTimer():

```
extern "C" JRI_PUBLIC_API(void)
native_AviPlayer_setTimeOut(JRIEnv* env, struct AviPlayer* self,
➥jint timeout)
{
 NPP instance = (NPP)self->getPeer(env);
 CPluginWindow* pPluginData = (CPluginWindow*)instance->pdata;
 pPluginData->GetAviStream().SetFrequency(timeout);
}
```

N O T E The timer in NPAvi is used in much the same way as the timer in CharFlipper is
used—it sets the pace for the playback, so that each frame pauses on-screen
long enough for the user to see it. The timer in an AVI movie, of course, runs on a much
shorter interval than the timer in CharFlipper. ■

***Java Interface* AviObserver**   Recall that the Java class AviPlayer includes a
private member of type AviObserver. To understand AviObserver start from a plug-
in member such as CAvi::OnStop(). When Windows sends the MM_MCINOTIFY
message, the WindowsProc dispatches CAvi::OnStop(). This method is
implemented by getting the Java peer object (with NPN_GetJavaPeer()) and then
retrieving a pointer to its observer. Finally, CAvi::OnStop() calls the observer's
onStop() method.

How the JavaScript and HTML Are Connected   The buttons of the form directly call methods of the Java applet. This form directs the function calls such as `play()` to the named plug-in.

Closing Down the Plug-In   When the interaction is over and the user is ready to leave NPAvi, Navigator calls `NPP_Destroy()`. Because there is only one instance, `NPP_Shutdown()` is called immediately after the instance is deleted. The implementation of `NPP_Destroy()` follows the standard pattern—it deletes pdata and resets that pointer to NULL:

```
// NPP_Destroy
//
// Deletes a plug-in instance and releases all of its resources.
//
NPError NP_LOADDS
NPP_Destroy(NPP instance, NPSavedData** save)
{
 CPluginWindow * pluginData = (CPluginWindow *)instance->pdata;
 delete pluginData;
 instance->pdata = 0;
 return NPERR_NO_ERROR;
}
```

Note that `NPP_Destroy` has hooks for all the usual plug-in features, including NPSavedData. Although the function isn't used here, it can be hooked up easily.

From Here...

Plug-ins consist of two cooperating objects. One object, the plug-in object, has methods that you, as the plug-in programmer, write. Navigator calls these methods to get information from the plug-in or to give it information. The other object, the Netscape peer object, is written by Netscape and lives "inside" Navigator. You call the peer object to get information from Navigator or to ask Navigator to take certain actions. Methods of the plug-in object start with "NPP_" and methods of the Netscape peer object start with "NPN_".

■ The next chapter, "Creating Plug-Ins," looks at creating plug-ins for Windows and Macintosh platforms.

- Chapter 5, "Programming Plug-Ins," looks plug-ins and HTML, as well as Simple and CharFlipper LiveConnect plug-ins.
- Chapter 6, "Developing Content for Plug-Ins," looks at LiveCache and CD-ROM developing.
- Chapter 8, "Calling Java Methods from Plug-Ins," shows how fields are accessed, Java names and parameters, as well as security issues.
- Chapter 9, "Calling the Plug-In from Java Methods," shows how to define a Plug-in Class as well as more about native methods and globals.

Part
II

Ch
3

CHAPTER 4

Creating Plug-Ins

As our civilization becomes increasingly dependent upon computers, many people foresee a shortage of programmers. Foresee? It's *here!* And those of us *in* the industry have to be the ones to do something about it.

One solution that seems to be firming up is the concept of *component architectures*. In this model, programmers build sophisticated software components—small tools that do various jobs. Then end users, or others who are not professional programmers, put these components together into an application.

With LiveConnect, Netscape gives sophisticated end users a way to control complex components (plug-ins and Java applets) from a relatively simple language—JavaScript—bringing component architecture to the Web. ∎

Small, Sharp Tools versus Monolithic Code

Small, sharp tools can be assembled into applications that are more powerful than monolithic code. In the "UNIX-style" versus "Microsoft-style" design war, history favors the little guy.

How to Manually Install a Plug-In

If you write plug-ins for all three major platforms, you should be aware of subtle differences.

How Netscape Loads Plug-Ins

You can use JavaScript to find out which plug-ins are on the client's machine.

How to Write an HTML Page that Checks for Your Plug-In

Have your Web site initiate a download.

About the Assisted Installation Process

Navigator will help your users find your site.

About MIME Type Conflict

If your plug-in conflicts with others, you may be able to walk users through a conflict resolution process.

Compound Documents

Object Linking and Embedding (OLE) technology is designed to allow users to build *compound documents*. With in-place activation (also known as *Visual Editing*) and OLE automation, the components of a compound document do more than just look good—they can be changed in place by the user or by other software. The distinction between "program" and "data" was never blurrier. This transition from a world in which end users have to think about which application they are using to one in which end users just manipulate their data (and let the system figure out which application to use) is known as *document-centric computing*.

Document-Centric Computing Meets the Web

This brings us back to the Web. Today, when a user wants to access the Web, he or she launches an application—Netscape. If they want to copy some content from a Web page to a word-processing document, they have to launch their word processor and copy (or drag) the contents from one window to the next. If Apple's Cyberdog is any indication, in the next generation of software the user may start by opening a document. They would put in text content by typing. They would put in graphics content by drawing. And they could put in Web content by... surfing?

In this scenario the embedded plug-in becomes an agent, controlled in part by the end user (through interaction) and in part by the page into which it is embedded. When copied or dragged into a compound document, the plug-in negotiates its content with this document, and either embeds its content or maintains a link through the browser back to the Net.

Although it may take a professional programmer to write a plug-in, the end user is fully able to assemble content into a compound document. So it is the end user who builds the solution (which was once called an application), using these professionally developed components.

The UNIX Way

There is adequate precedent for the success of this approach. The designers of UNIX started with a vision of "small, sharp tools" that could be connected together as needed. Do you need to see how many copies of the HTTP daemon are running on your Web server? The UNIX command `ps -ef` lists all of the processes. The command `grep httpd` scans its input (standard in) for the string "httpd," which is the name of the HTTP daemon. The UNIX tool `wc` counts things—`wc -l` counts lines. So the following line of code creates a one-time application where none existed before:

```
ps -ef ¦ grep httpd ¦ wc -l
```

Do you want to keep this little program around? Save this line in a file named, say, daemonCount.ksh. Make the file an executable program by typing the following:

```
chmod +x daemonCount.ksh
```

Also, make sure that daemonCount.ksh is in the path that your computer searches when you issue commands.

Now, when you type "daemonCount.ksh" this little application runs and returns the number of server processes. Hey, presto!

Figure 4.1 illustrates a typical document-centric component-based environment.

FIG. 4.1
In a component-based environment, the user's request is satisfied by small tools assembled for a specific purpose.

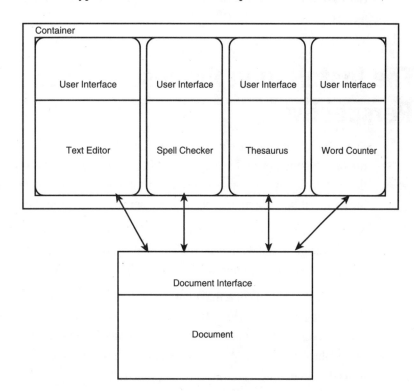

The Microsoft Way

Contrast this approach with, say, Microsoft Word. The flagship application of the world's largest software company has it all. Do you need an outline? It's right there on the View menu. Ready to spell-check? It's at the top of the list under Tools. Graphics? Spreadsheets? Databases? You can connect them all through Microsoft Office. Microsoft has tried to anticipate your every need. If they haven't, until recently, you were out of luck.

But only until recently. Microsoft has more to lose by encouraging component architectures because components can be written by smaller companies, potentially carving up part of Microsoft's pie. OLE 2 is a major step toward component architecture, and so are compound documents, especially with in-place activation. DLLs make it easier to add or change functionality after a product is fielded. ActiveX seems to be a big step toward components. Over time, perhaps driven by market pressures from software initiatives like OpenDoc, CommonPoint, and especially Netscape plug-ins, Microsoft is moving in the direction of component architecture.

The Installation Process: A User Perspective

Even though plug-ins are a great idea, installing them is a pain in the neck! During the beta-testing period for Navigator 3.0, developers' biggest complaint was that the installation process was arbitrary, cumbersome, and error-prone. As plug-ins have moved into the marketplace, end users say the same thing.

Netscape got the message. Although an improved installation routine didn't make it into Navigator 3.0, Netscape has made it a top priority in the new Netscape Communicator (the next generation of the Navigator was released in December, 1996).

When a user visits a page that contains non-native content, Navigator looks at its list of installed plug-ins and their MIME media types. If Netscape finds a matching MIME media type, it loads the library, calls NPP_Initialize(), instantiates a copy of the plug-in, calls NPP_New(), and starts the process that the rest of this book describes in detail.

If no plug-ins on the list match, Navigator looks at the list of helper applications. If none of *these* match, Navigator starts the installation process.

Navigator offers two kinds of installation—manual and assisted. You can use JavaScript to walk the user through the installation process, even offering some improvements over assisted installation.

Manual Installation

Although you won't often ask the user to install your plug-in manually, you will use this process many times while you develop the plug-in. Moreover, your installation pages and scripts automate this process, so you will want to know the details.

Generally, plug-ins must be installed in a special subdirectory, and they must be present when Navigator is started.

Windows   On Windows, the special plug-ins subdirectory must be named "plugins" and the plug-in files must have file names that begin with "np." Windows, of course, is not case-sensitive.

Macintosh   On the Macintosh, the special plug-ins subdirectory must be named "plug-ins" (note the hyphen). No special naming requirement is needed on the plug-in files.

OS/2 Warp   Under OS/2 Warp, the special plug-ins subdirectory must be named "plugins" but the plug-in files don't need special file names that begin with "np."

UNIX   UNIX uses a mechanism similar to the mechanism described for OS/2 Warp, Windows, and Macintosh. UNIX looks through the shared objects in the Plug-ins directory for libraries that advertise Netscape plug-in functions. When UNIX finds these libraries, it looks up the MIME types they handle and then links and loads the correct plug-in at runtime.

Assisted Installation

With Netscape Navigator, the best way to install a plug-in is to let Navigator help. If the plug-in is being loaded by using the <EMBED> tag, you can add the attribute PLUGINSPAGE=*url* to the tag. If a plug-in isn't found that can handle the MIME media type, Navigator puts up a dialog box that tells the user what is happening. Figure 4.2 shows this dialog box.

Part

II

Ch

4

FIG. 4.2
If Navigator cannot find a plug-in to handle the MIME media type of the incoming stream, it prompts the user to download the plug-in.

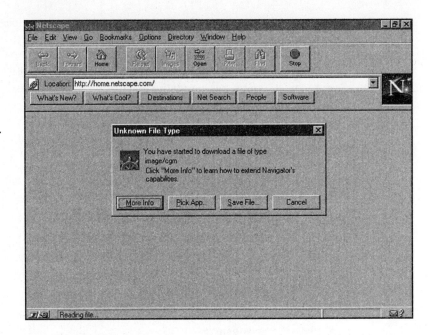

If the user chooses Cancel, then of course the installation process is terminated. If the user chooses to continue, however, Navigator follows the URL given in the PLUGINSPAGE attribute. When the user arrives at your page, you are in control of the download process.

TIP Navigator offers the assisted installation process the first time a particular non-native MIME type is encountered. After that it puts up the "missing plug-in" icon and proceeds. You may want to supply some JavaScript—to anyone who uses your MIME type—to supplement assisted plug-in with JavaScript. JavaScript, which will tell you if your plug-in is available on the client's machine, is coming up in the following section.

Adobe was among the first companies to use plug-ins—their current product, a version of the Acrobat Portable Document Format reader codenamed Amber, is one of the more advanced plug-ins available. Figure 4.3 shows the Web page on which Adobe begins the user download process.

ON THE WEB

You can find Amber at **http://www.adobe.com/acrobat/readstep.html**.

FIG. 4.3

Adobe's plug-in download site opens by describing the product and offers to download. It shows the user a 4-step process, which includes registering the plug-in, choosing the right version, downloading the software, and configuring the browser.

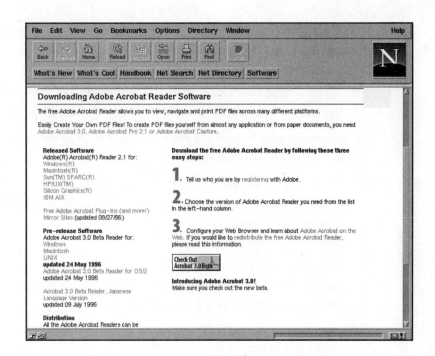

Note that Adobe takes advantage of the visit to capture registration information. Anything you can do to learn more about your client base can help you meet your organization's objectives.

NOTE At the Adobe site the registration step is optional. Although the site doesn't draw attention to this, it's entirely possible to download their software without registering.

You should decide whether your organization's objectives are best served by mandatory registration, or whether you want to allow visitors to bypass this step. ■

Here are some considerations that may help in the design of your download page:

■ Because you can read the browser type and, consequently, the platform ID in a CGI script or LiveWire program, you can default to the correct platform.

■ You should offer other versions of the plug-in (for example, a Macintosh user shouldn't be prohibited from downloading the Windows version, though doing so may be unusual).

- Because the plug-in is intended for Navigator, it's a safe bet that the visitor is using Navigator. You can enhance the page accordingly, including using JavaScript and Java, as desired.

- You can write your plug-in so that it "phones home" from time to time. This section contains a procedure for having your plug-in keep itself up-to-date.

You can design your plug-in and your download page to keep your plug-in up-to-date by taking the following steps:

1. Design the download page with some JavaScript that checks to see if your plug-in is already on the user's machine. (You will find more information on this subject in the following section.) If your plug-in isn't loaded, proceed with the download in the usual way.

2. If the user already has a copy of your plug-in, use JavaScript to start your plug-in. Have your download page tell your plug-in (in a private MIME media type) its current version on this platform.

3. Your plug-in compares the version it gets from the download page with its major and minor version numbers, tells the user if the plug-in version you are using is out-of-date, and offers to download the latest version. You may want to offer to take the user to a new page where you list the latest features. You can even make this feature list longer or shorter, depending upon how obsolete the user's copy of the plug-in is.

4. After the user has a chance to download the new version, write a record of the date and time to the user's hard drive. You can use a Netscape cookie, or you can write the information to a small file. In Windows 95, you might save the data in the system registry.

5. In your plug-in's `NPP_Initialize()`, check the date-time stamp to see how much time has passed since the user checked the download site. If too much time has elapsed, use `NPN_GetURL()` with `window` set to NULL to ask your site if a newer version exists.

6. If your plug-in discovers that it is obsolete, discreetly inform the user. You may want to enable a menu item in a pop-up menu, for example, that says `Download newer version`.

If you follow this procedure, make sure that you tell the user about it somewhere in the documentation, and consider giving them a way to turn off any auto-download of the newer version. Some users are quite uncomfortable with software writing to their hard drive or calling up Web sites without their permission.

It's a good idea to tell the user about the system requirements before they download the plug-in. On one of Adobe's Web pages, Adobe describes the minimum requirements a Windows machine needs to run Version 2 of their product. (See Figure 4.4.)

FIG. 4.4
Tell the user the minimum system requirements so they can make an intelligent choice about downloading the plug-in.

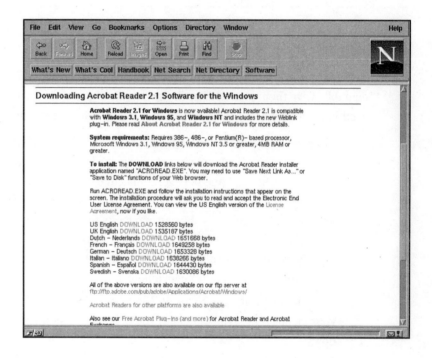

Part
II

Ch
4

ON THE WEB

You can find the Adobe Windows minimum requirements at **http://www.adobe.com/acrobat/windows.html**.

Note also that Adobe's download page tells the user the size of the file they are about to download, and includes detailed instructions about how to run the installation program. If you require the user to read and accept a license agreement as part of the installation process, link to a copy of the agreement here.

TIP All major platforms make it easy to "internationalize" your software. You can include help files, dialog text, and menu items in nearly any language. If your software is internationalized, provide a `<SELECT>` tag or other option on the download page to allow your users to request the right version.

If you're a really big firm, like Netscape, you may want to ask the user where they are physically located so that you can steer them to a server on their continent.

It is, after all, a *World Wide* Web.

Installation Scripts and Pages

In Navigator, you will often want the user to download an installation script or executable. Give them instructions in the download page about how to run it. This section points out a few considerations you may want to remember:

- Although Netscape discourages it, prepare for the possibility that the user may have more than one copy of Navigator installed. Netscape seems to always have at least one beta version active, not to mention versions of Netscape Navigator Gold. Many users may have three or four copies of the browser. When your install program looks for Navigator, consider allowing it to run until it finds *all* copies on the local drive. If more than one version already exists, put up a list that shows the path to each one, and ask the user where the plug-in should be installed.

- Consider carefully the issues of Windows compatibility. Think about having your installation script check for the presence of Win32s (on classic Windows).

- On a Windows 95 machine, make sure that you take advantage of the Wizard control. Users are used to running a setup program and launching a Wizard.

- On a Macintosh, offer native versions for both 68K and PowerPC Macintoshes. Mac users are used to being offered three choices: 68K, PowerPC, and "Fat Binaries" that work on either kind of machine (but take longer to download). Use Apple's single-button installer. If it's appropriate for your plug-in, offer a custom configuration option as well as the default "Easy Install."

■ Remember that UNIX is in many ways the least-restricted environment. UNIX comes in many flavors with subtle differences. Not all users will have the "standard" configuration. If you're not a UNIX expert, enlist the help of one. Remember that you may have to get more than one expert to span the UNIX world.

LiveConnect and Installation

New features in JavaScript make it easy to find out what plug-ins the user has on their machine. You can use this information to do the following:

■ Warn the user about potential MIME type conflicts

■ Direct the user to your download page from your content page

■ Offer the content in one of several formats, depending upon what MIME types the user's computer can read

How Navigator Loads Plug-Ins

When Navigator launches, it looks through the files in the plug-ins subdirectory. On Windows, it looks for certain fields in the VERSIONINFO resource. On the Mac, Navigator looks at STR# 128. When Navigator finds a plug-in, it reads the MIME type information and registers the plug-in for use with that type.

MIME Type Conflict

If your plug-in reads a common MIME type, you will inevitably find your software competing for registration with another plug-in. Even if your MIME type is unique, you may find that you are competing with an older version of your own plug-in.

Macintosh and UNIX users can specify which plug-in gets to handle which MIME type, although few users may be aware of it. On those platforms, the user goes to Options, General Preferences and chooses the Helpers tab. The user then can specify which plug-in handles each MIME type, just as they specify a helper application. Figure 4.5 shows the Helpers screen.

FIG. 4.5

Macintosh and UNIX
users can select
which plug-in gets to
handle each MIME
type.

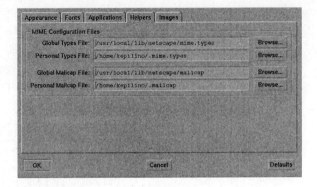

On Windows machines, the Helpers tab under Options, General Preferences
doesn't include a plug-in option. The last plug-in to load gets to handle the MIME
type. If you want to make sure that *your* plug-in will handle the data, use JavaScript
to discover the conflict and warn the user.

The *plugins* and *mimeTypes* Arrays

As each plug-in is registered, Navigator reads information from each plug-in into
an array named plugins. You can read this array with client-side JavaScript. A
JavaScript plugins object has the following four properties:

- name   The name of the plug-in
- filename   The name of the plug-in file on the disk
- description   The description of the plug-in, read from the plug-in's resources
- An array of MIME types that the plug-in can handle

Navigator also tracks how many plug-ins it has registered, so you can read the
length property of the plugins array.

If your plug-in is named "npQuux," you can easily check to see if it is registered as
follows:

```
var myPlugin = navigator.plugins["npQuux"];
if (myPlugin)
   --the plug-in is loaded
else
   --no quux here
```

Not only does Navigator track all registered plug-ins, it also maintains a list of which plug-in is assigned to handle which MIME type. (In a clever display of originality, Navigator's engineers choose to call this array "mimeTypes".) Recall that this assignment is a function of load order (on Windows) or of the user's selection (on Macintosh and UNIX machines). To see if your plug-in has been selected to handle your MIME type, write the following:

```
var myMIMEtype = navigator.mimeTypes["application/x-quux"];
if (myMIMEtype)
  if (myMIMEtype.enabledPlugin == navigator.plugins["npQuux"])
    --all is well. We are in control, here
  else
    --this machine uses someone else's plug-in to handle _our_ type
else
  --oops. This machine can't handle our type at all. They need our
plug-in.
```

If you find that the user isn't using your plug-in, you have several options (depending on your organization's objectives):

- You can allow them to proceed. After all, they can read the content with *someone's* plug-in.

- You may display a warning; if they're on a Mac or UNIX machine, you can ask them to reconfigure. If they're on a Windows machine, you can suggest that they remove the offending plug-in (give them `myMimetype.enabledPlugin.filename` to give them the full path).

- If the user doesn't have a plug-in that can read your MIME type, you can negotiate content. Perhaps your plug-in can read several MIME types. Use client-side JavaScript to find a format the user's machine *can* read, and write an appropriate link or <EMBED> tag into the page.

- Put up a notice to the user that tells them they need your plug-in, and write a link to your download site into the document.

The *embeds* Array

After a page with embedded plug-ins is up, JavaScript can read the embeds array of the current page. Each element of embeds is a Plugin object. Therefore, embeds[0] is associated with the plug-in that will handle the first <EMBED> tag on your page, embeds[1] is associated with the second <EMBED> tag, and so on. Chapter 10,

"JavaScript to Java Communication," describes JavaScript you can write to communicate from JavaScript back to your plug-in. This code routes messages to a Java object associated with your plug-in, addressed by the embeds array.

N O T E The embeds array is read-only. You cannot override the registered plug-in assignment at runtime. ▪

Creating Plug-Ins for Windows

As I mentioned previously, in order to create a Windows plug-in you need a C++ compiler, like Microsoft's Visual C++ 2.1 compiler.

Steps to Creating a Windows Plug-in:

1. Create a directory on your hard drive called "plug-in" for the plug-in project. You may call this directory anything you like. Download the Windows Sample Source Code to your plug-in directory. This file is a compressed file. Make sure you specify the plug-in directory in the save dialog box to save the file in the proper directory.

2. Decompress the file. If you're using pkunzip to decompress the file, it's important to use the -d flag to create the directory structure that is stored in the zip file. These two subdirectories, called AVI and shell, will then be created. The shell directory contains all the files you need to create a new Windows plug-in. The AVI directory contains example files for creating an AVI movie plug-in. See Table 4.1 for a listing of directory files.

3. Create a new subdirectory under your plug-in directory. You could call this "myplugin". Copy all the directories and files in the shell directory into your new subdirectory. Also copy any auxiliary plug-in-specific files you have created into this directory. You may have written code to implement receiving keyboard and mouse events. This code needs to be copied to your working plug-in directory.

4. Using your compiler, open the existing makefile in your working directory. For Windows 95 or Windows NT, make sure you open the makefile for 32-bit applications. There is also one for 16-bit applications.

5. Edit the resource file, NPDLL32.RC2, to include the correct information. You must change the MIME type and the file extension values. For example, if you were creating an AVI plug-in, your resource file would look like this:

```
VALUE "MIMEType",          "video/x-msvideo\0"

VALUE "FileExtents",       "AVI\0"

VALUE "FileOpenName",      "Video for Windows (*.AVI)\0"
```

To include multiple MIME types in the plug-in, use a vertical bar to delimit each value in the MIME type.

```
VALUE "MIMEType", "video/x-msvideo ¦ video/quicktime\0"
```

6. Save the resource file. This resource file allows Netscape to query the plug-in without having to load it in memory.

7. Open the file NPSHELL.CPP. This shell file is the framework for creating a new plug-in. You fill in the necessary code for basic plug-in functionality. In NPSHELL.CPP, write the code for the functions needed for your plug-in. See Chapter 3 , "Overview of Plug-In API," for more information on Netscape's Application Programming Interface.

 TIP Take a look at the NPSHELL.CPP file in the AVI directory. This is an example of how the NPSHELL.CPP file is used to create an AVI plug-in.

8. Save the NPSHELL.CPP file. Using your compiler, build the project. The file NPWIN32.DLL is created.

9. Copy this dll file into the plugins subdirectory of Navigator. If this directory doesn't exist, create it in the same location where netscape.exe is found. If the plug-in has files associated with it, create a subdirectory for those files.

10. Restart Navigator. When Netscape Navigator starts up, it checks for plug-in modules in the netscape\plugins directory. From the Help menu of Navigator, choose About Plug-ins. A list of all plug-ins in the directory is displayed. You should see your MIME type listed. You can now test your plug-in by creating an HTML document.

Part
II

Ch
4

N O T E The AVI directory of the Sample Source Code includes files that illustrate a basic plug-in for Netscape. The example utilizes Microsoft Video for Windows AVI player as both a 16-bit and 32-bit plug-in. The plug-in utilizes MCI calls for its video display. You must have Video for Windows installed in order to run this plug-in. The AVI plug-in illustrates what is known as a file-based plug-in. A file-based plug-in handles the data stream when it is completed, instead of while the stream is being transferred. ▪

Table 4.1 Sample Source Code Directory Files

File Name	Description
Shell Directory Listing	
npapi.h	The main plug-in header file that contains all plug-in and Netscape prototypes, including typedefs for all types and structures.
npupp.h	Procedure typedefs, including function creation and calling macros.
npshell.cpp	Shell implementation of all plug-in methods. This file also includes help on plug-in development. This is the file you edit to create your own plug-in.
npwin.cpp	For communication, it passes plug-in function pointers to Netscape and includes shell functions for Navigator entry points.
npdll32.def	Used by the linker to resolve export symbols for 32-bit plug-in entry points. There is also a file for 16-bit plug-in entry points.
npdll32.rc	Contains boilerplate Visual C++ symbols for 32-bit plug-ins. There is also a file for 16-bit plug-ins.
npwin32.mak	A Visual C++ 2.1 make file for 32-bit plug-ins. There is also a file for 16-bit plug-ins.
npdll32.rc2	Located in the res subdirectory, contains the resources for the MIME type supported by 32-bit plug-ins. There is also a file for 16-bit plug-ins.
AVI Directory Listing	
npapi.h	The main plug-in header file that contains all plug-in and Netscape prototypes, including typedefs for all types and structures.

File Name	Description
AVI Directory Listing	
npupp.h	Procedure typedefs, including function creation and calling macros.
npshell.cpp	The AVI implementation, including help with applicable plug-in methods.
npwin.cpp	For communication, it passes plug-in function pointers to Netscape and includes shell functions for Navigator entry points.
npavi32.def	Used by the linker to resolve export symbols for 32-bit plug-in entry points. There is also a file for 16-bit plug-ins.
npavi32.rc	Contains boilerplate Visual C++ symbols for 32-bit plug-ins. There is also a file for 16-bit plug-ins.
npavi32.mak	A Visual C++ 2.1 make file for 32-bit plug-ins. There is also a file for 16-bit plug-ins.
npavi32.rc2	Located in a subdirectory, it contains the resources for the AVI MIME type for the implementation of 32-bit plug-ins. There is also a file for 16-bit plug-ins.
npavi.h	Specific to the AVI example, it contains the class definitions for the AVI application class.
npavi.cpp	Specific to the AVI example, includes the AVI application class implementation.
cavi.h	Specific to the AVI example, contains the class definitions for the AVI class.
cavi.cpp	Specific to the AVI example, includes the implementation of the AVI class.
plugwind.h	Specific to the AVI example, made up of the class declaration for the plug-in Window class.
plugwind.cpp	Specific to the AVI example, includes the implementation of the plug-in Window class.
resource.h	Specific to the AVI example, contains the boilerplate Visual C++ symbols for MFC-based plug-ins.
stdafx.h	Specific to the AVI example, contains the boilerplate Visual C++ symbols for MFC-based plug-ins.
stdafx.cpp	Specific to the AVI example, is a standard MFC-based file that contains information used by precompiled headers.

Part
II

Ch
4

Creating Plug-Ins for Macintosh

As mentioned previously, in order to create a Macintosh plug-in you need a C++ compiler, like CodeWarrior 9, and the application Stuffit Expander that is included with the Navigator. You also need a resource editor, like Resourcer or ResEdit.

Steps to Creating a Macintosh plug-in:

1. Download the Macintosh plug-in SDK. If you have Stuffit Expander already installed, the folder PluginSDK is automatically created. The SDK contains the following:

   Classes—Contains moz_30.zip, the Navigator class file.

   Common—Source code for utility classes used in multiple examples, and which can be reused.

   Examples—Example plugin projects, including MacTemplate, on which you can base your own projects.

   Include—The header and stub files required for all Navigator plug-ins.

2. Next, duplicate the MacTemplate folder and call it "myplugin". You can name this folder anything you prefer. The folder contains the shell files that provide a compilable framework for creating a plug-in. You fill in the necessary code for basic plug-in functionality.

3. Copy any auxiliary plug-in specific files you have created into this directory. You may have written code to implement receiving keyboard and mouse events. This code needs to be copied to your working plug-in directory.

4. In the folder myplugin, rename the file MacTemplate68K.u to Myplugin68K.u and delete these four files: MacTemplatePPC, MacTemplate68K, MacTemplatePPC.xSYM, and MacTemplate68k.SYM. These files are automatically created again when you build your plug-in. Using a resource editor (your choice), open the file MacTemplate.rsrc. You must edit and change the MIME type and file extension values by editing str #128. First, change string #1 to MIME type and string #2 to extension. Save the resource file. The resource file allows Netscape to query the plug-in without having to load it in memory.

5. Open the file Myplugin68K.u. Using your compiler, open macshell.cpp. This is the compilable shell file.

6. Using the Save As command, copy and rename npshell.cpp as myplugin.cpp in the folder myplugin:Source. In myplugin.cpp, write the code for the functions needed for your plug-in. See Chapter 3, "Overview of Plug-In API," for more information on Netscape's Application Programming Interface. Save the myplugin.cpp file.

7. Change the Preferences associated with myplugin.cpp by choosing Preferences from the Edit menu. Select 68k Project Preferences and make these necessary changes:

   Rename the file name to myplugin68K.

   Rename they sym name to myplugin68K.sym.

   Save the settings

8. Using your compiler, build the project. Notice that the file myplugin68K is created.

9. If you want to create a fat PowerPC native application, open the file mypluginppc.u and use the Project menu to:

   Remove the file MacTemplate68K.

   Add the file myplugin68K. This ensures that your plugin can run on both PowerPC and 68K code.

   Delete npshell.cpp.

   Add the file myplugin.cpp.

   Now recompile the project.

10. Drag the file myplugin68K into the plugins folder of Navigator. If this folder doesn't exist, create it in the same location where the file netscape.exe is found. If the plug-in has files associated with it, place the files in a separate folder. Restart Navigator. When Netscape Navigator starts up, it checks for plug-in modules in the netscape\plugins directory.

11. From the Help menu of Navigator, choose About Plug-ins. A list of all plug-ins in the directory is displayed. You should see your MIME type listed. You can now test your plug-in by creating an HTML document.

Part

II

Ch

4

Navigator Communicator

One of the biggest objections to plug-ins has been how complex it is to find the right plug-in and download it. Navigator Communicator will largely automate this process.

Using the <EMBED> tag with the PLUGINSPAGE attribute will serve as a good starting point for auto-download. Use this attribute on any pages you write that include embedded data.

From Here...

From the beginning, Netscape Navigator has supported helper applications that allow users to access data types other than the ones built into Navigator. The mechanism for describing these data types is the MIME-compliant media type.

Navigator 2.0 and 3.0 support in-line plug-ins, allowing programmers to write native code to read data and present it inside the Netscape window. Navigator 3.0 and Communicator also includes LiveConnect, which integrates plug-ins, JavaScript, and Java. Now all programming techniques for the client can be brought together into an integrated solution.

Starting with Navigator Communicator, Netscape is supporting automated downloading and installation of plug-ins, making the use of plug-ins even more transparent to the end user.

You can write JavaScript on your content pages and in your download site, which ensures that users do not get a "Plug-in Not Present" message. Rather, your pages can negotiate with the user's machine to find a compatible format, or offer to take the user to your download site.

- Chapter 3, "Overview of Plug-In API," looks at API organization, plug-in, and Netscape methods.
- The next chapter, "Programming Plug-Ins," looks at plug-ins and HTML, as well as Simple and CharFlipper LiveConnect plug-ins.

- Chapter 6, "Developing Content for Plug-Ins," looks at LiveCache and CD-ROM developing.
- Chapter 8, "Calling Java Methods from Plug-Ins," shows how fields are accessed, Java names and parameters, as well as security issues.
- Chapter 9, "Calling the Plug-In from Java Methods," shows how to define a plug-in class, as well as more about native methods and globals.

Part

II

Ch

4

CHAPTER 5

Programming Plug-Ins

What is a great way to add additional features and enhanced functionality to Netscape Navigator? Plug-ins, of course! Plug-ins extend the capabilities of Netscape Navigator through integration of multimedia and interactive modules. Plug-ins are native to the specific platform where Netscape Navigator is installed. Utilities like compression, Multimedia applications like Live3D and Macromedia Shockwave, and database management applications all extend the plug-in technology that is now available to Internet users.

Plug-ins complement platform-native inter-application architectures such as OLE and OpenDoc, as well as programming languages like Java. Unlike Java Applets, which you can read extensively about in Chapter 10, "JavaScript to Java Communication," plug-ins (using existing tools) are designed to be simple and relatively easy to control. ■

How to Read a Plug-In's Source

By tracing the flow of control between Navigator and the plug-in, you can get a good idea of what the plug-in does when.

How JavaScript Can Send a Message to a Plug-In

"Officially," JavaScript can only talk to Java, but Netscape has made it almost trivial to set up a Java "peer" object for the plug-in.

How Java "Native" Classes Are Implemented in C and C++

This chapter covers these native classes, which are the key to letting Java call the plug-in's methods.

How to Read Characters from a Stream

CharFlipper is one of Netscape's principle stream-reading example plug-ins.

About the Netscape Class Library

Netscape has written a small set of "helper classes" to get you started programming plug-ins.

Integrating Plug-Ins with HTML

Although only experienced programmers are writing plug-ins and Java applets, almost anyone can learn to write JavaScript or HTML. As a programmer, you can give the user a certain amount of control over your plug-in by passing parameters through the <EMBED> tag. For example, NPP_New() passes a description of the parameters in argc, argn, and argv. You can read more about NPP methods in Chapter 3, "Overview of Plug-In API." If the HTML author writes the following, for example, your plug-in can read these parameters:

```
<EMBED SRC="http://www.somemachine.com/myFile.tst" HEIGHT=100
➥WIDTH=100
  AUTOSTART=True LOOP=False AUTOSCALE=Often>
```

What it *does* with these parameters is, of course, determined by you as the programmer.

Integrating Plug-Ins by Using LiveConnect

There is now a simpler way to get messages into a plug-in. The current techniques hook platform-native controls such as menus and pushbuttons into your plug-in. This approach has the advantage of looking familiar to the user. It also gives you a great deal of control over the appearance of your plug-in. (For example, a pop-up menu that appears when the user right-clicks the mouse may offer a dozen or more menu items, and yet it doesn't clutter the screen when not in use.)

Sometimes, however, you'll be happy to have a little HTML form with some buttons that tell the plug-in to "Start" or "Stop." Netscape provides all this flexibility and more through the technology that we now know as LiveConnect.

There is a distinction between interacting and controlling within a plug-in. Here's an example: If your plug-in downloads a drawing from the Web and allows you to annotate it and post it back to the Web, you need to use native controls. For example, you probably want a pop-up menu (perhaps triggered by the right mouse button) that allows you to zoom, save, and revert.

If your plug-in is simpler, such as a video player, and you want to allow the HTML author to add buttons to the page like "Start" and "Stop," LiveConnect may be faster and easier to implement. You can do more complex tasks with LiveConnect. Many plug-ins will want to use both native controls and LiveConnect. It's up to you to decide how to best design your plug-in.

Building a Simple Plug-In

The sample applications included with the Windows version of the Netscape plug-in Software Development Kit (SDK) are a tour de force of plug-in programming. They include calls to Java code and allow the user to play AVI movies. Unfortunately, so much is going on in these sample applications that the novice plug-in programmer can be overwhelmed.

Traditionally, the first program a C or C++ programmer writes in a new environment is one to put up the words, "Hello, world!" Such a simple program serves to check out the compiler and development environment, because the code itself is trivial. This chapter shows you how to build a "Hello, world!" plug-in—a plug-in that just shows these words to the user.

After "Hello, world!" is working, you can use this plug-in as a foundation for showing more of the calls a plug-in and Navigator can exchange.

The Development Process

This chapter uses Microsoft's Visual C++ 4.0 Standard Edition under Windows 95 as the sample development environment. You can use this environment to develop applications for Windows computers as well as for the Macintosh.

This chapter concentrates on the plug-in rather than the application environment. There are some notes showing how Macintosh plug-ins differ from plug-ins for Windows. For more information on writing plug-ins for Windows environments other than Windows 95, see Chapter 4, "Creating Plug-Ins."

 TIP Visual C++ 4.0 Standard Edition does not allow the developer to link Microsoft Foundation Classes (MFC)statically. The consequences are that you must provide (or the user must already have) the MFC dynamic link library (DLL) on the target machine.

continues

continued

> If you're developing plug-ins for general release, you may prefer to link MFC statically. You can use the linker in the Visual C++ 4.0 Professional Edition, as well as in some non-Microsoft development environments, to link the MFC library to your plug-in.

If you're developing plug-ins for an intranet that only has Windows computers, you may be able to get by with a Windows-only plug-in. If you're developing for the Internet, consider releasing versions of your plug-in for all major platforms. This chapter shows how to develop a generic plug-in, using Windows 95 and Microsoft's Visual C++ as the development environment.

The "Simple Plug-In"

Despite its name, the "Simple Plug-In" that Netscape supplies with the Plug-in Software Development Kit (SDK) is far from simple. It includes a full implementation of the major methods, including LiveConnect. LiveConnect (described in more detail in Part III, "Live-Connecting Plug-Ins with Java," and Part IV, "LiveConnect Communication in JavaScript") is Netscape's integration technology that allows your plug-in to communicate with Java and JavaScript.

How the Plug-In Works

To get an idea of what Simple does, start by compiling the plug-in and running it. This chapter uses the Windows version of the plug-in, but Netscape supplies a version for the Mac as well. See Chapter 2, "LiveConnect Components," for information on how the SDK is further organized, including example templates and demos, as well as Chapter 4, "Creating Plug-Ins," for creating Macintosh plug-ins.

Compiling the Plug-In   Netscape uses Microsoft's Visual C++ on Windows and MetroWorks' Code Warrior on the Macintosh. You can simplify the installation process if you use the same environment they do.

In Visual C++'s Developer Studio, choose File, Open Workspace and open NPSimple32.mdp in the Examples\Simple\Windows subdirectory of the Plugins SDK directory. After the project opens, choose Build, Build **NPSimp32.dll**. The project should compile and link with no errors or warnings.

Moving the Files into Position   Copy the Java class file Simple.class from the Examples\Simple subdirectory of the Plugins SDK directory to the Navigator plug-ins directory.

Copy the NPSimp32.dll file, which you just built, to the plug-ins directory and re-start Navigator. Make sure that you're using a version of Navigator that is at least at v3.0b5, or you won't see all the features of this plug-in working.

Running the Plug-In   When Navigator restarts, it examines the files in the plug-ins directory and registers plug-ins based on their MIME media type. Chapter 4, "Creating Plug-Ins," describes this process in more detail.

After Navigator is up, use File, Open File in Browser to open Examples\Simple\Testing\SimpleExample.html. You'll probably want to bookmark this page while you learn about plug-ins.

Choose Options, Show Java Console and make sure that this item is checked. The Java Console is a small window to which your Java classes can send messages. When it opens, you'll see that your Simple plug-in has already been busy. If you have enough room on-screen, try to position your windows so that you can see both the Java Console and the plug-in's part of the Navigator window. Figure 5.1 shows the SimpleExample.html and the Java Console.

Part
II

Ch
5

FIG. 5.1

Simple writes to both the Java Console and the Navigator window.

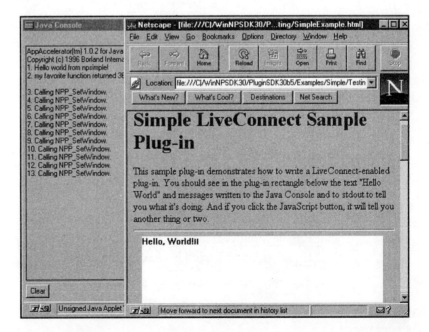

Notice that Simple wrote "Hello, World!" to its Navigator window. To see that Simple is listening to JavaScript as well, click the "Click Me" button a few times while watching the Java Console.

Understanding Flow of Control

Although you may not want to ship Simple as a finished product, Simple is rich enough to have hooks for many of the actions that you can perform with a more sophisticated plug-in.

Follow Navigator As you saw when you ran Simple, a plug-in has two interfaces—one to Navigator and another to the user. Because the plug-in cannot do anything with the user until most of its Navigator functions are called, you start by tracing the flow of control between Navigator and Simple. Follow along in Figure 5.2.

FIG. 5.2
Navigator makes a series of calls to the plug-in to get things started.

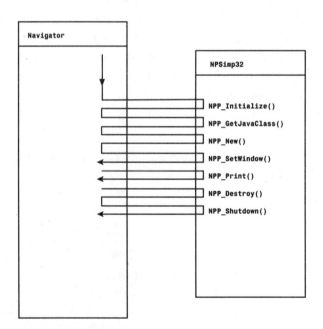

How Simple Is Called Return to Microsoft Developer Studio and use it to open SimpleExample.html. This file isn't part of the project—you need to use File, Open to open it. The plug-in is loaded because of the following line:

```
<EMBED type=application/x-simple-plugin name=simple1 width=400
➥height=300>
```

This line tells us that Simple doesn't read a stream from the Net. The TYPE attribute forces Navigator to load this plug-in by specifying the MIME media type. Notice also that the plug-in has a name—Simple1. This name is used by JavaScript later, in the section that reads as follows:

```
<form>
<input type=button value="Click Me"
  onclick='document.simple1.doit("Hello from JavaScript!")'>
</form>
```

NP_Initialize()   When Navigator sees the <EMBED> tag, it looks up the plug-in that is registered to handle MIME type application/x-simple-plugin. Navigator finds NPSimp32 and loads this library into its address space. Then it exchanges entry points. The first method it calls is NP_Initialize()—a function written by Netscape to get the plug-in started. Use Microsoft Developer Studio's ClassView to open this function. (It's in the Globals folder because it's not part of any class. The implementation is in the npwin.cpp file in the Common directory of the SDK.) Here's NP_Initialize().

```
// NP_Initialize
//
//      called immediately after the plugin DLL is loaded
//
NPError WINAPI NP_EXPORT
NP_Initialize(NPNetscapeFuncs* pFuncs)
{
    // trap a NULL ptr
    if(pFuncs == NULL)
        return NPERR_INVALID_FUNCTABLE_ERROR;

    g_pNavigatorFuncs = pFuncs; // save it for future reference

    // if the plugin's major ver level is lower than the Navigator's,
    // then they are incompatible, and should return an error
    if(HIBYTE(pFuncs->version) > NP_VERSION_MAJOR)
        return NPERR_INCOMPATIBLE_VERSION_ERROR;

     // We have to defer these assignments until g_pNavigatorFuncs is
     ⇒set
    int navMinorVers = g_pNavigatorFuncs->version & 0xFF;

     if( navMinorVers >= NPVERS_HAS_NOTIFICATION ) {
         g_pluginFuncs->urlnotify = NPP_URLNotify;
     }
```

Part
II

Ch
5

```
#ifdef WIN32 // An ugly hack, because Win16 lags behind in Java
    if( navMinorVers >= NPVERS_HAS_LIVECONNECT ) {
#else
    if( navMinorVers >= NPVERS_WIN16_HAS_LIVECONNECT )
#endif // WIN32
        g_pluginFuncs->javaClass = Private_GetJavaClass();
    }

    // NPP_Initialize is a standard (cross-platform) initialize
    ➥function.
    return NPP_Initialize();
}


  // NPP_Initialize is a standard (cross-platform) initialize
  ➥function.
  return NPP_Initialize();
}
```

Most of `NP_Initialize()` is very standard stuff. All implementations of `NP_Initialize()` should check their incoming parameters to make sure that Navigator has done its job.

Before exiting, `NP_Initialize()` checks to make sure that your version of Navigator is new enough to include notification and LiveConnect. If so, the function fills these slots in the function table.

NPP_GetJavaClass()   If your plug-in isn't using LiveConnect, you don't need to do much with `NPP_GetJavaClass()`—just return `NULL`.

If you want to support LiveConnect, you need to include an `NPP_GetJavaClass()` function similar to the one in Simple, as follows:

```
/*
** NPP_GetJavaClass is called during initialization to ask your
** plugin what its associated Java class is. If you don't have one,
** just return NULL. Otherwise, use the javah-generated "use_" func
** tion to both initialize your class and return it. If you can't
** find your class, an error will be signaled by "use_" and will
** cause the Navigator to complain to the user.
*/
jref NPP_GetJavaClass(void)
{
#ifdef __MC68K__
    return NULL;
#else
```

```
      struct java_lang_Class* myClass;
      env = NPN_GetJavaEnv();
      if (env == NULL)
        return NULL;   /* Java disabled */
      myClass = use_Simple(env);
      if (myClass == NULL) {
        /*
        ** If our class doesn't exist (the user hasn't installed it)
        ** then don't allow any of the Java stuff to happen.
        */
        env = NULL;
      }
      return myClass;
#endif
}
```

N O T E If you're writing a plug-in for the Macintosh, make sure that you include the
following lines:

```
#ifdef __MC68K__
      return NULL;
#else
    .
    .
    .
```

Netscape doesn't support LiveConnect on the 680X0 Macintosh, but they do support it
on the Power Macintosh.

It's important to note that NPP_GetJavaClass() calls NPN_GetJavaEnv() to put a
pointer to the Java runtime environment into env. If this step succeeds, the plug-in
calls a function named use_Simple(). use_Simple() is a function written by an automated tool (javah) based on our Java class, Simple. use_Simple() performs certain
initializations and connections in the Java Runtime Interface. As a plug-in programmer, you don't have to be familiar with too many Java details yet. Figure 5.3 illustrates the flow of control between the Java runtime and the plug-in during
NPP_GetJavaClass().

FIG. 5.3
The plug-in and the
Java runtime interface
work together closely
to initialize the peer
object.

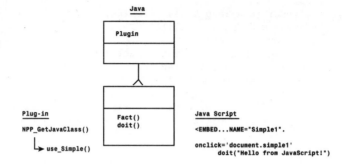

NPP_New()   Now Navigator is ready to make the plug-in instance. Open
NPP_New() with Classview. Note the following line:

```
instance->pdata = NPN_MemAlloc(sizeof(PluginInstance));
```

This line is a "heads-up" that the designer chose to associate a PluginInstance
with the instance's pdata. Recall that pdata points to a block of Navigator memory
that will be passed back to your plug-in on every NPP call. Inside the function the
programmer uses This to point to this instance.

Simple and most other Netscape sample plug-ins use the structure PluginInstance
to hold the data passed through pdata. Netscape defines PluginInstance in
npsimple.c:

```
#ifdef XP_PC
typedef struct _PlatformInstance
{
    HWND                fhWnd;
    WNDPROC             fDefaultWindowProc;
} PlatformInstance;
#endif /* XP_PC */

#ifdef XP_UNIX
typedef struct _PlatformInstance
{
    Window              window;
    Display *           display;
    uint32              x, y;
    uint32              width, height;
} PlatformInstance;
#endif /* XP_UNIX */
```

```
#ifdef XP_MAC
typedef struct _PlatformInstance
{
    int                     placeholder;
} PlatformInstance;
#endif /* macintosh */

typedef struct _PluginInstance
{
    NPWindow*               fWindow;
    uint16                  fMode;
    char*                   fOutString;
    PlatformInstance        fPlatform;
} PluginInstance;
```

Although Simple doesn't store anything special in `PluginInstance`, this structure is custom in each plug-in because most plug-ins *will* store instance-specific data in the structure.

Here's Simple's version of `NPP_New()`:

```
NPError
NPP_New(NPMIMEType pluginType,
    NPP instance,
    uint16 mode,
    int16 argc,
    char* argn[],
    char* argv[],
    NPSavedData* saved)
{
    NPError result = NPERR_NO_ERROR;
    PluginInstance* This;
    char factString[60];
    const char* defaultText = "Hello World!";
    JRIEnv* env = NPN_GetJavaEnv();

    if (instance == NULL) {
        return NPERR_INVALID_INSTANCE_ERROR;
    }
    instance->pdata = NPN_MemAlloc(sizeof(PluginInstance));
    This = (PluginInstance*) instance->pdata;
    if (This == NULL) {
        return NPERR_OUT_OF_MEMORY_ERROR;
    }
    /* mode is NP_EMBED, NP_FULL, or NP_BACKGROUND (see npapi.h) */
    This->fWindow = NULL;
    This->fMode = mode;
    This->fOutString = NPN_MemAlloc( strlen( defaultText ) + 1 );
    strcpy( This->fOutString, defaultText );
```

```
PlatformNew( This );        /* Call Platform-specific
⟳initializations */

    /* PLUGIN DEVELOPERS:
     *     Initialize fields of your plugin
     *     instance data here.  If the NPSavedData is non-
     *     NULL, you can use that data (returned by you from
     *     NPP_Destroy to set up the new plugin instance).
     */

/* Show off some of that Java functionality: */
if (env) {
    jint v;

    /*
    ** Call the DisplayJavaMessage utility function to cause
    ** Java to write to the console and to stdout:
    */
    DisplayJavaMessage(instance, "Hello world from npsimple!",
-1);

    /*
    ** Also test out that fancy factorial method. It's a static
    ** method, so we'll need to use the class object in order
    ** to call it:
    */
    v = Simple_fact(env, class_Simple(env), 10);
    sprintf(factString, "my favorite function returned %d\n",v);
    DisplayJavaMessage( instance, factString, -1 );
}

return result;
}
```

After you define `PluginInstance` for your plug-in, the following lines provide a
formula to open nearly every plug-in:

```
instance->pdata = NPN_MemAlloc(sizeof(PluginInstance));
This = (PluginInstance*) instance->pdata;
if (This == NULL)
  return NPERR_OUT_OF_MEMORY_ERROR;
```

In the following line from `NPP_New()`, `env` is a global pointer to a `JRIEnv`:

```
if (env)
```

If all went well in `NPP_GetJavaClass()`, `env` points to the Java runtime environment.
To show that all this works, the Simple plug-in makes a series of gratuitous calls to
Java, writing its results to the Java Console. You'll see these calls to the Java Con-
sole scattered around the plug-in.

Note that if the Java runtime is successfully set up, the plug-in goes on to call a Java method on class Simple (Simple_fact()). The return value of that function is a Java int—a jint. Chapter 8, "Calling Java Methods from Plug-Ins," shows an entire table of these C/C++ names for Java native types.

DisplayJavaMessage( ) DisplayJavaMessage() is one of the larger and more interesting functions in this plug-in. Its parameters include a char pointer and an int (for length), as follows:

```
/*
** This function is a utility routine that calls back into Java to
** print messages to the Java Console and to stdout (via the native
** method, native_Simple_printToStdout, defined below).  Sure, it's
** not a very interesting use of Java, but it gets the point across.
*/
void DisplayJavaMessage(NPP instance, char* msg, int len)
{
  jref str, javaPeer;
  JRIEnv* env = NPN_GetJavaEnv();

  if (!env) {
    /* Java failed to initialize, so do nothing. */
    return;
  }

  if (len == -1)
    len = strlen(msg);

  /*
  ** Use the JRI (see jri.h) to create a Java string from the input
  ** message:
  */
  str = JRI_NewStringUTF(env, msg, len);

  /*
  ** Use the NPN_GetJavaPeer operation to get the Java instance that
  ** corresponds to our plug-in (an instance of the Simple class):
  */
  javaPeer = NPN_GetJavaPeer(instance);

  /*
  ** Finally, call our plug-in's big "feature" — the 'doit' method,
  ** passing the execution environment, the object, and the java
  ** string:
  */
  Simple_doit(env, javaPeer, str);
}
```

The function calls the Java Runtime Interface (JRI) to allocate a string in Java:

```
jref str;
str = JRI_NewStringUTF(env, msg, len);
```

Then the function calls `NPN_GetJavaPeer()` to get a Java reference (`jref`) to its own peer object. Because the peer is known to be an instance of Java class `Simple`, the plug-in calls the C stub of its peer class and runs `Simple_doit()`. In following sections of this chapter, you'll read about Java class `Simple` and its `doit()` method.

Figure 5.4 traces the flow of control between the plug-in and the Java runtime.

FIG. 5.4

Netscape illustrates how the plug-in calls Java, with `DisplayJavaMessage()`.

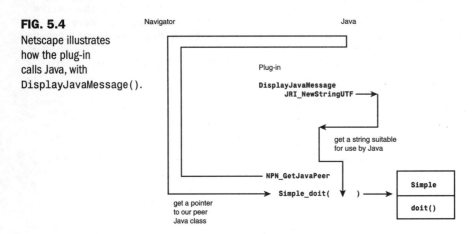

NPP_SetWindow() Because there's no stream associated with this plug-in, you don't have to worry about `NPP_NewStream()`, `NPP_WriteReady()`, or `NPP_Write()`. These functions are available in this plug-in, but they do nothing useful.

The next call the plug-in expects is `NPP_SetWindow()`. Find the place in `NPP_SetWindow()` that reads as follows:

```
NPP_SetWindow(NPP instance, NPWindow* window)
{
    NPError result = NPERR_NO_ERROR;
    PluginInstance* This;

    if (instance == NULL)
        return NPERR_INVALID_INSTANCE_ERROR;

    This = (PluginInstance*) instance->pdata;
```

```
/*
 * PLUGIN DEVELOPERS:
 *      Before setting window to point to the
 *      new window, you may wish to compare the new window
 *      info to the previous window (if any) to note window
 *      size changes, etc.
 */
result = PlatformSetWindow( This, window );

This->fWindow = window;
return result;
}
```

This code does the work of saving off the old WindowProc (into This->fDefaultWindowProc) and installing the new PluginWindowProc. Now that PluginWindowProc is installed as the WindowProc, any messages sent to our window by Windows are passed to your plug-in (and directed to PluginWindowProc). Figure 5.5 shows how subclassed windows work.

FIG. 5.5
After a window is subclassed, the new WindowProc has first shot at reading any messages.

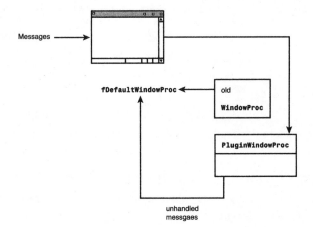

SetProp() is a Windows API call that adds a new entry to the property list of the window. This call puts a link in your Navigator-supplied hwnd back to your pdata. Recall that there can be more than one copy of our plug-in running at a time. By tying your instance data to the window, you can always find your own windowProc and your own data.

PluginWindowProc()   Farther down in the same file (npsimple.c) is PluginWindowProc(), which is the callback function the programmer defined to handle messages to our window. In this simple plug-in, the only message handled in PluginWindowProc() is WM_PAINT. All other messages are routed back to the default windowProc.

The WM_PAINT handler consists of just five lines, as follows:

```
LRESULT CALLBACK PluginWindowProc( HWND hWnd, UINT Msg, WPARAM
wParam, LPARAM lParam)
{
     PluginInstance* This = (PluginInstance*) GetProp(hWnd,
gInstanceLookupString);

     switch( Msg ) {
        case WM_PAINT: {
             PAINTSTRUCT paintStruct;
             HDC hdc;

             hdc = BeginPaint( hWnd, &paintStruct );
             TextOut(hdc, 0, 0, This->fOutString, strlen(
             ➡This->fOutString )-1 );

             EndPaint( hWnd, &paintStruct );
             break;
        }
        default: {
             This->fPlatform.fDefaultWindowProc( hWnd, Msg, wParam,
             ➡lParam);
        }
     }
     return 0;
}
#endif /* XP_PC */
```

When a WM_PAINT message comes to this plug-in, it sets up a device context (so it has someplace to draw), draws the string "Hello, World!", deallocates the device context, and exits.

NPP_Print()   What will happen if the user selects **Print**? Because the plug-in is embedded, NPP_Print() gets called only once—when printInfo->mode is NP_EMBED. In this case the plug-in runs the following code and returns:

```
NPWindow* printWindow =
   &(printInfo->print.embedPrint.window);
void* platformPrint =
   printInfo->print.embedPrint.platformPrint;
```

These lines retrieve the window into which the plug-in is to draw and the device context of the printer, but they don't do anything with them! If you want to complete the task, use TextOut to send "Hello, World!" to the printer's device context. You can use the WM_PAINT handler in PluginWindowProc as a starting point.

LiveConnect Details

Because Simple doesn't get a stream, there's not much else for it to do as far as Navigator is concerned. If the user resizes the window, Navigator obligingly sends another NPP_SetWindow()—you can watch this happen in the Java Console. All the user interaction, such as it is, comes through LiveConnect. Recall from Figure 5.3 the interaction between JavaScript, Java, and the plug-in.

Examining the Java Code

Recall that to install Simple, you copied a file named simple.class into the plug-in directory. The Java compiler, javac, turns Java classes (in .java files) that are human-readable into .class files, which contain bytecodes for the Java Virtual Machine. If there's a simple.class, you should look for a human-readable simple.java—and you find it in the source subdirectory:

```
import netscape.plugin.Plugin;

class Simple extends Plugin {
  /*
   ** A plug-in can consist of code written in java as well as
   ** natively. Here's a dummy method.
   */
  public static int fact(int n) {
    if (n == 1)
      return 1;
    else
      return n * fact(n-1);
  }
  /*
   ** This instance variable is used to keep track of the number of
   ** times we've called into this plug-in.
   */
  int count;

  /*
   ** This native method will give us a way to print to stdout from
   ** java instead of just the java console.
   */
  native void printToStdout(String msg);

  /*
   ** This is a publicly callable new feature that our plug-in is
   ** providing. We can call it from JavaScript, Java, or from native
   ** code.
```

Part II
Ch 5

```
   */
   public void doit(String text) {
     /* construct a message */
     String msg = "" + (++count) + ". " + text + "\n";
     /* write it to the console */
     System.out.print(msg);
     /* and also write it to stdout */
     printToStdout(msg);
   }
 }
```

Although you may not be a Java programmer, you can read the definition of the Java function `fact()` from this file. It's a simple function of the sort commonly used to teach recursion in freshman programming classes. You also will recognize `doit()`, the star of the show on the Java console.

fact() `fact()` is a simple (and not very efficient) implementation of the factorial function. Its function here is to show how to call a native Java function.

count Remember back on the Java Console that each line had a number? This little `int` here is responsible for that task. `count` gets managed by `doit()`, which will be described a bit later in this chapter.

printToStdout() On a Windows machine we don't think much about standard out, and it's difficult to actually see that this function is running. Still, this function shows how Java can call native (C/C++) code that is back in the plug-in.

Note the word `native` in the following function definition:

```
native void printToStdout(String msg);
```

This keyword tells Java to look for the definition of this function in a C or C++ function. Now go back over to the ClassView tool and search through the Globals section. Here you find a function `native_Simple_printToStdout()`. The header for this function was produced by the Java Runtime Interface of javah. The programmer added the following one-line implementation:

```
const char* chars = JRI_GetStringUTFChars(env, a);
```

Here `env` is the Java runtime environment, and `a` is the Java string to be printed. Both variables are passed in as parameters from Java.

doit()   Simple's "big feature" is `doit()`. This function is called when the user clicks on the button on the HTML page. The next section shows how messages get from JavaScript to this Java class. This section shows how `doit()` does its work:

```
public void doit(String text) {
String msg = "" + (++count) + "   " + text + "\n";
System.out.print(msg);
printToStdout(msg);
}
```

The first line of the function uses the plus operator to concatenate a series of strings. The sequence starts with an empty string, so that the finished result is a string. After the message is built, it is sent to the console by using the `print` method of the System's `out` class. Finally, the program sends a copy of the message to standard out (for what it's worth). Figure 5.6 illustrates this process.

FIG. 5.6

The `doit()` function, such as it is, is one of the few pieces of complexity in Simple.

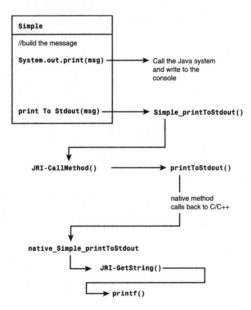

How the JavaScript and HTML Are Connected

Recall that the HTML file contained the following tiny form:

```
<form>
<input type=button value="Click Me"
  onclick='document.simple1.doit("Hello from JavaScript!")'>
</form>
```

This form directs a function call, doit(), to the named plug-in. LiveConnect does not allow direct communication between a plug-in and JavaScript. But because Simple, the plug-in, has an associated Java class (also known as Simple), all is well. The JavaScript handler onClick calls doit() on the named plug-in Simple1. That method gets picked up by Java, which calls the Java method doit(). Java, in turn, handles the message construction and the write to the system console internally, but calls the native method printToStdout back in the plug-in. Figure 5.3, shown earlier in this chapter, traces the flow of control between JavaScript, the Java peer object, and the plug-in.

Closing Down the Plug-In

When the interaction is over and the user is ready to leave Simple, Navigator calls NPP_Destroy(). Because there is only one instance, NPP_Shutdown() is called immediately after the instance is deleted.

NPP_Destroy()   NPP_Destroy() is the place to undo the allocations made in NPP_New(). Simple's implementation of NPP_Destroy() calls NPN_MemFree(), passing it the pdata pointer it's been carrying from one function call to the next. Finally it displays a message through Java to the Java console and then exits. Here's Simple's version of NPP_Destroy():

```
NPError
NPP_Destroy(NPP instance, NPSavedData** save)
{
  PluginInstance* This;
  if (instance == NULL)
    return NPERR_INVALID_INSTANCE_ERROR;
  This = (PluginInstance*) instance->pdata;

  /* PLUGIN DEVELOPERS:
   *  If desired, call NP_MemAlloc to create a
```

```
     *   NPSavedDate structure containing any state information
     *   that you want restored if this plugin instance is later
     *   recreated.
     */
    DisplayJavaMessage(instance, "Calling NPP_Destroy.", -1);

        if (This != NULL) {
          NPN_MemFree(instance->pdata);
          instance->pdata = NULL;
        }
    return NPERR_NO_ERROR;
    }
```

> **CAUTION**
>
> Always remember to free pdata in NPP_Destroy(). If you don't, you'll leak memory out of Navigator and eventually crash the browser. Detecting the cause of such leaks can be time-consuming and is frustrating to the end user (who naturally will blame Netscape for the supposedly buggy browser).

NPP_Shutdown()   Just as NPP_Destroy() undoes the work of NPP_New(), so NPP_Shutdown() is the counterpart of NPP_Initialize(). NPP_Shutdown() verifies that this plug-in has been running with a Java environment. Because it has, it severs the link between Java class Simple and the plug-in. Here's how simple it is to disconnect from the JRI:

```
    * NPP_Shutdown:
     * Provides global deinitialization for a plug-in.
     *
     * This function is called once after the last instance of your
    plug-in is destroyed.
     * Use this function to release any memory or resources shared across
     * all instances of your plug-in. You should be a good citizen and
     * declare that you're not using your java class any more. This
     * allows java to unload it, freeing up memory.

    void
    NPP_Shutdown(void)
    {
```

```
        JRIEnv* env = NPN_GetJavaEnv( );

        if (env) {
            unuse_Simple(env);
            unuse_netscape_plugin_Plugin( env );
        }
    }
```

N O T E The plug-in actually connected to the Java class as part of
`NPP_GetJavaClass( )`, but because this function is called just after
`NPP_Initialize( )`, it's reasonable to use `NPP_Shutdown( )` to undo
`NPP_GetJavaClass`'s actions. ■

The CharFlipper Plug-In

The CharFlipper plug-in is considerably more complex than the Simple plug-in you
have just examined.

In this section you will learn that:

■ CharFlipper is one of Netscape's principal stream-reading example plug-ins.

■ Netscape has written a small set of "helper classes" to get you started
programming plug-ins.

■ You can avoid long, tedious `WindowsProcs` by using MFC's message map.

■ The CharFlipper plug-in reads from its stream far faster than a human can
keep up with. Here, a timer is used to slow down the demonstration.

Introduction to CharFlipper in Action

To get an idea of what CharFlipper does, start by compiling and running the
plug-in. This chapter uses the Windows version of the plug-in, but Netscape also
supplies a version for the Mac. See Chapter 2, "LiveConnect Components," for
information on how the SDK is further organized.

Compiling the Plug-In   Netscape uses Microsoft's Visual C++ on Windows and MetroWorks' Code Warrior on the Macintosh. You can simplify the installation if you use the same environment they do.

In Visual C++'s Developer Studio, choose File, Open Workspace and open CharFlipper.mdp in the Examples\CharFlipper\Windows subdirectory of the Plugins SDK directory. After the project opens, choose Build, Build **NPFlip.dll.**

This project has a few problems—it should compile without errors, but six warnings are issued. These warnings don't affect the running of the plug-in, but they are troublesome. If you choose to build one of your plug-ins around CharFlipper, start by fixing these warnings.

Moving the Files into Position   Copy the Java class file TimeMediaPlugin.class to the Navigator plug-ins directory.

Copy the NPFlip.dll file, which you just built, to the plug-ins directory and restart Navigator. Make sure that you are using a version of Navigator version that is at least at 3.0b5, or you won't see all the features of this plug-in working.

Running the Plug-In   When Navigator restarts, it examines the files in the plug-ins directory and registers plug-ins based on their MIME media type. Chapter 4, "Creating Plug-Ins," describes this process in more detail.

After Navigator is up, use File, Open File to open Examples\CharFlipper\Testing\CharFlipperExample.html. You probably will want to bookmark this page while you learn about plug-ins.

As soon as it opens, CharFlipper goes to work. Figure 5.7 shows the CharFlipper.html user interface.

Part
II

Ch
5

FIG. 5.7
CharFlipper reads from a stream and writes to the window. It's also listening to JavaScript, waiting for a user to press a button.

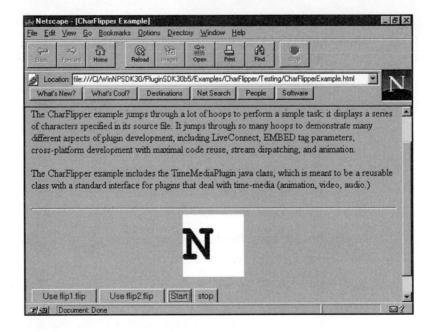

CharFlipper begins to display its data right way. You can use the controls to stop and restart the display or to change the plug-in from one data file to another.

Flow of Control

CharFlipper is rich enough to have hooks for many of the things you might do with a more sophisticated plug-in.

Follow Navigator

As you saw when you ran Simple, a plug-in has two interfaces—one to Navigator and another to the user. Because the plug-in can do nothing with the user until most of its Navigator functions are called, start by tracing the flow of control between Navigator and CharFlipper. Follow along in Figure 5.8.

FIG. 5.8
Navigator makes a
series of calls to the
plug-in to get things
started.

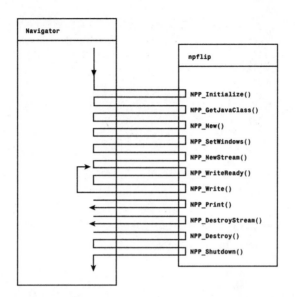

Navigator

npflip

NPP_Initialize()

NPP_GetJavaClass()

NPP_New()

NPP_SetWindows()

NPP_NewStream()

NPP_WriteReady()

NPP_Write()

NPP_Print()

NPP_DestroyStream()

NPP_Destroy()

NPP_Shutdown()

How CharFlipper Is Called   Return to Microsoft Developer Studio and use it to
open CharFlipperExample.html. That file isn't part of the project—you'll need to
use File, Open to open it. The plug-in is loaded because of the line

```
<EMBED SRC="flip1.flip" ALIGN=CENTER WIDTH=100 HEIGHT=100
➥speed=60 autostart=true loop=true name ="flipper">
```

Unlike Simple, CharFlipper reads a stream. The stream (in this case, a file) has the
series of characters that will be displayed.

Because this stream is a local file, no server is needed to translate the file extension into a MIME type. Instead, Navigator looks at the file extensions registered
by each plug-in and determines that files with suffix .flip get handled by
CharFlipper.

Like Simple in the first section, this plug-in has a name: `flipper`. This name gets
used by JavaScript later in this section of code:

Part
II

Ch
5

```
<form>
<input    type=button
          onclick="document.flipper.SetSource('flip1.flip');"
          value="Use flip1.flip">
<input    type=button
          onclick="document.flipper.SetSource('flip2.flip');"
          value="Use flip2.flip">
<input    type=button
          onclick="document.flipper.Start();"
          value=Start>
<input    type=button
          onclick="document.flipper.Stop();"
          value=stop>
</form>
```

Note, too, the private parameters that are passed through <EMBED>. The plug-in reads these parameters back out in NPP_New().

NPP_Initialize()   When Navigator sees the <EMBED> tag, it looks up the plug-in that registered to handle files with the .flip suffix. It finds npFlip and loads this library into its address space. Then it exchanges entry points.

The first method it calls for which you, as the programmer, are responsible is NPP_Initialize(). Use Microsoft Developer Studio's ClassView to open this function. (It's in the Globals folder because it's not part of any class.)

If you're not using Microsoft Visual C++, you may find it difficult to find NPP_Initialize() and the other standard plug-in functions. This is because CharFlipper is built with Netscape's plug-in framework. Look in the Examples/ FrameWork directory of the Plug-In SDK. The file that holds the implementation of the class CNetscapePlugin, CNctscapcPlugin.cpp, also holds tiny implementations of the standard plug-in entry points. For example, here is the definition of NPP_Initialize():

```
//----------------------------------------------------------------
// NPP_Initialize:
//----------------------------------------------------------------
NPError NPP_Initialize(void)
{
        NPError error = InitializeNetscapePlugin();
        return error;
}
```

Notice that `NPP_Initialize()` is simple—it merely uses a call to the `InitializeNetscapePlugin()` function. This function in turn calls the static method `Initialize()` for the class `CCharFlipper()`. Unlike Simple, CharFlipper takes advantage of object technology.

Find `CCharFlipper` toward the top of ClassView. Double-click the tag (not the button to the left) to open the class definition. As shown in the following section, `CCharFlipper` is derived from Netscape's class library class, `CNetscapePlugin`.

Expand the `CCharFlipper` class using FileView and find the `Initialize()` member. This member, too, is simple because it calls Netscape's framework member, `CNetscapePlugin::Initialize()`. Here's the definition of `CCharFlipper::Initialize()`:

```
//----------------------------------------------------------------
// CCharFlipper::Initialize
//----------------------------------------------------------------
NPError
CCharFlipper::Initialize( void )
{
    return CNetscapePlugin::Initialize();
}
```

So this plug-in initializes itself by calling the default `Initialize()` routine in the framework. This method is defined in CNetscapePlugin.h, also in the Framework directory:

```
class CNetscapePlugin : public CNetscapeMemObject {
    public:
        static NPError Initialize( void ) { return NPERR_NO_ERROR; };
        .
        .
        .
}
```

NPP_GetJavaClass()   Just as `NPP_Initialize()` ends up back at `CNetscapePlugin::Initialize()`, so `NPP_GetJavaClass()` ends up having its work done by a global function, `InitializeJavaClass()`, shown in the following code. This function calls the `use` members for the two Java classes employed in this plug-in (`TimeMediaPlugin` and `netscape.plugin.Plugin`), and then returns the Java reference for TimeMediaPlugin.

```
jref InitializeJavaClass(void)
{
    jref theRef = NULL;
    JRIEnv* env = NPN_GetJavaEnv();
    theRef = TimeMediaPlugin::_use( env );
    netscape_plugin_Plugin::_use( env );
    TimeMediaPlugin::_register(env);
    return theRef;
}
```

Figure 5.9 shows the hierarchy of classes that control startup.

FIG. 5.9

Very little of the work of the Netscape functions actually gets done in these functions.

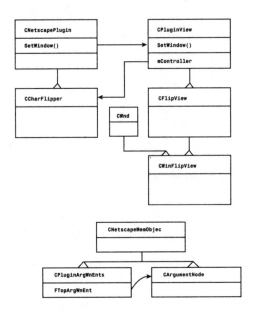

NPP_New()   Now Navigator is ready to make the plug-in instance. Open NPP_New() with ClassWizard. (If you're not using Visual C++, you can find it in at Examples/Framework/CNetscapePlugin.cpp.) In this case, you find that the work is done by CreateNetscapePlugin(), which is simply a convenient wrapper for the real plug-in: CCharFlipper(). Here's the framework's definition of NPP_New():

```
//-----------------------------------------------------------
// NPP_New:
//-----------------------------------------------------------
```

```
NPError NP_LOADDS
NPP_New(NPMIMEType pluginType,
        NPP instance,
        uint16 mode,
        int16 argc,
        char* argn[],
        char* argv[],
        NPSavedData* saved)
{
  if (instance == NULL)
    return NPERR_INVALID_INSTANCE_ERROR;

  // Had to perform the (const char *[]) casts MSVC++ is retarded.
  CPluginArguments* theArgs = new CPluginArguments( argc,
                                                    (const char
                                                    **)argn,
                                                    (const char
                                                    **)argv );
  CNetscapePlugin* thePlugin = CreateNetscapePlugin( instance,
                                                     mode,
                                                     theArgs,
                                                     saved );

  if( thePlugin == 0 )
    return NPERR_OUT_OF_MEMORY_ERROR;
  return NPERR_NO_ERROR;
}
```

CreateNetscapePlugin( ) is defined in CharFlipperFactory.cpp:

```
CNetscapePlugin* CreateNetscapePlugin( NPP instance,
                                       uint16 mode,
                                       CPluginArguments* adoptedArgs,
                                       NPSavedData* saved )
{
    return new CCharFlipper( instance, mode, adoptedArgs );
}
```

So indirectly, NPP_New() calls the CCharFlipper() constructor, which initializes the class to the proper values:

```
CCharFlipper::CCharFlipper( NPP instance,
                            uint16 mode,
                            CPluginArguments* adoptedArgs )
  : CNetscapePlugin( instance, mode, adoptedArgs ),
    mCurrentChar(' '),
    mText( 0 ),
    mTextLength( 0 ),
    mTextIndex( 0 ),
    mTimeLastFlipped( 0 )
{
```

```
        SetSpeed( mArgs->ArgumentValueAsInt( kCharFlipperArgs_Speed,
        ➥ kDefaultSpeed ) );
        SetRunning( mArgs->ArgumentValueAsBool(
kCharFlipperArgs_Autostart,
        ➥kDefaultAutostart ));
        SetLooping( mArgs->ArgumentValueAsBool(
kCharFlipperArgs_Looping,
        ➥kDefaultLooping ));
    }
```

There is considerable delegation in this design, allowing the arguments to be de-
coded easily. Class CCharFlipper has a data member, mArgs, which is an instance
of class CPluginArguments (another Netscape-supplied class from the class
library). CPluginArguments, in turn, has members such as
AcceptArgumentValueAsInt() and AcceptArgumentValueAsBool(), which parse the
parameters into a form understandable by CCharFlipper.

NPP_SetWindow()
NPP_SetWindow() quickly gets through to
CNetscapePlugin::SetWindow(). CNetscapePlugin's mView member is initialized
here. mView is a pointer to a CPluginView, which has the following definition:

```
class CPluginView {
  public:
    CPluginView( CNetscapePlugin* controller );
    virtual ~CPluginView();
    virtual NPError SetWindow( NPWindow* window )
virtual void Paint() {};
    CNetscapePlugin* GetController();
  protected:
    CNetscapePlugin* mController;
};
```

Netscape's model is based on the View/Controller model, like the MVP architecture used at Taligent. The Netscape CPluginView class is useful—it encapsulates
the Paint routines from MS-Windows.

Figure 5.10 illustrates how the components of NPP_SetWindow() communicate.

FIG. 5.10
NPP_SetWindow() is part of a complex hierarchy of structures and classes.

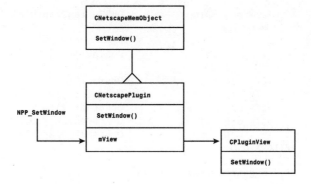

Both CFlipView and CWinFlipView are derived from CPluginView:

```
class CFlipView : public CPluginView
{
public:
    CFlipView( CCharFlipper* inController );
    virtual ~CFlipView();

    // CFlipView methods
    virtual void        SetChar( char inChar );
    CCharFlipper*        GetFlipper();

protected:
    char                mCurrentChar;
};
class CWinFlipView : public CWnd, public CPluginView {
    public:
                            CWinFlipView( CCharFlipper*
inController );
        virtual             ~CWinFlipView();

        virtual WNDPROC*    GetSuperWndProcAddr();

    //{{AFX_MSG( CMainWindow )
        afx_msg void        OnPaint();
        afx_msg void        OnPaletteChanged(CWnd* pWnd);
        afx_msg void        OnLButtonDown(UINT flags, CPoint
        ➥point);
```

```
        afx_msg void            OnRButtonDown(UINT flags, CPoint
        ➥point);

        afx_msg void            OnPlay();

        afx_msg void            OnStop();
        afx_msg void            OnRewind();
        afx_msg void            OnForward();
        afx_msg void            OnFrameBack();
        afx_msg void            OnFrameForward();
    //}}AFX_MSG

        DECLARE_MESSAGE_MAP()

    protected:
        char                    mLastCharacter;
};
```

Note that CWinFlipView is derived not only from CPluginView but also from CWnd:

```
    public CWnd, public CPluginView
```

This class's primary role is to serve as a "gateway" into the Windows message system.

NPP_NewStream(), NPP_WriteReady(), and NPP_Write()   Netscape's class
CNetscapeStream fully encapsulates Netscape's concept of a stream. In
NPP_NewStream() the designer builds a new stream based on the CNetscapePlugin
pointer controller.

```
//-----------------------------------------------------------------
// NPP_NewStream:
//-----------------------------------------------------------------
NPError NP_LOADDS
NPP_NewStream(NPP instance,
              NPMIMEType type,
              NPStream *stream,
              NPBool seekable,
              uint16 *stype)
{
  if (instance == NULL)
    return NPERR_INVALID_INSTANCE_ERROR;
  CNetscapePlugin* controller = (CNetscapePlugin*) instance->pdata;
  CNetscapeStream* theStream = controller->CreateStream(type,
                                                        stream,
                                                        seekable,
                                                        *stype );
```

```
  if( theStream == 0 )
    return NPERR_OUT_OF_MEMORY_ERROR;
  *stype = theStream->GetStreamType();
  return NPERR_NO_ERROR;
}
```

The stream is left at its default `stype` (`NP_NORMAL`). `NPP_WriteReady()` and
`NPP_Write()` just call their underlying `CNetscapeStream` counterparts.

```
//------------------------------------------------------------------
// NPP_WriteReady:
//------------------------------------------------------------------
int32 NP_LOADDS
NPP_WriteReady(NPP instance, NPStream *stream)
{
  if (instance == NULL)
    return -1;
  CNetscapeStream* theStream = CNetscapeStream::EvolveStream( stream );
  if( theStream == 0 )
    return -1;
  return theStream->WriteReady();
}


//------------------------------------------------------------------
// NPP_Write:
//------------------------------------------------------------------
int32 NP_LOADDS
NPP_Write(NPP instance,
          NPStream *stream,
          int32 offset,
          int32 len,
          void *buffer)
{
  if (instance == NULL)
    return -1;
  CNetscapeStream* theStream = CNetscapeStream::EvolveStream( stream );
  if( theStream == 0 )
    return -1;
  return theStream->Write( offset, len, buffer );
}
```

This approach is a bit naive, but considering that the application only reads a short
file and the buffer size is 256 MB, the designer need not be too aggressive in looking for buffer overflow.

NPP_Print()   Like Simple, `NPP_Print()` is not fully hooked up. There is, however,
a tantalizing set of hooks for a future programmer to use:

```
// ------------------------------------------------------
// NPP_Print:
// ----------------------------------------------------------------
void NP_LOADDS
NPP_Print(NPP instance, NPPrint* printInfo)
{
  if(printInfo == NULL)    // trap invalid parm
    return;
  if (instance != NULL)
  {
    CNetscapePlugin* This = (CNetscapePlugin*) instance->pdata;
    This->Print( printInfo );
  }
}

// ----------------------------------------------------------------
// CNetscapePlugin::Print
// ----------------------------------------------------------------
void
CNetscapePlugin::Print( NPPrint* printInfo )
{
  if(printInfo == NULL)    // trap invalid parm
    return;
  if (printInfo->mode == NP_FULL)
  {
    NPBool printResult = PrintFull( printInfo->print.fullPrint );
    printInfo->print.fullPrint.pluginPrinted = printResult;
    ➥// Do the default
  }
  else // If not fullscreen, we must be embedded
  {
    PrintEmbeded( printInfo->print.embedPrint );
  }
}
```

LiveConnect Details

So far you have seen a lot of encapsulation but nothing written to the screen.
CharFlipper, even more so than Simple, is a creature of LiveConnect. Figure 5.11
shows the interaction between JavaScript, Java, and the plug-in.

FIG. 5.11
Although the plug-in
and JavaScript cannot
talk directly, the Java
peer object is quick
and easy to set up.

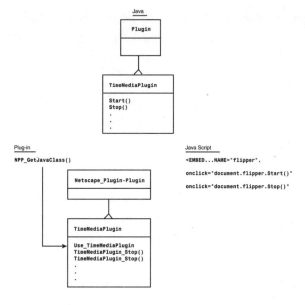

Examining the Java Code

Netscape intends the Java class `TimeMediaPlugin` to become a general-purpose tool
for use with time-based content. A look at the Java code reveals that all of the real
work is done in native methods:

```java
class TimeMediaPlugin extends Plugin {
  public void SetSource(java.net.URL inSourceURL) {
    SetSourceNative( inSourceURL.toString() );
  }
  public void SetSource(java.lang.String inSourceString) {
    SetSourceNative( inSourceString );
  }
  public native void SetSourceNative( java.lang.String inSourceString
);
  public native void Start();
  public native void Stop();
  public native boolean IsRunning();
  public native void Loop( boolean inLoop );
  public native boolean IsLooping();

  // speed is in 60ths of a second
  public native void SetSpeed( int inSpeed );.
  public native int GetSpeed();
}
```

"Native" Java methods are the methods implemented outside of Java, usually in a language like C or C++. Netscape supplies a tool, javah, which reads Java files and writes function stubs. When javah reads the following line:

```
public native void Start();
```

in class TimeMediaPlugin, it writes a series of function definitions in _gen/ TimeMediaPlugin.h, including the following:

```
extern JRI_PUBLIC_API(void)
native_TimeMediaPlugin_Start(JRIEnv* env, struct
TimeMediaPlugin*self);
```

The plug-in programmer then writes an implementation of the native functions. The Netscape programmer has put these implementations in the file TimeMediaNatives.cpp. For example, native_TimeMediaPlugin_Start() is implemented as follows:

```
extern JRI_PUBLIC_API(void)
native_TimeMediaPlugin_Start(JRIEnv* env, struct TimeMediaPlugin* self)
{
  NPP instance = (NPP) (self->getPeer(env));
  CCharFlipper* flipper = (CCharFlipper*) instance->pdata;
  flipper->StartAtFrame( 0 );
}
```

This function calls CCharFlipper::StartAtFrame() with inFrame set to zero. If that function passes its internal tests, CCharFlipper::SetRunning() is set to TRUE and the flipper begins to flip.

 T I P When tracing through large amounts of code, particularly in an object-oriented system where so many small functions call other small functions, it's good to be able to tell the system, "Show me where this function is used," or "Show me who defines this function." To get this kind of information from Microsoft, C++ rebuilds the project with "browse into" turned on.

Triggering the Plug-In with Periodic Events

Your desktop computer can read streams quickly, even those coming in through a dial-up connection. If the plug-in displayed each character and immediately "flipped" to the next, you'd see only a blur as characters passed from the stream to the screen. To solve this problem, CharFlipper keeps each character on the screen until a timer tells the program to move on to the next character.

Examine `CCharFlipper::HandleTimePassed()`. As long as `isRunning` remains true, this function looks at the time and the current speed and decides whether or not it's time to read another character. If so, the character is received from the `(GetNextChar()` buffer and displayed in the `(SetChar())` view.

Finally `Paint()` is called. `Paint()` simply invalidates the rectangle and waits while Windows comes back through to dispatch the `WM_PAINT` message.

```
CCharFlipper::HandleTimePassed()
{
  NPBool isRunning = GetRunning( );
  if( isRunning ) {
    unsigned long currentTicks = GetNormalSysTime();
    long speed = GetSpeed();
    if( mTimeLastFlipped <= ( currentTicks - speed ) ) {
      mTimeLastFlipped = currentTicks;
      mCurrentChar = GetNextChar();
      ((CFlipView*)mView)->SetChar( mCurrentChar );
      mView->Paint();
    }
  }
}
```

Note also that CharFlipper handles mouse-down messages. The generic `HandleMouseClick()` simply toggles the running state:

```
void
CCharFlipper::HandleMouseClick()
{
  NPBool isRunning = GetRunning();
  SetRunning( ! isRunning );
}
```

What triggers `HandleTimePassed()`? If you compiled the project with "Build browse info file" turned on in the Build Settings, you can right-click the mouse on `HandleTimePassed()` and find that this function is triggered by a timer.

A similar inquiry on `SetTimer()` reveals that the timer is set in `CWinFlipView::SetWindow()`. Every 10 milliseconds this timer sends a `WM_TIMER` message.

Figure 5.12 illustrates the process of producing and consuming timer messages.

FIG. 5.12
Use a periodic timer if you're looking for something that can happen at any time.

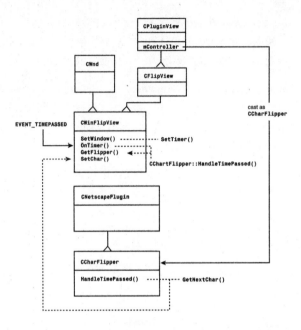

CharFlipper also is the first Netscape-supplied plug-in to use MFC and the message map. Examine the message maps in WinFlipView.cpp and CWinFlipView.cpp.

`CWinFlipView::OnTimer()`, in turn, calls `CharFlipper::HandleTimePassed()`, as follows:

```
void CWinFlipView::OnTimer(UINT nIDEvent)
{
    // TODO: Add your message handler code here and/or call default
    if( nIDEvent == EVENT_TIMEPASSED ) {
        GetFlipper()->HandleTimePassed();
    }
    CWnd::OnTimer(nIDEvent);
}
```

How the JavaScript and HTML Are Connected

Recall that the HTML file held a form:

```
<form>
<input    type=button
          onclick="document.flipper.SetSource('flip1.flip');"
          value="Use flip1.flip">
<input    type=button
          onclick="document.flipper.SetSource('flip2.flip');"
          value="Use flip2.flip">
```

```
<input    type=button
          onclick="document.flipper.Start();"
          value=Start>
<input    type=button
          onclick="document.flipper.Stop();"
          value=stop>
</form>
```

This form directs the function calls such as start(), stop(), and setSource() to the named plug-in. Because CharFlipper, the plug-in, has an associated Java class (TimeMediaPlugin), all is well.

The JavaScript handler onClick calls start or one of the other functions on the named plug-in flipper. This method gets picked up by Java, which calls the Java method start().

Java, in turn, calls the native method named start, which is back in the plug-in. Figure 5.3, which appeared earlier in this chapter, traced the flow of control between JavaScript, the Java peer object, and the plug-in.

Closing Down the Plug-In

When the interaction is over and the user is ready to leave CharFlipper, Navigator calls NPP_Destroy(). Because there is only one instance, NPP_Shutdown() is called immediately after the instance is deleted.

NPP_Destroy() is in Examples/Framework/CNetscapePlugin.cpp:

```
//-----------------------------------------------------------------
// NPP_Destroy:
//-----------------------------------------------------------------
NPError NP_LOADDS
NPP_Destroy(NPP instance, NPSavedData** save)
{
  if (instance == NULL)
    return NPERR_INVALID_INSTANCE_ERROR;
  CNetscapePlugin* thePlugin = (CNetscapePlugin*) instance->pdata;
  if (thePlugin == 0)
    return NPERR_INVALID_PLUGIN_ERROR;
  NPError result = thePlugin->SaveData( save );
  delete thePlugin;
  return result;
}
```

Note that because CharFlipper is designed with Netscape's class library, the code has hooks for all the usual plug-in features, such as the use of NPSavedData. Although the function isn't used here, it could be hooked up easily in CCharFlipper::SaveData().

From Here...

In this chapter you built complete Windows plug-ins, using Microsoft's Visual C++ on Windows. These plug-ins were shown to be quite complete in terms of functionality, including support for LiveConnect.

- The next chapter, "Developing Content for Plug-Ins," looks at LiveCache and CD-ROM developing.

- Chapter 7, "The Java Runtime Interface," looks at Java platform support for native methods and Java classes.

- Chapter 8, "Calling Java Methods from Plug-Ins," shows how fields are accessed and discusses Java names and parameters, as well as security issues.

- Chapter 9, "Calling the Plug-In from Java Methods," shows how to define a Plug-in class and tells you more about native methods and globals.

CHAPTER 6

Developing Content for Plug-Ins

Multimedia publishers are currently developing products that are a mix of online and CD-ROM content, called hybrid technology. This chapter contemplates this technology and what it means for those who are new to developing and publishing content.

This is the information age, so it comes as no surprise that there are great advantages to combining retrieval software with up-to-date real-time online information. Large volumes of offline information (CD-ROMs) can be combined with online access (the Web) to supply the user with quicker search and retrieval methods while having the counterpart of great graphics, video, and sound. In other words, the best of both worlds. ▪

How You Can Customize LiveCache

This not only improves your own system performance, but also decreases network time lag as well.

CD-ROM Developing

There are currently very powerful changes happening in the world of CD-ROMs and online hybrids.

Rewritable CD-ROMs

CD-RW gives users the ability to write, rewrite, and erase files on CDs.

Product Development Rights and Protections

Content acquisition is an important process that encompasses such things as requiring third-party licenses and releases.

Major Offerings in the Protection and Rights Arena

See what the leading companies are offering in the way of technology protection and rights.

LiveCache

With all the new interest in hybrid CD-ROM/Web development products, Netscape's LiveCaching technology preloads multimedia files on a CD into its browser cache.

LiveCache enables programmers to create a cache that can be customized and can be found on a CD-ROM as well as on your local computer system. Content developers now have a much easier way of letting users download video, audio, and any other kinds of multimedia content that would be much too slow to download over a network. Users can now load a CD-ROM that contains Web content and then go to the corresponding Web site for interaction with new Web pages. This can now be done without slowing down your network and frustrating your users.

Cache Preferences

If you're running a Windows or Unix machine, you'll find your cache size and preferences in the Network/Cache panel. If you're running a Macintosh, the disk cache size is already set in the Memory panel. You can access this info by choosing Get Info from the File menu within the Finder mode. The cache preferences can be found in the Netscape Preferences folder inside the System Folder on your Mac.

A cache only temporarily stores the page information on your computer. By choosing a link, or entering a new URL, or reloading a page, Netscape Navigator looks at the server to see if any changes or updates have been made before loading a page from your cache. If there are any changes, the Navigator loads a new version of the page over the network. If there are no changes, the Navigator can load a copy from your cache much quicker.

When a page is loaded by the Navigator, the document information is temporarily stored in both the memory and disk cache. Of course, the information is retrieved much more quickly from the memory cache, but the cache is emptied each time you exit Netscape. The disk cache, though, can be maintained on your local hard drive, and pages are still retrieved quicker than when directly loaded from the Network. However, keep in mind that the disk cache is taking up hard drive space. This not only improves your own system performance, but also decreases network time lag as well.

Setting Up LiveCache

To set up LiveCache, follow these steps recommended by Netscape:

1. Clear your memory and disk caches.

2. Set the memory cache to zero.

3. Set the disk cache to your preferred size (recommended 2000-5000KB).

4. You can enter the following code in any HTML document that will now use your new cache setting:

   <META HTTP-EQUIV="Ext-cache"CONTENT="name=MyCache; instructions=Intructions to Your User">

5. Now when Netscape Navigator loads an HTML document that includes the line of code above, a File Open dialog box will appear. The user will find the cache file called fat.db. After the cache file is opened by the user, all other files with that same tag (.htm or .html) will now use this cache file. (See Figure 6.1.)

FIG. 6.1
HTML document showing the File Open dialog box where cache file fat.db can be opened and used by same tag files.

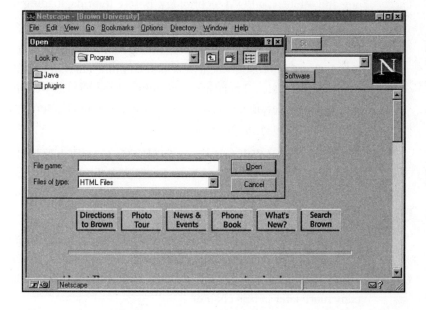

Part

II

Ch

6

T I P The preferable size of the cache should increase your Navigator's performance. However, a cache that is increased too much can restrict the performance of other applications. A better configuration may be to increase your memory cache to the size your system usually doesn't use, and then to increase your disk cache to anywhere between 2000KB and 5000KB. You'll know if the cache is too large if you exit Navigator and there is quite a time lag.

CD-ROM Developing

There are currently some powerful changes going on in the world on CD-ROMs and online hybrids. Big players like Intel, Microsoft, and Netscape have been moving forward with new technology that holds a bright future for hybrid CD-ROMs and Web development.

As mentioned previously, hybrid technology is the merging of online Web technology and offline CD-ROM technology. Before hybrids, loading multimedia content over a phone live was a very arduous and time-consuming task.

Early on, Microsoft pushed this technology forward with Microsoft Complete Baseball and Microsoft Encarta, which combine current CD-ROM content with new online updates. There are currently catalog CDs as well that, when combined with online ordering and product updates, are a quick alternative to loading a whole catalog over the network.

The beginning of Web content on CD-ROMs (CD/Web hybrids) included HTML page content with embedded links to the Web directly from the CD. These make it easier for users to find you on the Web, and keep the cumbersome content on the CD-ROM.

As you can expect, there now are new Web-based tools that make this kind of union and more powerful kinds of hybrids possible. The first company that provided custom software for this purpose is Teleshuttle. We'll talk about this company more later in this chapter.

Developing Tools

There are several new tools that have emerged within the past year that are now becoming quite integrated into hybrid CD/Web technology. The first tool, CD caching of Web content, was already discussed at the beginning of this chapter.

The second tool is known as *parallel searching*. Parallel searching enables searching of both the local CD content and remote Web content as if the search request were a single request only. Two software companies, Verity and Personal Library Software, were the first to move forward with this search capability, but there are now companies cropping up all the time and jumping on the hybrid bandwagon.

The third tool, offline access facilities, allows users to update CD-ROM content by downloading new Web content to their own local hard drive. They can then browse this content offline, without any further need to connect to a network. Netscape's Inbox Direct is one of several software packages available today that does this quite well.

These tools allow for a seamless integration between the CD-ROM and the Web. Users load a CD-ROM first and then interact with the Web, or access the Web first and then integrate it with a preloaded CD cache. Either way, this new technology is a quicker and easier way of accessing Web content.

The CD/Web Hybrid Future

The next few years should showcase new markets for this hybrid technology. The competition will be getting fierce, which will increase the amount of multimedia software available and bring the prices down as well.

Integrating multimedia content is also useful to the client/server market, when combined with authoring and developing tools. Vendors now have resources for developing content like never before. Macromedia is a leader in the authoring tool market. (See Figure 6.2.) Two of its major authoring products, Director and Authorware, bring new competition to the authoring arena and could be a client/server force in the near future.

Part
II

Ch
6

FIG. 6.2
Macromedia's Web
site.

ON THE WEB

You can find Macromedia at **http://www.macromedia.com/**.

Oracle's authoring tool, called Oracle Media Objects (OMO), is like Director—
fully compatible across Windows and Macintosh platforms. While Macromedia's
Director can be purchased for about $800, OMO lists for about $500. (See Figure
6.3.)

OMO is very similar to HyperCard, but is much faster. Hypercard users will find it
very easy to use, especially since Hypercard is strictly for Macintosh platforms.
Most content developing tools, like Adobe's Photoshop, seem to be priced around
or below $500.

ON THE WEB

You can find Oracle at **http://www.oracle.com/**.

FIG. 6.3
Oracle's Web site.

Developing Cross-Platform Tools and Objects

When developing multimedia content, a major consideration is developing for cross-application environments. For instance, client/server environments provide ease-of-use across application environments and have the benefit of being object-oriented as well. Macromedia's Authorware, which now includes SQL access, is an incredible tool that gives users analysis capabilities and ease-of-use features. Sysbase's Gain Interplay also offers great ease-of-use features and offers client/server cross-platform developing.

The current and future hybrid CD/Web technology will provide users with new ways of connecting to online services or accessing interactive Web pages while running media, like video and graphics, all very easy to use and in real time.

While only a programmer can use Macromedia's Director quickly, Apple Media Tool (see Figure 6.4) enables someone less experienced to program a product. With a relatively simple point-and-click interface, you can easily and quickly create designs and integrate media productions. Multimedia users that have little programming experience will find more and more authoring tools that are beginner-friendly.

Part
II

Ch
6

FIG. 6.4

Apple Media Tool Web page.

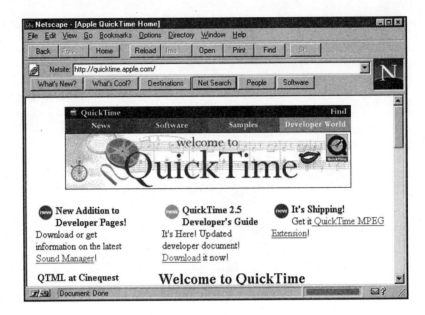

ON THE WEB

You can find Apple Media Tool at **http://quicktime.apple.com/**.

For those of us that want a more advanced object-oriented programming tool, Kaleida's ScriptX creates interactive multimedia content that is more complex and difficult to use. ScriptX is really more of an object-oriented language than a tool, and is definitely not beginner-friendly.

ON THE WEB

You can find Kaleida's ScriptX at **http://www.iis.forthnet.gr/MVres/ScriptXstep1.html**.

Of course, this will also create more competition in the authoring and developing market arena in the future. The bigger the competition, the better the product and the lower the price.

Teleshuttle

Teleshuttle links CD-ROMs and other local media with up-to-date online information. Software is prepared as an essential component of CD-ROMs or disks that are embedded to allow users access to information, communication, and entertainment as well.

This essential hybrid component provides a technology business environment for searching and retrieving information that crosses over to either a network or the Web. (See Figure 6.5.)

FIG. 6.5
Teleshuttle Web site
is a valuable resource
for distributed media
content.

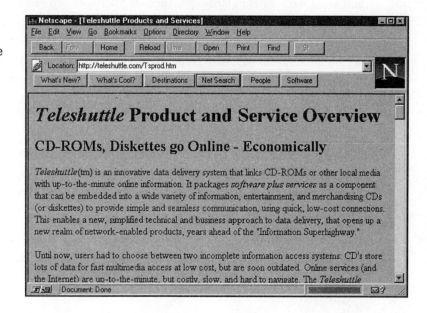

Teleshuttle's software packages offer publishers and developers the following:

- A packaged communications software module

  Works with their CD-ROMs or disks through an Application Programming Interface (API) that controls requests.

- An operations server

  Transporter module connects to a remote server, and a Drop-in Utility Transporter does not need program integration.

- User support services

  Mouse driven, requires very little browsing experience from users.

ON THE WEB

You can find Teleshuttle at **http://www.teleshuttle.com/Tsprod.htm**.

Part
II

Ch
6

RadMedia's PowerMedia

RadMedia's PowerMedia Web multimedia presentation software combines a set of authoring tools for standard Netscape and Microsoft browsers. PowerMedia is cross-platform Web communications and presentation software that can create and publish dynamic multimedia presentations on a CD-ROM, over an intranet, or across the Internet. HTML 3.0 documents can be created that contain hyperlinks to other documents, Java applets, and other multimedia software.

PowerMedia has the ease-of-use of a desktop publisher, as well as the power of a full Web publishing tool using essential multimedia effects.

Training courses can be designed using PowerMedia, and classes can be taken over the Net to train users and employees alike. The same presentations can be distributed on CD-ROM format or can be accessed by the user over an intranet or the Internet itself.

PowerMedia's architecture technology is derived from RadMedia's New Tsunami Architecture and merges HTML, HTTP, Java, and Netscape standards. PowerMedia is compatible with Windows 95, UNIX, and Macintosh as well. (See Figure 6.6.)

FIG. 6.6
RadMedia Web site.

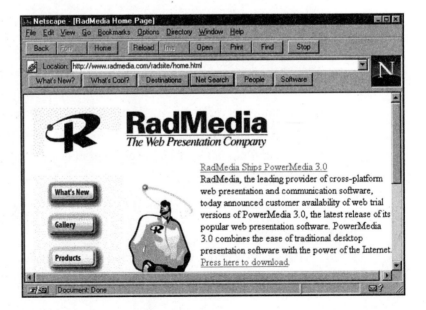

PowerMedia consists of the following four components:

■ PowerStart

A set of presentation start-up functions, including storyboarding tools, templates, styles, table of contents, demos, and tutorials.

■ PixelPerfect HTML

One-button publishing of Web and multimedia content in a WYSIWYG style. Content can be combined in a variety of ways: HTML, graphics, dynamic images, Java applets, and in-line plug-ins.

■ LiveDoc Publishing

Enables interactive user control with live dynamic media in the form of Java, multimedia, and Web content. Uses embedded Java applets that can be run by the user or can be run automatically.

■ WebSmart Authoring and Delivery

Enables authors and developers to use the Web as a content and media library. With a mouse click, link directly to any URL on the Web. You can import directly into PowerMedia from the Web, and you can create SmartObjects with any media and links and then use them again and again.

N O T E RadMedia has quite a library of LiveDoc Java applets. It's a great resource to find animated applets, live data feeds, synchronized audio and video, and database linking. ■

RadMedia offers a 30-day trial version of PowerMedia (it times-out after 30 days) and can be downloaded directly from their Web site (see the following "On the Web"). Full versions are available for Windows 95 and NT for $199, and UNIX (Solaris, IRIX, HP-UX and AIX) for $499. Versions are available in English, French, German, and Japanese.

Part

II

Ch

6

ON THE WEB

You can find RAD Power Media at **http://www.radmedia.com/radsite/home.html**.

SuperCard

SuperCard, published by Allegiant Technologies, Inc., offers a 30-day trial version (times-out after 30 days) for the Macintosh. Documentation is provided for you electronically. You can download the software directly from their Web site (see the "On the Web" later in this section). There's a Windows version in the works, but at the time of this writing it's still under construction. (See Figure 6.7.)

FIG. 6.7
SuperCard Web site.

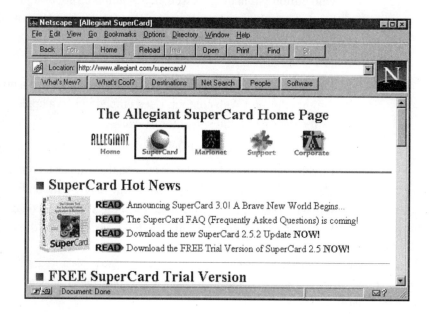

SuperCard is an authoring tool that lets users create and design content that can run with a distributable Player or as a standalone application. Script editing cannot be done while running the trial version.

SuperCard consists of the following eight components:

- Quick Start Tutorial

  Contains a basic SuperCard tutorial on its editing environment, which consists of SuperEdit and Runtime Editor. An Adobe Acrobat (PDF) file is included that can be viewed with the Adobe Acrobat Reader.

- Applications

  Includes SuperCard TV, Bridger, and SuperEdit TV

- SC Pouch

  Contains the Runtime Editor, SuperCard Prefs, SharedFile project, and utility palettes for specialized Runtime functions

- SuperCard Documentation

  Contains full Adobe Acrobat (PDF) versions of standard retail documentation

- Help Folder

  Contains a complete SuperTalk Language Reference project, third-party services and support, and SuperCard tips and techniques

- Samples

  Contains sample SuperCard projects that instruct you on SuperCard functions. You'll learn about fields, windows, buttons, graphics, menus, and sounds

- Standalone Maker

  Used for creating mouse-driven (clickable) standalone project applications

- SuperCard Tutorial

  Contains the SuperCard Tutorial Guide in Adobe Acrobat (PDF) format

NOTE SuperCard can only run on a Macintosh with a 68020 processor or greater. System 7.0 or higher is also required. Version System 6 is not supported.

ON THE WEB

You can find SuperCard at **http://www.allegiant.com/supercard/**.

Part
II

Ch
6

Rewritable CD-ROMs

Five well-known companies, Sony (**www.sony.com**), Mitsubishi, Hewlett-Packard (**www.hp.com**), Phillips (**www.phillips.com**), and Ricoh (**www.ricoh.co.jp/index_e.html**) all have plans for rewritable CD-ROM drives known as CD-RW. CD-RW allows users the capability to write, rewrite, and erase files on CD-ROMs. All this can be done by using a mouse, without the need of additional recording software. At the time of this writing, CD-RW drives are expected for the first quarter of 1997 and should be priced at approximately $500-$700.

CD-RW discs will not be readable by current CD-ROM drives due to their use of new phase-change technology and their decreased reflectivity. There are new multiread CD-ROMs that can play (only) CD-RW discs and cost about the same as current CD-ROM drives. CD-RW drives will also be backward-compatible with all current CD drive technology (CD-ROM, CD-R, and CD-RW). Media discs for CD-RW drives will cost $25 and up.

Microsoft, Apple, and Unix are working on enabling UDF (Universal Disk Format—enables packet writing) software to seamlessly integrate into computer operating systems, instead of running on top of the standard operating system as it does currently.

The rewritablity and relatively low cost of CD-RW drives could result in thousands of units sold by the end of 1997, and possibly millions by the year 2000.

Product Development Rights and Protections

Multimedia products are a colossal combination of text, video, and audio material. This section focuses on some of the major hurdles you may encounter when creating such vast multimedia products as CD-ROMs, interactive software, and games.

Content acquisition is an important process that includes requiring third-party licenses and releases, and it takes a lot of effort to track down the proper people in authority who can grant those necessary licenses and other rights. Keep in mind, it's pretty common for a multimedia product to require many different licenses and agreements.

An important goal of a multimedia developer should be to find a way to keep the costs of this product-protection process to a minimum, while also evaluating what the outcome would be if the developers' rights were breached. This section is meant to give you good information and resources to help you make some of these difficult decisions governing your rights and protections.

Content Licensing

This section gives you an overview of important terms and ideas to keep in mind when stipulating a multimedia content license. Keep in mind that this section is not meant to take the place of important legal advice when you're actually writing and enforcing a content license. In other words, I'm not your legal adviser!

What Is the Content?   The first and foremost step is to identify what portions of your content need to be licensed. It's a good idea to include a copy of the actual licensed work describing the product.

What About Limitations?   Multimedia developers can place limitations on the rights they grant to a license; however, safeguard your product by making sure your product rights are quite comprehensive in spectrum. A comprehensive use of rights should consider the following:

- Licensing rights must be detailed—what rights are specifically granted to the multimedia developer?
- The owner of content licenses should have exclusive right to reproduce, adapt, publish, and display that particular content freely and openly to the public.
- Additional rights can be obtained under trademark and privacy laws as well.

What About the Future?   The content license should also be clear about any future technology, whether or not the technology is currently known, and how the developer rights should include this technology even if this technology is still tentative.

What About the Length?   A multimedia product developer should look for the longest-term rights possible. Why? Obviously, this increases the amount of profits received from the product, and helps to ensure that the developer reclaims its investment.

What About Payment?   Before agreeing to any particular fees or royalties, a developer should know the current industry standard for his or her product. Fees can be fixed and paid out in one lump sum or over a period of time. Whereas royalties allow both the licensor and licensee to share in the success (or failure) of that product.

Part
II
Ch
6

What About Receiving Credit for Your Work?   Who doesn't want to receive credit where credit is due? Developers and authors usually like to receive credit, in writing, directly associated with their multimedia product content.

Major Offerings in the Protection and Rights Arena

We also wanted to include a section describing the technology protection and rights that leading companies are offering. Each company discussed in this section will be reviewed concerning their copyright protection and technology rights.

AT&T Secure Communications Systems   In 1995, through the combined effort of AT&T Secure Communications Systems, Bell Laboratories, and VLSI Technology, a market metering technology called IVES (Information Vending Encryption System) was created. IVES demonstrates metering technology by protecting digital content, rights management, and usage metering.

IVES is an advanced metering technology that encompasses such electronic technology as electronic commerce, electronic publishing, electronic news, video-on-demand, software distribution, program licensing, and program use metering. See Table 6.1 for descriptions of IVES-Supported Security Services.

Table 6.1.   IVES Supported Security Services

Security Service	Description
(SSI) Security Service Interface	Calls that access IVES services
Secure network communications	Means for secure messaging across protocols; a network, including secure addressing
Security applications protocols	Application-dependent protocols, such as methods for dispensing entitlements the service is supporting
IVES Authentication protocols	Methods for securely and reliably identifying system entities
Key management	Cryptographic key generation, distribution, and maintenance methods supporting the various security functions

Security Service	Description
Local, off-chip memory	Capabilities for storing protection mechanisms information, including digital cash balances in security containers of arbitrary size, off-chip
Security kernel	Atomic security services that cannot be interrupted or interfered with
Physical layer security	Silicon-layer anti-tamper, memory protection, bus isolation protection

IVES architecture is based on a cryptographic key management system that uses a secure coprocessor, the RSA public key encryption system for authenticating permissions, and also triple DES (Data Encryption Standard) with key cache for content encryption and/or decryption. Besides security technology, IVES also provides communications protocols for data and audio compression as well.

Many electronic devices, such as computers, servers, CD-ROMs, and video games, can apply IVES chip technology. Application Programming Interface (API) developing can be incorporated also.

CD-MAX, Inc. CD-MAX, Inc. supplies copyright protection and usage billing services to content developers and patented technology providers.

During content development and before the actual development of the CD-ROM, CD-MAX encrypts the CD-ROM content to manage content and metering. A security program has to be installed on the user's machine to effectively decrypt the CD-ROM content so the user can then have full access to it. CD-MAX system versions are available for Windows, Unix, and Macintosh operating systems.

CD-MAX will supply to the developer/publisher the actual program that does the content encryption. The program can be changed relative to the developer's software and therefore is unique.

The CD-MAX's encryption program can only be accessed if the security program is loaded and running on the user's system. The user can access the program from the CD-ROM itself or from a disk included with the CD-ROM.

A file that is protected is created at the time of installation, and includes necessary security keys and information. The security keys can be updated online directly from CD-MAX as well.

Developers and publishers can select many different types of charges. You can choose certain functions that can be metered and then billed. Functions like downloading and printing are quite common usages that are billed. Different ways of customer payment choices can be formulated as well.

N O T E   In 1995, CD-MAX was granted, for its copyright protection and usage billing services, an unrestricted export license that enables their technology to be freely exported and used anywhere, with the exception of Cambodia, Cuba, Libya, North Korea, and Vietnam.

CD-MAX's security and metering services are media-independent and multi-platform as well. This is an important design factor to note, especially with CD-MAX's capability to be used across networks and the Internet.

ON THE WEB

You can find CD-MAX, Inc. at **http://www.cais.net/**.

Infosafe Systems, Inc.   Infosafe Systems, Inc., offers protection and metering utilizing a hardware-based technology. Their proprietary technology does combine both software and hardware protection. A device box called the Infosafe-Mark III connects via a Small Computer System Interface (SCSI) directly to the user's computer or multi-user server. Infosafe is compatible with both Windows and Macintosh systems. The software provided with their device box doesn't modify the existing operating system in any way.

Infosafe's Mark III also is equipped with a modem and phone line that you can use with other online devices like fax communications. The modem is used by Infosafe to transmit usage information to the publisher, and different customer payment options can be set up as well.

The developer can choose portions of content information that can be sold and separately priced. Each portion of information, called a packet, is encrypted with a separate encryption key and placed on a media, like a CD-ROM, and packaged together with unencrypted indices that can then access the encrypted packet of information.

An example from the user's point of view: if you provided an online newspaper and periodical service, a user could browse through article abstracts or read full articles without being charged. Maybe you would only charge your customers per download or per article printed.

ON THE WEB

You can find Infosafe Systems, Inc. at **http://www.infosafe.com/**.

Wave Systems Corporation   The Wave Systems Corporation has both CD-ROM and network versions of their encryption metering technology. The Wave System consists of a control and metering device called the WaveMeter, data preparation and information control, search programs, and the WaveNet. See Table 6.2 for WaveMeter components and their descriptions.

Table 6.2.   WaveMeter Application Process

Application Process	Description
The WaveMeter	Microprocessor-based device that decrypts and tracks usage data
Data Preparation	Information, volume, article, or page that is prepared and protected by the Wave System
Information Control	The information now encrypted can be delivered to the user by CD-ROM, across networks, or the Internet.
Search and Retrieval	WSC does not provide its own end-user search application. With Application Programming Interfaces (APIs), developers and design their own functions that suit their product.
WaveNet	WaveNet is an information transaction data communications system, processed through the WaveMeter, started by the user.

The WaveMeter is a microprocessor-based system that decrypts and tracks usage data. It's physically hooked up to a standalone computer or computer network server. A user starts WaveMeter via modem by dialing into the WaveNet, which is a Wave System Corporation online system. The user then uses a credit card to set up a credit account which credits a dollar amount to the WaveMeter usage system. Companies can set up credit accounts directly with WaveNet instead of using a credit card. Once credit is established directly or by credit card, the user then receives keys for the purchasing of databases.

Once the WaveMeter is started and initialized, the user can look through and buy information using third-party search-and-retrieval programs. Once purchase information is filled out (on the entry screen), the WaveMeter decrypts this information packet to be downloaded or printed by the user.

The Wave System handles data preparation by executing four important steps:

1. The developer or publisher groups the packet of information for purchase.
2. The developer or publisher decides on the price of each packet of information purchased. There is a WaveNet interface that allows for the updating of prices.
3. For search and retrieval purposes, abstracts and keywords need to be defined. The abstracts and keywords are not encrypted and can be searched by the user.
4. Finally, the packets of information to be protected must now be encrypted. This encryption process is fully automated and the Wave System complies with the Data Encryption Standard (DES).

The encrypted content can now be retrieved by the user through many different methods: CD-ROMs, across networks, across satellites, and across the Internet.

N O T E The Wave System Corporation was granted an unrestricted export license that enables their technology to be freely exported and used in any non-Communist countries. This is because the WaveMeter doesn't let the user actually control the encryption keys or the WaveMeter device itself.

ON THE WEB

You can find Wave Systems Corporation at **http://www.wavesys.com/**.

From Here...

Hybrid technologies enable publishers and developers to distribute their products across the Web while much of the content resides on local CD-ROMs. There is no limit to what the future may hold for this technology. From catalog CD links to the Web for product information, to pricing, to searching and retrieving up-to-date online resources, this is assuredly the information age.

- The previous chapter, "Programming Plug-Ins," looks at plug-ins and HTML, as well as Simple and CharFlipper LiveConnect plug-ins.
- The next chapter, "The Java Runtime Interface," looks at Java platform support for native methods and Java classes.
- Chapter 8, "Calling Java Methods from Plug-Ins," shows how fields are accessed and discusses Java names and parameters, as well as security issues.
- Chapter 9, "Calling the Plug-In from Java Methods," shows how to define a plug-in class and tells you more about native methods and globals.

Part
II

Ch
6

Live-Connecting Plug-Ins with Java

The Java Runtime Interface

Netscape LiveConnect is based on a key technology called the Java Runtime Interface (JRI). The JRI allows native methods to be written so that they stay relative to any changes anticipated in new releases of Java classes, the Java runtime, or the Navigator. This ensures that any plug-ins developers write today will still run well into the future. ■

Java Platform Support for Native Methods

Java runtime clients can be native methods that respond to Java operations called from the Java runtime.

Java Classes and Native Methods

The JRI decouples native methods from the Java classes they manage.

JRI Reflection Module

The JRI Reflection Module is a way to ascertain reflective information on Java classes and methods.

JRI Embedding Module

The JRI Embedding Module defines the mechanism that enables Java runtimes to be embedded in application programs.

JRI Compiler Module

The JRI Compiler Module determines the programming interface that invokes the class compiler.

Introduction to JRI

The JRI is the standard interface to Java. JRI enables native methods to operate against any Java platform supporting JRI.

JRI prevents Java classes from affecting native methods when upgrading Java classes. Runtime providers can enhance their runtime without changing their clients.

Java runtime clients can be either native methods that are called from Java operations or applications implementing functions. Applications that run applets in performing their functions, like Netscape Navigator, use Java runtime.

The JRI is the device that implements the Java runtime. This does not exclude the existing interfaces that are internal to a runtime, like a compiler.

It is the JRI that allows Netscape Navigator plug-ins to define Java classes and to call native C functions. The JRI, along with Netscape Navigator application programming interface (API), is what allows plug-ins to be accessed in a Java environment.

Netscape Navigator Version 3.0 and Later Includes Borland's Java JIT Compiler

Netscape enhanced its Java support when they struck a deal with Borland International, Inc., to include the Borland JIT compiler, AppAccelerator, for Windows 95.

Although the Java programming language produces dynamic live Web pages, users and developers have complained of its slow compile time. AppAccelerator translates Java bytecodes into machine code (Intel in this case), allowing programs to execute 5-10 times faster. The JIT compiler will entice more developers to create Java programs and, given its fast compile time, will enable users to use Java applets without further time delays.

Java Platform Support for Native Methods

Java runtime clients can be native methods that respond to Java operations called from the Java runtime. They can also be applications that implement particular functions and are also called from the Java runtime. Netscape Navigator is one such application that runs applets and operates programming or developing environments that function with the Java runtime.

The JRI is the interface between Java operations and applications. JRI extracts the information from the Java runtime. This is necessary for runtime independence. However, additional interfaces like a "just-in-time" compiler could be utilized as well.

N O T E The javah that is provided with the Java Development Kit (JDK) has the interfaces that are necessary in implementing native methods. These important interfaces all integrate with the JRI. The new javah version is enhanced in the following ways:

- Native methods can be written that are Java object-independent.
- C programmers will find that the macros used to call methods and access fields are very similar to C.
- Each Java class has a C++ class defined so that call methods to JRI operations are inlined calls. ▨

JRI Native Method Interface

The JRI Native Method Interface Module delineates the start of native method operations. It is the most basic interface to the Java runtime. It offers the native method programmer the ability to load classes, access fields, create instances, call arrays, and set up new native methods as well.

There are operations that are included in the current version of JRI (version 0.6). These operations are not included:

▨ Operations to control threads and perform synchronization

▨ Operations to initialize the runtime and construct execution environments

These operations are provided for through the JRI Embedding Interface, which is explained later in this chapter. They are also provided for by system-dependent native method implementation.

▶ For more information on integrating native methods with plug-ins, **see** Chapter 9, "Calling the Plug-In from Java Methods."

There have been changes to the JRI (version 0.6) since Netscape Navigator 3.0b5. These changes include the following:

- ▣ `JRI_NewScalarArray` now has an elementSig parameter describing the element type of the array.

- ▣ `JRI_CopyString` and `JRI_CopyStringUTF` have been replaced by the garbage collected versions: `JRI_GetStringChars` and `JRI_GetStringUTFChars`.

- ▣ `JRI_CallMethod`, `JRI_CallMethodA`, `JRI_CallMethodV`, `JRI_CallStaticMethod`, `JRI_CallStaticMethodA`, and `JRI_CallStaticMethodV` have been divided into separate functions for each of the primitive types instead of returning a `JRIValue` union type.

- ▣ Field and method "thunks" have been replaced by field and method IDs.

Java Classes and Native Methods

The JRI decouples native methods from the Java classes they manage. This is what enables native code to run in spite of revisions to the Java classes. For instance, a superclass can be revised without affecting the functioning of its subclass.

The Java runtime can provide for as many of the JRI as necessary, and allows applications using the JRI to operate on any subsytems accessible at the time.

The JRI Native Method Module is the minimum support required for the JRI. The other modules are optional and are discussed later in this chapter.

The JRI also offers many implementation types of Java runtime. These include the layout, object's lifetime, object model and garbage collection execution.

Debuggers and IDEs (Interactive Development Environments) can be implemented for Java runtimes through the JRI as well. This enables debuggers and development tools to be linked with application programs. This is currently known as an embedded development environment, and it's what enables a programmer to develop and debug a Java program within the actual application program it needs to work in. You can see how this makes a lot of sense. The JRI Debugging Module and the debugger architecture and interface are discussed later in this chapter.

Loading Classes

The JRI allows native methods to be written so that they stay relative to any changes anticipated in new releases of Java classes. Java classes are loaded by what is known as the Java class loader (no kidding). This loading is done in such a way that when loading an applet, for example, the applet is kept separate from system resources and other applets. The following sections show examples of loading classes and throwing exceptions as well.

JRI_LoadClass Loads a class file from a buffer and returns a java class object or NULL if an exception occurs.

```
jref
JRI_LoadClass(JRIEnv* env, const char* buf, jsize bufLen);
```

Throws:

OutOfMemoryError if insufficient memory is available.

ClassFormatError if the class data does not specify a valid class.

JRI_FindClass Returns a class object. If the name begins with an array, the array class is returned. This is a higher-level routine than the JRI_LoadClass and searches by the CLASSPATH environment. If the class cannot be found, it returns NULL.

```
jref
JRI_FindClass(JRIEnv* env, const char* name);
```

Throws: Nothing.

Exceptions

The Java language uses *exceptions* to provide error-handling capabilities for its programs. An exception is an event occurring during the execution of a program that disrupts the normal flow of instructions. Now that you understand what exceptions are and the advantages of using exceptions in your Java programs, let's start writing some Java code to put exceptions to use.

JRI_Throw Causes a java.lang.Throwable object to be thrown.

```
void
JRI_Throw(JRIEnv* env, jref obj);
```

Part
III

Ch
7

Throws:

> IllegalAccessError if obj is not an instance of java.lang.Throwable.

JRI_ThrowNew   Constructs an exception from the specified class with the message specified by message and causes it to be thrown.

```
void
JRI_ThrowNew(JRIEnv* env, jref clazz, const char* message);
```

Throws:

> NullPointerException if clazz is NULL.

> IllegalAccessError if clazz does not specify a class.

> IllegalAccessError if clazz is not a subclass of java.lang.Throwable.

JRI_ExceptionOccurred   Returns the exception object. Returns NULL if there is no exception thrown.

```
jref
JRI_ExceptionOccurred(JRIEnv* env);
```

Throws: Nothing.

JRI_ExceptionDescribe   Prints an exception and a backtrace of the stack to stderr for debugging.

```
void
JRI_ExceptionDescribe(JRIEnv* env);
```

Throws: Nothing.

JRI_ExceptionClear   Clears the current exception being thrown, and returns the last thrown object, exception, or error.

```
void
JRI_ExceptionClear(JRIEnv* env);
```

Throws: Nothing.

Global References

JRI_NewGlobalRef   Creates a new global reference that refers to the object by the ref parameter.

```
JRIGlobalRef
JRI_NewGlobalRef(JRIEnv* env, jref ref);
```

Throws:

> OutOfMemoryError if insufficient memory is available.

JRI_DisposeGlobalRef   Disposes of a global reference.

```
void
JRI_DisposeGlobalRef(JRIEnv* env, JRIGlobalRef globalRef);
```

Throws:

> NullPointerException if globalRef is NULL.

JRI_GetGlobalRef   Returns a local reference to the object the global reference refers.

```
jref
JRI_GetGlobalRef(JRIEnv* env, JRIGlobalRef globalRef);
```

Throws: Nothing.

JRI_SetGlobalRef   Sets a global reference to the object referred to by value.

```
void
JRI_SetGlobalRef(JRIEnv* env, JRIGlobalRef globalRef, jref value);
```

Throws:

> NullPointerException if globalRef is NULL.

JRI_IsSameObject   Tests if two references refer to the same object.

```
jbool
JRI_IsSameObject(JRIEnv* env, jref r1, jref r2);
```

Throws: Nothing.

Object Operations

JRI_NewObject   Constructs a new Java object and returns a reference. Will return NULL if the object cannot be constructed.

```
jref
JRI_NewObject(JRIEnv* env, jref clazz, JRIMethodID methodID, ...);
```

Throws:

> NullPointerException if clazz is NULL.

> IllegalAccessError if clazz does not specify a class.

InstantiationException if the class is an interface or abstract.

OutOfMemoryError if insufficient memory is available.

JRI_NewObjectA   Constructs a new Java object from an array of parameters and returning a reference. Returns NULL is the object cannot be constructed.

```
jref
JRI_NewObjectA(JRIEnv* env, jref clazz, JRIMethodID methodID,
➥JRIValue* args);
```

Throws:

NullPointerException if clazz is NULL.

IllegalAccessError if clazz does not specify a class.

InstantiationException if the class is an interface or abstract.

OutOfMemoryError if insufficient memory is available.

JRI_NewObjectV   Constructs a new Java object from a va_list of parameters. Returns NULL if the object cannot be constructed.

```
jref
JRI_NewObjectV(JRIEnv* env, jref clazz, JRIMethodID methodID, va_list args);
```

Throws:

NullPointerException if clazz is NULL.

IllegalAccessError if clazz does not specify a class.

InstantiationException if the class is an interface or abstract.

OutOfMemoryError if insufficient memory is available.

JRI_GetObjectClass   Returns the class of an object.

```
jref
JRI_GetObjectClass(JRIEnv* env, jref obj);
```

Throws: Nothing.

JRI_IsInstanceOf   Tests whether an object is an instance of a class.

```
jbool
JRI_IsInstanceOf(JRIEnv* env, jref obj, jref clazz);
```

Throcks:

>   NullPointerException if obj or clazz is NULL.
>
>   IllegalAccessError if clazz does not specify a class.

Accessing Fields of Objects

JRI_GetFieldID   Returns a field ID for a field of a class.

```
JRIFieldID
JRI_GetFieldID(JRIEnv* env, jref clazz, const char* name, const char*
➥sig);
```

Throws:

>   NullPointerException if clazz is NULL.
>
>   IllegalAccessError if clazz does not specify a class.
>
>   NoSuchFieldError if the specified field cannot be found.
>
>   OutOfMemoryError if insufficient memory is available.

JRI_GetField   Returns the value of a field of an object.

```
NativeType
JRI_GetField(JRIEnv* env, jref obj, JRIFieldID fieldID);
```

Throws:

>   NoSuchFieldError if the specified field does not exist or is declared static.
>
>   NullPointerException if obj is NULL.
>
>   OutOfMemoryError if insufficient memory is available.

JRI_SetField   Sets the value of a field of an object.

```
void
JRI_SetField(JRIEnv* env, jref obj, JRIFieldID fieldID, NativeType
➥value);
```

Throws:

>   NoSuchFieldError if the specified field does not exist or is declared static.
>
>   NullPointerException if obj is NULL.
>
>   OutOfMemoryError if insufficient memory is available.

Calling Dynamic Methods of Objects

JRI_GetMethodID   Returns a method ID for a method of a class.

```
JRIMethodID
JRI_GetMethodID(JRIEnv* env, jref clazz, const char* name, const
➥char* sig);
```

Throws:

NullPointerException if clazz is NULL.

IllegalAccessError if clazz does not specify a class.

NoSuchMethodError if the specified method cannot be found.

OutOfMemoryError if insufficient memory is available.

JRI_CallMethod   Calls a dynamic or interface method on a Java object according to the method ID specified.

```
NativeType
JRI_CallMethod(JRIEnv* env, jref obj, JRIMethodID methodID, ...);
```

Throws:

NullPointerException if obj is NULL.

NoSuchMethodError if the specified method cannot be found.

OutOfMemoryError if insufficient memory is available.

JRI_CallMethodA   Calls a dynamic or interface methods on a Java object according to the method ID specified.

```
NativeType
JRI_CallMethodA(JRIEnv* env, jref obj, JRIMethodID methodID,
➥JRIValue* argArray);
```

Throws:

NullPointerException if obj is NULL.

NoSuchMethodError if the specified method cannot be found.

OutOfMemoryError if insufficient memory is available.

JRI_CallMethodV   Calls a dynamic or interface method on a Java object according to the method ID specified.

```
NativeType
JRI_CallMethodV(JRIEnv* env, jref obj, JRIMethodID methodID, va_list
➥args);
```

Throws:

> NullPointerException if obj is NULL.
>
> NoSuchMethodError if the specified method cannot be found.
>
> OutOfMemoryError if insufficient memory is available.

Class Operations

JRI_IsSubclassOf   Determines whether the first class is a subclass of the second or has the second class as one of its interfaces.

```
jbool
JRI_IsSubclassOf(JRIEnv* env, jref clazz, jref super);
```

Throws:

> NullPointerException if clazz or super is NULL.
>
> IllegalAccessError if clazz or super does not specify a class.

Accessing Static Fields of Classes

JRI_GetStaticFieldID   Returns a field ID for a static field of a class.

```
JRIFieldID
JRI_GetStaticFieldID(JRIEnv* env, jref clazz, const char* name, const
➥char* sig);
```

Throws:

> NullPointerException if clazz is NULL.
>
> IllegalAccessError if clazz does not specify a class.
>
> NoSuchFieldError if the specified field cannot be found.
>
> OutOfMemoryError if insufficient memory is available.

JRI_GetStaticField   Returns the value of a static field of a class.

```
NativeType
JRI_GetStaticField(JRIEnv* env, jref clazz, JRIFieldID fieldID);
```

Throws:

> NoSuchFieldError if the specified field does not exist or is not declared static.

Part
III

Ch
7

NullPointerException if clazz is NULL.

IllegalAccessError if clazz does not specify a class.

OutOfMemoryError if insufficient memory is available.

JRI_SetStaticField Sets the value of a static field of a class.

```
void
JRI_SetStaticField(JRIEnv* env, jref clazz, JRIFieldID fieldID,
➡NativeType value);
```

Throws:

NoSuchFieldError if the specified field does not exist or is not declared static.

NullPointerException if clazz is NULL.

IllegalAccessError if clazz does not specify a class.

OutOfMemoryError if insufficient memory is available.

Calling Static Methods of Classes

JRI_GetStaticMethodID Returns a method ID for a static method of a class.

```
JRIMethodID
JRI_GetStaticMethodID(JRIEnv* env, jref clazz, const char* name,
➡const char* sig);
```

Throws:

NullPointerException if clazz is NULL.

IllegalAccessError if clazz does not specify a class.

NoSuchMethodError if the specified method cannot be found.

OutOfMemoryError if insufficient memory is available.

JRI_CallStaticMethod Calls a static method on a Java class object according to the method ID specified.

```
NativeType
JRI_CallStaticMethod(JRIEnv* env, jref clazz, JRIMethodID methodID,
➡...);
```

Throws:

NullPointerException if clazz is NULL.

NoSuchMethodError if the specified method cannot be found.

OutOfMemoryError if insufficient memory is available.

JRI_CallStaticMethodA   Calls a static method on a Java class object according to the method ID specified.

```
NativeType
JRI_CallStaticMethodA(JRIEnv* env, jref clazz, JRIMethodID methodID,
➥JRIValue* args);
```

Throws:

NullPointerException if clazz is NULL.

NoSuchMethodError if the specified method cannot be found.

OutOfMemoryError if insufficient memory is available.

JRI_CallStaticMethodV   Calls a static method on a Java class object according to the method ID specified.

```
NativeType
JRI_CallStaticMethodV(JRIEnv* env, jclazz clazz, jmethodID methodID,
➥va list args);
```

Throws:

NullPointerException if clazz is NULL.

NoSuchMethodError if the specified method cannot be found.

OutOfMemoryError if insufficient memory is available.

Registering Native Methods

JRI_RegisterNatives   Registers native methods with a class.

```
void
JRI_RegisterNatives(JRIEnv* env, jref clazz, char** nameAndSigArray,
➥void** nativeProcArray);
```

The native methods must have the following signature:

```
typedef void (*JRI_NativeMethodProc)(JRIEnv* env, jref classOrObject,
➥...);
```

Throws:

NullPointerException if clazz is NULL.

IllegalAccessError if clazz does not specify a class.

NoSuchMethodError if a specified method cannot be found or is not native.

OutOfMemoryError if insufficient memory is available.

JRI_UnregisterNatives   Unregisters native methods of a class.

```
void
JRI_UnregisterNatives(JRIEnv* env, jref clazz);
```

Throws:

NullPointerException if clazz is NULL.

IllegalAccessError if clazz does not specify a class.

JRI Reflection Module

The JRI Reflection Module is a way to ascertain reflective information on Java classes and methods. For instance, class and method access privileges, superclasses and interfaces, and information about fields and methods can be determined.

Reflection Module Types

JRIReflectionEnv denotes the type of a JRI reflection environment. The JRIReflectionInterface type specifies the operations available on a reflection environment.

```
typedef struct JRIReflectionInterface    JRIReflectionInterface;
typedef const JRIReflectionInterface*    JRIReflectionEnv;
```

JRIAccessFlags   Reflection Environment

Beginning Code

```
typedef enum JRIAccessFlags {
/* Field and Method Access */
```

▓ JRIAccessPublic   = 0x0001

▓ JRIAccessProtected   = 0x0002

▓ JRIAccessPrivate   = 0x0004

▓ JRIAccessStatic   = 0x0008

■ JRIAccessFinal   = 0x0010

■ JRIAccessSynchronized   = 0x0020

■ JRIAccessNative   = 0x0100

   /* Class Access */

■ JRIAccessInterface   = 0x0200

■ JRIAccessAbstract   = 0x0400

Ending Code

```
} JRIAccessFlags;
```

JRI_GetClassCount   Returns the number of classes currently loaded into the Java runtime instance associated with the environment.

```
jsize
JRI_GetClassCount(JRIReflectionEnv* env);
```

JRI_GetClass   Returns the class object currently loaded into the Java environment at a particular index ranging from 0 to the value returned by the JRI_GetClassCount minus 1. Returns NULL if the index is invalid.

```
jref
JRI_GetClass(JRIReflectionEnv* env, jsize index);
```

JRI_GetClassName   Returns the name of a class.

```
char*
JRI_GetClassName(JRIReflectionEnv* env, jref clazz);
```

JRI_VerifyClass   Verifies a class. Returns true if the class passes verification.

```
jbool
JRI_VerifyClass(JRIReflectionEnv* env, jref clazz);
```

JRI_GetClassSuperclass   Returns the superclass of a class. NULL is returned for the class java.lang.Object.

```
jref
JRI_GetClassSuperclass(JRIReflectionEnv* env, jref clazz);
```

JRI_GetClassInterfaceCount   Returns the number of interfaces implemented by the class.

```
jsize
JRI_GetClassInterfaceCount(JRIReflectionEnv* env, jref clazz);
```

Part

III

Ch

7

JRI_GetClassInterface   Returns the interface associated with a class by index ranging from 0 to the value returned by `JRI_GetClassInterfaceCount` minus 1.

```
jref
JRI_GetClassInterface(JRIReflectionEnv* env, jref clazz, jsize
➥index);
```

JRI_GetClassFieldCount   Returns the number of fields that are defined by a class.

```
jsize
JRI_GetClassFieldCount(JRIReflectionEnv* env, jref clazz);
```

JRI_GetClassFieldInfo   Returns information about a field of a class by index ranging from 0 to the value returned by `JRI_GetClassFieldCount` minus 1.

```
void
JRI_GetClassFieldInfo(JRIReflectionEnv* env, jref clazz, jsize
➥fieldIndex, char* *fieldName, char* *fieldSig, JRIAccessFlags
➥*fieldAccess, jref *fieldClass);
```

JRI_GetClassMethodCount   Returns the number of methods defined by a class.

```
jsize
JRI_GetClassMethodCount(JRIReflectionEnv* env, jref clazz);
```

JRI_GetClassMethodInfo   Returns information about a method of a class by index. Returns NULL if the method is not declared native or if no native method is currently registered.

```
void
JRI_GetClassMethodInfo(JRIReflectionEnv* env, jref clazz, jsize
➥methodIndex, char* *methodName, char* *methodSig, JRIAccessFlags
➥*methodAccess, jref *methodClass, void* *methodNativeProc);
```

The Reflection Module Structure

There's a specific order in which the methods must appear in the JRI Reflection Module's jump-table. The signatures of the methods have a corresponding type that ends with _t. See the following for the order of methods that must appear in the Reflection Module's jump-table:

```
struct JRIReflectionInterface {
    void*                    Reserved0;
    void*                    Reserved1;
    void*                    Reserved2;
    JRI_GetClassCount_t      GetClassCount;
    JRI_GetClass_t           GetClass;
```

```
        JRI_GetClassName_t              GetClassName;
        JRI_VerifyClass_t               VerifyClass;
        JRI_GetClassSuperclass_t        GetClassSuperclass;
        JRI_GetClassInterfaceCount_t    GetClassInterfaceCount;
        JRI_GetClassInterface_t         GetClassInterface;
        JRI_GetClassFieldCount_t        GetClassFieldCount;
        JRI_GetClassFieldInfo_t         GetClassFieldInfo;
        JRI_GetClassMethodCount_t       GetClassMethodCount;
        JRI_GetClassMethodInfo_t        GetClassMethodInfo;
    };
```

JRI Embedding Module

The JRI Embedding Module defines the mechanism that enables Java runtimes to be embedded in application programs. The mechanism that initializes a Java runtime instance is included as well to construct the execution environment.

N O T E   There have been changes made to the JRI version 0.6. This version corresponds to Netscape Navigator version 3.0b5. The change is to the `JRI_NewEnv` function. The classLoader parameter has been eliminated. Instead, a separate routine that provides this function was created, called `JRI_SetClassLoader`. ◼

Runtime Instances Types

The `JRIRuntimeInstance` denotes:

```
        typedef struct JRIRuntimeInterface    JRIRuntimeInterface;
        typedef const JRIRuntimeInterface*    JRIRuntimeInstance;
```

`JRIRuntimeInstance` represents the type of a Java runtime instance. A runtime instance incorporates all the heap and loaded classes of a Java runtime. The runtime instance performs as an independent environment for users of JRI operations. The execution environments are created relative to the runtime instance. The operations on the runtime instance are determined by the `JRIRuntimeInterface` type.

JRI_NewRuntime   Creates a new Java runtime instance and returns NULL if the runtime cannot be initialized.

```
        JRIRuntimeInstance*
        JRI_NewRuntime(JRIRuntimeInitargs* initargs);
```

Part
III

Ch

7

NOTE Because it doesn't need an object to route through, this operation is known as a hard entry implementation into the JRI. There are some JRI implementations that cannot provide more than one Java runtime instance for each application, usually depending on the way global variables are utilized. NULL will be returned if any following calls are made to the JRI_NewRuntime.

JRIRuntimeInitargs

```
typedef struct JRIRuntimeInitargsStruct {

/* Required arguments */

short                    majorVersion;

short                    minorVersion;

jsize                    initialHeapSize;

jsize                    maxHeapSize;

JRICollectionStartProc   collectionStartProc;

JRICollectionEndProc     collectionEndProc;

JRIVerifyMode            verifyMode;

/* Implementation-dependent arguments follow... */

} JRIRuntimeInitargs;
```

This type of the initialization arguments to the JRI_NewRuntime. Certain Java runtime implementations could need other parameters to be passed so that they may be properly initialized. For instance, the majorVersion must be initialized to 1 and minorVersion must be initialized 0 for the version of the JRI.

The other parameters are as follows:

- initialHeapSize

  The initialHeapSize parameter specifies the initial heap size of the runtime instance.

- maxHeapSize

  The maxHeapSize parameter specifies the maximum size to which the heap can grow.

■ collectionStartProc

The `collectionStartProc` parameter specifies procedures to invoke when a collection starts.

■ collectionEndProc

The `collectionEndProc` parameter specifies procedures to invoke when a collection ends.

The following types illustrate these procedures:

```
typedef void
  (* JRICollectionStartProc)(JRIRuntimeInstance* runtime);

typedef void
  (* JRICollectionEndProc)(JRIRuntimeInstance* runtime);
```

The `verifyCode` parameter must be initialized to one of the values specified by the `JRIVerifyMode`. `JRIVerifyNone` specifies that no classes are verified at the time they are loaded. `JRIVerifyRemote` specifies that only classes loaded from a class loader will be verified. `JRIVerifyAll` makes sure that all classes should be verified when loaded, regardless of how they're loaded.

```
typedef enum JRIVerifyMode {
    JRIVerifyNone,
    JRIVerifyRemote,
    JRIVerifyAll
} JRIVerifyMode;
```

JRI_DisposeRuntime   Disposes a Java runtime instance, including classes and all associated data structures.

```
void
JRI_DisposeRuntime(JRIRuntimeInstance* runtime);
```

JRI_SetIOMode   Sets the I/O mode of a Java runtime instance.

```
void
JRI_SetIOMode(JRIRuntimeInstance* runtime, JRIIOModeFlags mode);
```

The following example describes possible I/O modes:

```
typedef enum JRIIOModeFlags {
JRIIOMode_Unrestricted    = ~0,
    JRIIOMode_None            = 0,
    JRIIOMode_AllowStdin      = 0x01,
    JRIIOMode_AllowStdout     = 0x02,
```

```
            JRIIOMode_AllowSocket        = 0x04,
            JRIIOMode_AllowFileInput     = 0x08,
            JRIIOMode_AllowFileOutput    = 0x10
        } JRIIOModeFlags;
```

JRI_SetFSMode   Sets the `filesystem` mode of a Java runtime instance.

```
        void
        JRI_SetFSMode(JRIRuntimeInstance* runtime, JRIFSModeFlags mode);
```

The following example describes possible filesystem modes:

```
        typedef enum JRIFSModeFlags {
            JRIFSMode_Unrestricted,      /* no C level filesystem checks */
            JRIFSMode_None               /* no filesystem access allowed */
        } JRIFSModeFlags;
```

JRI_SetFSMode   Sets the `runtime` mode of a Java runtime instance. This is the lowest-level security check that's done by the C implementation of the native runtime methods.

```
        void
        JRI_SetRTMode(JRIRuntimeInstance* runtime, JRIRTModeFlags mode);
```

The following example describes possible runtime modes:

```
        typedef enum JRIRTModeFlags {
            JRIRTMode_Unrestricted,      /* no C level runtime checks */
            JRIRTMode_None               /* no runtime access allowed */
        } JRIRTModeFlags;
```

Execution Environments

JRI_NewEnv   Creates a new instance of the JRI Native Method interface, and returns NULL if the runtime fails to create an execution environment.

```
        JRIEnv*
        JRI_NewEnv(JRIRuntimeInstance* runtime, void* thread);
```

JRI_DisposeEnv   Disposes an execution environment, including any allocated global references relative to it.

```
        void
        JRI_DisposeEnv(JRIEnv* env);
```

JRI_GetRuntime   Returns the runtime instance associated with the execution environment.

```
        JRIRuntimeInstance*
        JRI_GetRuntime(JRIEnv* env);
```

JRI_GetThread   Returns the native thread object associated with the execution environment.

```
void*
JRI_GetThread(JRIEnv* env);
```

JRI_SetClassLoader   Sets the class loader associated with an execution environment. You use this class when invoking methods from native code.

```
void
JRI_SetClassLoader(JRIEnv* env, jref classLoader);
```

Sets the class loader associated with an execution environment. This class loader is used when invoking methods from native code. This can influence the security policy of other methods when invoked through the following JRI operations:

- JRI_CallMethod
- JRI_CallMethodA
- JRI_CallMethodV
- JRI_CallStaticMethod
- JRI_CallStaticMethodA
- JRI_CallStaticMethodV
- JRI_NewObject
- JRI_NewObjectA
- JRI_NewObjectV

The Embedding Module Structure

There's an order to which the methods must appear in the JRI Embedding Module's jump-table. The signatures of methods are noted by a corresponding type ending with _t:

```
struct JRIRuntimeInterface {
    void*                    Reserved0;
    void*                    Reserved1;
    void*                    Reserved2;
    JRI_DisposeRuntime_t     DisposeRuntime;
    JRI_SetIOMode_t          SetIOMode;
    JRI_SetFSMode_t          SetFSMode;
    JRI_SetRTMode_t          SetRTMode;
    JRI_NewEnv_t             NewEnv;
```

Part

III

Ch

7

```
        JRI_DisposeEnv_t                DisposeEnv;
        JRI_GetRuntime_t                GetRuntime;
        JRI_GetThread_t                 GetThread;
        JRI_SetClassLoader_t            SetClassLoader;
};
```

JRI Compiler Module

The JRI Compiler Module determines the programming interface that invokes the class compiler.

Compiler Module Types

```
typedef struct JRICompilerInterface    JRICompilerInterface;
typedef const JRICompilerInterface*     JRICompilerEnv;
```

JRICompilerEnv denotes the type of a JRI compiler environment. The JRICompilerInterface type denotes the operations that are available on a compiler environment.

JRI_CompileClass   Compiles Java source code for a class.

```
void
JRI_CompileClass(JRICompilerEnv* env, const char* classSrc, jsize
↪classSrcLen, jbyte* *resultingClassData, jsize *classDataLen);
```

The Compiler Module Structure

As you can figure out, there's also an order in which the methods must appear in the JRI Compiler Module's jump-table. The signatures of methods are declared by a corresponding type ending with _t:

```
struct JRICompilerInterface {
    void*                   Reserved0;
    void*                   Reserved1;
    void*                   Reserved2;
    JRI_CompileClass_t      CompileClass;
};
```

JRI Debugger Module

It's the JRI that defines the routines for implementing an interactive Java development environment. These routines are independent from the Java runtime, and can be an optional subset of the JRI that the particular application program can test before it's actually run.

This is very helpful, because it means that the runtime systems necessary to be deployed can be kept to a minimum, while still defining the subset of the JRI that needs to be executed.

Inspecting Stack Frames Types

The JRIDebuggerEnv denotes the type of debugging environment. This debugging environment is necessary to check and control the Java execution environment.

```
typedef struct JRIDebuggerInterface      JRIDebuggerInterface;
typedef const JRIDebuggerInterface*      JRIDebuggerEnv;
```

JRI_GetFrameCount   Returns the number of stack frames associated with the debugging environment.

```
jsize
JRI_GetFrameCount(JRIDebuggerEnv* env);
```

JRI_GetFrameInfo   Returns stack frame information associated with the debugging environment.

```
jbool
JRI_GetFrameInfo(JRIDebuggerEnv* env, jsize frameIndex, jref
➥*methodClass, jsize *methodIndex, jsize *pc, jsize *varsCount);
```

JRI_GetVarInfo   Returns a local variable or argument of a stack frame.

```
void
JRI_GetVarInfo(JRIDebuggerEnv* env, jsize frameIndex, jsize varIndex,
➥char* *name, char* *signature, jbool *isArgument, jsize
➥*startScope, jsize *endScope);
```

Part
III

Ch
7

JRI_GetSourceInfo   Returns source file information associated with the class of the method specified by frameIndex.

```
void
JRI_GetSourceInfo(JRIDebuggerEnv* env, jsize frameIndex, const char*
➥*filename, jsize *lineNumber);
```

JRI_GetVar   Returns the value of a local variable or formal parameter of the specified method.

```
NativeType
JRI_GetVar(JRIDebuggerEnv* env, jsize frameIndex, jsize varIndex);
```

JRI_SetVar   Sets the value of a local variable or formal parameter of the specified method.

```
void
JRI_SetVar(JRIDebuggerEnv* env, jsize frameIndex, jsize varIndex,
➥NativeType value);
```

Controlling Execution

JRI_StepOver   Enables the interpreter to move forward to the next instruction.

```
void
JRI_StepOver(JRIDebuggerEnv* env);
```

JRI_StepIn   Enables the interpreter to move forward to the next instruction. If this next instruction is a method call, it enters the method and then the execution stops at the first instruction of the method.

```
void
JRI_StepIn(JRIDebuggerEnv* env);
```

JRI_StepOut   Enables the interpreter to continue until current methods return and stops execution right after the method call.

```
void
JRI_StepOut(JRIDebuggerEnv* env);
```

JRI_Continue   Enables the execution to continue.

```
void
JRI_Continue(JRIDebuggerEnv* env);
```

JRI_Return   Returns a value from the current method without completing its execution.

```
void
JRI_Return(JRIDebuggerEnv* env, jsize frameIndex, JRIValue value);
```

The Debugging Module Structure

Again, there's an order in which the methods must appear in the JRI Debugging Module's jump-table. The signatures of methods are declared by a corresponding type that ends with _t:

```
struct JRIDebuggerInterface {
        void*                       Reserved0;
        void*                       Reserved1;
        void*                       Reserved2;
        JRI_GetFrameCount_t         GetFrameCount;
        JRI_GetFrameInfo_t          GetFrameInfo;
        JRI_GetVarInfo_t            GetVarInfo;
        JRI_GetSourceInfo_t         GetSourceInfo;
        JRI_GetVar_t                GetVar;
        JRI_GetVarBoolean_t         GetVarBoolean;
        JRI_GetVarByte_t            GetVarByte;
        JRI_GetVarChar_t            GetVarChar;
        JRI_GetVarShort_t           GetVarShort;
        JRI_GetVarInt_t             GetVarInt;
        JRI_GetVarLong_t            GetVarLong;
        JRI_GetVarFloat_t           GetVarFloat;
        JRI_GetVarDouble_t          GetVarDouble;
        JRI_SetVar_t                SetVar;
        JRI_SetVarBoolean_t         SetVarBoolean;
        JRI_SetVarByte_t            SetVarByte;
        JRI_SetVarChar_t            SetVarChar;
        JRI_SetVarShort_t           SetVarShort;
        JRI_SetVarInt_t             SetVarInt;
        JRI_SetVarLong_t            SetVarLong;
        JRI_SetVarFloat_t           SetVarFloat;
        JRI_SetVarDouble_t          SetVarDouble;
        JRI_StepOver_t              StepOver;
        JRI_StepIn_t                StepIn;
        JRI_StepOut_t               StepOut;
        JRI_Continue_t              Continue;
        JRI_Return_t                Return;
};
```

ON THE WEB

For more information on the Java Runtime Interface (JRI), see Netscape's JRI documentation located at **http://home1.netscape.com/eng/jri/**.

For information on Netscape's client Java package class libraries for calling JavaScript and plug-ins from Java, see **http://home1.netscape.com/newsref/std/java-security~_faq.html**.

From Here...

In this chapter you learned how Java supports native methods. Java runtime clients can be native methods that respond to Java operations called from the Java runtime. You use the JRI Reflection Module to ascertain reflective information on Java classes and methods. It's the JRI Embedding Module that defines the mechanism enabling Java runtimes to be embedded in application programs. The JRI Compiler Module determines the programming interface that invokes the class compiler. Last, but not least, it's the JRI Debugger Module that defines the routines for implementing an interactive Java development environment.

- Chapter 8, "Calling Java Methods from Plug-Ins," shows how fields are accessed and discusses Java names and parameters, as well as security issues.

- Chapter 9, "Calling the Plug-In from Java Methods," shows how to define a plug-in class and tells you more about native methods and globals.

Calling Java Methods from Plug-Ins

It's relatively easy to understand how to call Java methods from plug-ins. First you need to have the new javah version, which is the Java Runtime Interface (JRI) from Netscape. You need to run the JRI version of javah on any class files for any methods you will call. The header files you need to call Java (for C and C++) will then be generated. Chapter 7, "The Java Runtime Interface," covers this JRI version of javah in more detail. ▪

How to Access Fields

Netscape's Java Runtime Interface (JRI) of javah creates accessor macros using a straight naming convention.

Accessing Static Fields

You access static fields much like you would access nonstatic fields, from a class object.

Accessing Methods

You access methods much like you would access static fields.

Overloaded Methods

Two or more methods can have the same name as long as they take different parameters.

Java Names and Parameters

Netscape's version of javah transforms Java variables into C/C++ variables with a new Java-specific type.

Security

Java has extensive security support to allow you to create tamper-free systems.

Using Naming Conventions to Access Java Class Fields

In accessing fields, Netscape's Java Runtime Interface (JRI) of javah creates accessor macros using a straight naming convention. This naming convention is used for all Java class fields. With this naming convention, `get_` or `set_` precedes the package and class name.

```
ResultType
get_ClassName_fieldName(JRIEnv* env, ClassName* self);

void
set_ClassName_fieldName(JRIEnv* env, ClassName* self,
                        ResultType value);
```

When accessing a field, the type of object is indicated by the class name. You can use the name of the struct, as in `struct ClassName*`, instead of including any other header files.

The type indicating the Java class is really a C++ class and has the same name. You can access fields directly through in-line functions.

```
class ClassName : ... {
    ResultType      // get method
    fieldName(JRIEnv* env) { ... }

    void            // set method
    fieldName(JRIEnv* env, ResultType value) { ... }
    ...
}
```

The plug-in talks to Java through Netscape's Java Runtime Interface. Figure 8.1 illustrates the JRI.

Netscape has defined the Java Runtime Interface to allow native code (such as a plug-in) to call Java methods.

FIG. 8.1

The plug-in connects to the Java Runtime Interface, which handles communications with Java.

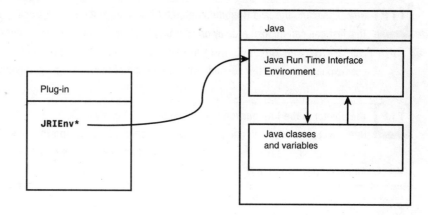

ON THE WEB

The full specification of the Java Runtime Interface is available online as part of the Netscape Plug-in SDK at **http://home.netscape.com/eng/mozilla/3.0/handbook/ plugins/index.html**.

CAUTION

javah doesn't do a very good job of protecting the privacy of data members in Java classes. You'll be able to access private members from inside your plug-in. Avoid this temptation, and use accessor methods and other public methods exclusively.

By restricting yourself to public methods, your plug-in is less likely to need maintenance when the implementation of the Java class changes.

To call the `increment()` method of the Java class `count`, just write the following:

```
count->increment(env);
```

Here, `env` is the result of the function `NPN_GetJavaEnv()`. `NPN_GetJavaEnv()` has the following specification:

```
JavaEnv* NPN_GetJavaEnv(void);
```

Typically you call `NPN_GetJavaEnv()` once, in `NPP_Initialize()`.

Netscape starts the Java Runtime Interpreter when you first call `NPN_GetJavaEnv()`. This first call can impose a delay on your plug-in. If you're sure that your plug-in needs to call Java, call `NPN_GetJavaEnv()` in `NPP_Initialize()` and get it out of the way. The user expects to wait a few seconds when he or she accesses the plug-in content anyway.

 The pointer to the Java environment is thread-specific. If you call it in `NPP_Initialize()` you can use it in any instance, but if you spawn a new thread, you need to call `NPN_GetJavaEnv()` for this thread and reserve the new `JavaEnv` pointer for use in this thread only.

NPP_GetJavaClass() Example

If you want to support LiveConnect, you may want to include an `NPP_GetJavaClass()` function similar to the one in Simple, as follows:

```
/*
** NPP_GetJavaClass is called during initialization to ask your
plugin
** what its associated Java class is. If you don't have one, just
return
** NULL. Otherwise, use the javah-generated "use_" function to both
** initialize your class and return it. If you can't find your class,
an
** error will be signaled by "use_" and will cause the Navigator to
** complain to the user.
*/
jref NPP_GetJavaClass(void)
{
#ifdef __MC68K__
    return NULL;
#else
    struct java_lang_Class* myClass;
    env = NPN_GetJavaEnv();
    if (env == NULL)
      return NULL;                  /* Java disabled */
    myClass = use_Simple(env);
    if (myClass == NULL) {
      /*
       ** If our class doesn't exist (the user hasn't installed it)
then
       ** don't allow any of the Java stuff to happen.
       */
      env = NULL;
    }
    return myClass;
#endif
}
```

N O T E If you're writing a plug-in for the Macintosh, make sure that you include the following lines:

```
#ifdef __MC68K__
        return NULL;
#else
    .
    .
    .
```

Netscape doesn't support LiveConnect on the 680X0 Macintosh—they do support it on the Power Macintosh. ▮

Chapter 5, "Programming Plug-Ins," goes into depth on LiveConnect. This chapter shows why Navigator is calling this function and why you might want a Java class. For now, just note that `NPP_GetJavaClass()` calls `NPN_GetJavaEnv()` to put a pointer to the Java runtime environment into env. If this step succeeds, the plug-in calls a function named `use_Simple()`. `use_Simple()` is a function written by an automated tool (javah) based on our Java class, Simple. `use_Simple()` performs certain initializations and connections in the Java Runtime Interface. As a plug-in programmer, you don't have to be familiar with too many Java details yet.

Accessing Static Fields from a Class Object

You access static fields in much the same way you would access nonstatic fields. You access them from a class object, rather than from an instance. For example, in C++ you might do the following:

```
java_lang_Class* systemClass = java_lang_System::_class(env);
java_io_PrintStream* o = java_lang_System::out(env, systemClass);
```

Or from C:

```
java_lang_Class* systemClass = class_java_lang_System(env);
java_io_PrintStream* o = java_lang_System_out(env, systemClass);
```

TIP Even though you're accessing static Java object fields in C++ through static member functions, they still have to be passed to the Java class object. Passing the class object keeps it from potential multiple lookups.

Accessing Methods

You access methods in much the same way you would access static fields. You can call the substring method of the String* class. This call first gets the substring of the string str from characters 3 through 7. The result is then assigned to the substring variable. See the following example:

```
java_lang_String* sub = str->substring(env, 3, 7);
```

Overloaded Methods

Recall that most object-oriented languages, including both C++ and Java, support overloaded methods. That is, two or more methods can have the same name, as long as they take different parameters. (Sets of parameters are called *signatures*.) In C++, the compiler performs *name mangling* to make sure that the internal names are unique. Netscape's javah appends an index to all but the first occurrence of a name. If you have three functions named foo, javah produces foo, foo_1, and foo_2. To find out which name to call for which signature, just check the header file output by javah. Without the use of an index on all but one of the names, the function name "foo" would be ambiguous. For this reason the index is sometimes known as a "disambiguating index."

For instance in C++, in the String class there are several methods with the name indexOf:

```
jint indexOf(JRIEnv* env, jint a);
jint indexOf_1(JRIEnv* env, jint a, jint b);
jint indexOf_2(JRIEnv* env, java_lang_String *a);
jint indexOf_3(JRIEnv* env, java_lang_String *a, jint b);
```

If you have overloaded methods, first declare the one you plan to use most frequently from your plug-in. In this way, the declared version of the method will not have an index.

Similarly, if you have a Java-implemented version of a method and a native (such as C or C++) version of the same method, put the declaration of the native method first. This way you don't have to worry about index names when you write the native implementation.

 Because javah uses the underscore followed by a number to disambiguate overloaded methods, it performs name-mangling on Java methods with an underscore in their name. Save yourself a headache—don't use underscores in Java method names.

Java Names and Parameters

As mentioned earlier, Netscape also supplies a new version of javah, named the JRI (Java Runtime Interface) version, which writes a C/C++ header file from a Java class. In the example below, to control the count class previously described from your plug-in, start by typing (or including in the makefile) the following:

```
javah -jri -classpath pathTojava_30Andclasses.zip count
```

The result of running javah is a header file for class count. Recall that count has one public data member, i. javah produces in-line accessor functions:

```
jint i(JRIEnv* env);
```

and:

```
void i(JRI* env, jint);
```

to get and set this data member.

Note that javah has transformed the Java int into a variable of type jint. Table 8.1 shows the JRI definitions of the Java primitive types. Netscape's version of javah transforms Java variables into C/C++ variables with a new Java-specific type.

Table 8.1 RI Definitions of Java Primitive Types

Java Type	C/C++ Type	Size
boolean	jbool	1 byte
byte	jbyte	1 byte
char	jchar	2 bytes
short	jshort	2 bytes
int	jint	4 bytes
long	jlong	8 bytes
float	jfloat	4 bytes
double	jdouble	8 bytes

These sizes are defined through a series of #ifdefs in the file jri_md.h, which is included in the header file jri.h. Make sure that your compiler sets up the proper preprocessor symbols for your target machine, so your code gets the right size types.

CAUTION

Make sure that you use the JRI types described in Table 8.1 when talking to Java methods. If you use the compiler's types (in other words, int), you run the risk of a size mismatch when you move to a new compiler or a new platform.

LiveConnect Details

As seen in Chapter 5, "Programming Plug-Ins," to install the example Simple, you copy a file named simple.class into the plug-in directory. The Java compiler, javac, turns Java classes (in .java files) that are human-readable into .class files, which contain bytecodes for the Java Virtual Machine. If there's a simple.class, you should look for a human-readable simple.java—and you find it in the source subdirectory. Here is an example:

```java
import netscape.plugin.Plugin;

class Simple extends Plugin {
  /*
   ** A plug-in can consist of code written in java as well as
   ** natively. Here's a dummy method.
   */
  public static int fact(int n) {
    if (n == 1)
      return 1;
    else
      return n * fact(n-1);
  }
  /*
   ** This instance variable is used to keep track of the number of
   ** times we've called into this plug-in.
   */
  int count;

  /*
   ** This native method will give us a way to print to stdout from
java
   ** instead of just the java console.
   */
  native void printToStdout(String msg);

  /*
   ** This is a publicly callable new feature that our plug-in is
   ** providing. We can call it from JavaScript, Java, or from native
   ** code.
   */
  public void doit(String text) {
    /* construct a message */
    String msg = "" + (++count) + ". " + text + "\n";
    /* write it to the console */
    System.out.print(msg);
    /* and also write it to stdout */
    printToStdout(msg);
  }
}
```

▶ For more information on LiveConnect examples, **see** Chapter 5, "Programming Plug-Ins."

JavaScript Details

You can communicate from JavaScript to the applet by making sure that the applet has a name. Figure 8.2 illustrates this mechanism. You can better understand this mechanism by looking at the following listing. Suppose that you had a Java class like count, shown in Listing 8.1.

FIG. 8.2
The HTML author assigns the applet a name so JavaScript can talk to it.

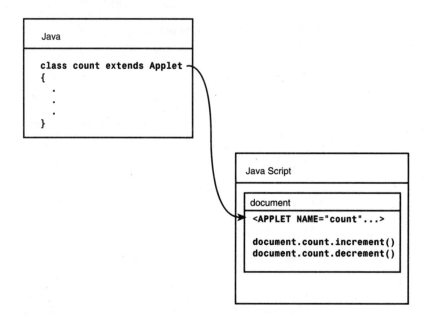

Listing 8.1   count.java—A Simple Java Class that Accepts Two Commands

```java
import java.applet.*;
import java.awt.*;
public class count extends Applet
{
  int i;
  public void init()
  {
    I = 0;
  }
  public void paint (Graphics g)
  {
    g.drawString("The count is" + i, 10, 50);
  }
  public void increment()
```

```
{
  I++;
  repaint();
}
public void decrement()
{
  I--;
  repaint();
}
}
```

You can install count on your Web page, as is shown in Listing 8.2.

Listing 8.2   count.html—A Web Page with a Controllable Applet

```
<HTML>
<HEAD>
<TITLE>Test count/TITLE>
</HEAD>
<BODY>
<H1>Test the Count Applet</H1>
<APPLET NAME="count" CODE="count.class" WIDTH=100, HEIGHT=100></
APPLET>
<FORM>
<INPUT TYPE="Button" VALUE="Increment" NAME="IncrementButton"
➥onClick="document.count.increment()">
<INPUT TYPE="Button" VALUE="Decrement" NAME="DecrementButton"
➥onClick="document.count.decrement()">
</FORM>
</BODY>
</HTML>
```

Now that you know how Java and JavaScript can talk, you just have to get the plug-in to talk to Java.

Talking to the Plug-In

When you add plug-ins to an HTML page, JavaScript puts them into an array named embeds. For example, if the following is the first <EMBED> tag on your page, JavaScript shows the associated plug-in in document.embeds[0]:

```
<EMBED SRC="http://www.somemachine.com/myFile.tst HEIGHT=100
WIDTH=100>
```

From JavaScript, you can access `document.embeds.length` to find out how many plug-ins are on the page.

N O T E Because full-page plug-ins are, by definition, on a page with no JavaScript (and no HTML!), it only makes sense to talk about controlling embedded plug-ins. ■

To make a plug-in visible from inside Java, your Java class must use `netscape.plugin.Plugin`. Netscape provides a file `java_30` with Netscape version 3.0 and java 301 with Netscape version 3.01. This file contains three Java packages, `java`, `sun`, and `netscape`:

- `java`
- `sun`
- `netscape.applet`
- `netscape.net`
- `netscape.javascript`
- `netscape.plugin`

The `java` and `sun` packages are replacements to packages of the same name in the Sun 1.0.2 Java Development Kit (JDK). They include security enhancements necessary for LiveConnect. Netscape and Sun are working together to ensure that these new packages are included in a future release of the Sun JDK. Also see the following section, "Security."

N O T E To use the Netscape-supplied packages with the JDK compiler, add the path of the `java_30` and `classes.zip` to the compiler's `classpath`. You can either specify a CLASSPATH environment variable or use the `-classpath` command line option when you run javac.

T I P As a plug-in programmer, you have a C++ development environment such as Microsoft Visual C++ handy. Don't waste time running javac from the command line. Put your plug-in's Java proxy class in the makefile and automatically call javac each time your plug-in is rebuilt. If you use Visual C++, just add the javac command line (with the `-classpath` option) to the Custom Build settings.

While setting up the makefile, add the call to javah described in the following section. It will save you time later.

▶ For more information about LiveConnect plug-ins, Java, and JavaScript, **see** Chapter 10, "JavaScript to Java Communication."

N O T E It seems that Microsoft Internet Explorer 3.0 only partially supports LiveConnect. Internet Explorer does support calling in Java applets from JavaScript. However, unlike Netscape 3.0, Internet Explorer does not support calling Java packages directly from JavaScript.

For example, the following code produces an "Unknown object java" error under Internet Explorer:

```
java.lang.System.out.println("Hello World");
```

Security

Because Java was designed with native support for client/server applications, security is obviously an issue. Java has extensive security support to allow you to create tamper-free systems. Java uses a public-key encryption scheme to provide authentication, and its new pointer model makes it impossible to overwrite secure areas of memory.

Java contains multiple layers of security, each serving to filter out harmful code. The four layers of security built into Java and Netscape are as follows:

- The Java language and compiler
- Java bytecode verification and strong type information
- Java's class loader
- Restrictions on local file system and network access

    ▶ For detailed information on Java's four layers of security, **see** Chapter 10, "JavaScript to Java Communication."

ON THE WEB

The Java Development Team also has an online overview of the security features inherent to applets. It is available, at **http://www.javasoft.com/sfaq/index.html**.

Other Resources

ON THE WEB

Sun maintains a complete set of documentation on Java at **http://www.javasoft.com**. At this site, you can find everything from language documentation to tutorials. Yahoo has a rather extensive index of pointers to Java resources. You can find this listing at **http://www.yahoo.com/Computers_and_Internet/Programming_Languages/Java/**

Again, for more information about plug-ins, take a look at the Plug-in Developer's Guide located at **http://home1.netscape.com/eng/mozilla/3.0/handbook/plugins/index.html**.

From this handbook, you can access documentation on calling Java methods from plug-ins at **http://home1.netscape.com/eng/mozilla/3.0/handbook/plugins/wr2.htm**, as well as documentation on calling plug-in native methods from Java at **http://home1.netscape.com/eng/mozilla/3.0/handbook/plugins/wr3.htm**.

From Here...

You learned in this chapter that it's relatively easy to call Java methods from plug-ins. You know that you need to have the new javah version, which is the Java Runtime Interface (JRI) from Netscape. You need to run the JRI version of javah on any class files for any methods you will call. The header files you use to call Java (for C and C++) can then be generated. Netscape's version of javah transforms Java variables into C/C++ variables with a new Java-specific type. Java also has extensive security support to allow you to create tamper-free systems. You also learned a little bit about LiveConnect and JavaScript, which is elaborated on in Part IV, "LiveConnect Communication in JavaScript."

- The next chapter, "Calling the Plug-In from Java Methods," looks at defining a plug-in class and implementing native methods.
- Chapter 5, "Programming Plug-Ins," looks at sample LiveConnect examples like Simple and CharFlipper.
- Chapter 7, "The Java Runtime Interface," looks at Java platform support for native methods and Java classes.

■ Chapter 10, "JavaScript to Java Communication," looks at accessing Java directly, as well as controlling applets and plug-ins.

■ Chapter 11, "Java to JavaScript Communication," looks at accessing JavaScript objects and properties, as well as calling JavaScript methods.

■ Chapter 12, "Netscape Packages," looks at using Netscape packages, as well as a quick Netscape package reference.

Part

III

Ch

8

CHAPTER 9

Calling the Plug-In from Java Methods

As you saw in the previous chapter, you can call Java methods from plug-ins. You can also define native methods that both Java and JavaScript can call. These native methods are written in C code rather than in Java.

Native methods give you lower-level functionality and improved performance when implementing plug-ins. This cannot be done with code directly written in Java. Plug-ins appear to Java as instances of netscape.plugin.Plugin class. You'll read about this class further in Chapter 12, "Netscape Packages." ■

Defining a Plug-In Class

You can define native methods in Java that are implemented in C or C++.

Implementing Native Methods

Follow the javah naming conventions (rather than C++ name mangling) when implementing the native methods.

DisplayJavaMessage() Example

DisplayJavaMessage() is one of the larger and more interesting functions in Simple plug-in.

NPAvi and Native Methods

Much of the work of NPAvi is implemented back in the plug-in through native methods.

Java Class TimeMediaPlugin

The Java class TimeMediaPlugin has become a good tool for use with time-based content. A look at the Java code reveals that all of the real work is done in native methods.

Defining and Using a Plug-In Class

You can define native methods in Java that are implemented in C or C++. These methods give your Java applet access to low-level library routines in the operating system and can be more efficient than Java alone. Figure 9.1 illustrates a Java class calling its native method.

FIG. 9.1

Java invokes a native method, allowing access to the operating system.

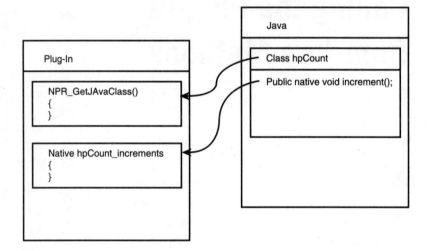

Just as calls by the plug-in to Java are made through the C or C++ header files produced by javah, Java methods call the plug-in by calling a Java peer of the plug-in. This peer is of type `netscape.plugin.Plugin`.

If you instantiate a Java object of type `Plugin`, your Java method will be able to refer to the plug-in but will not be able to call any plug-in specific methods. If you derive a new Java class from `Plugin`, you can define native methods in the derived class that correspond to these plug-in methods you want to expose to Java.

A Plug-In Developer Should Consider the Following When Supplying a Java Class for a Plug-In:

- Don't supply a Java class

  The plug-in would then be invisible to other Java applets. The plug-in can still call to Java, but will not have an object to represent it.

- Supply the default class `Plugin`

  This should be done first when the plug-in has an associated Java object and does not define any Java or native methods.

- Supply a subclass of `Plugin`

  This should be done when the plug-in is implementing native methods.

Suppose that you want to write a plug-in that does the same work as count. The new plug-in will be named npCount. For convenience, call the Java peer class npCount as well. Besides the `increment()` and `decrement()` methods defined for count, npCount has a new method, `post()`, which calls `NPN_PostURL()` and sends the current count back to a CGI script or LiveWire application on the Web site. The file shown in Listing 9.1 implements npCount.

Listing 9.1   npCount.java—A Java Peer Class for the npCount Plug-In

```
import netscape.plugin.Plugin;
class npCount extends Plugin
{
  public native void increment();
  public native void decrement();
  public native boolean post();
}
```

Compile npCount.java with javac, and run the latest JRI version of javah on it, as follows:

```
javah -jri -classpath pathTonpcount npCount
javah -jri -stubs -classpath pathTonpcount npCount
```

The second call to javah builds C stubs for the native methods. These stubs include a special initializer for each Java class. The initializer sets up the interface between Java and your plug-in. Be sure to call the initializer before you use the class! (If you have other Java classes with native methods outside of your plug-in, call their initializers, too.)

For npCount, the initializer is specified by the following line:

```
extern java_lang_Class* init_npCount(JRIEnv* env);
```

You can add initialization code to this init_ method. You can add balancing code to the Java peer's destroy() method. This method is called just before NPP_Destroy() is called on the instance. You also can check (from Java) to see if the native instance is still active by calling isActive(), which returns a boolean.

For Navigator to set up your Java peer class, it calls your plug-in's implementation of NPP_GetJavaClass(). NPP_GetJavaClass() is specified as follows:

```
jref NPP_GetJavaClass(void);
```

For npCount, a reasonable implementation of NPP_GetJavaClass() is:

```
jref NPP_GetJavaClass()
{
  return init_npCount(NPN_GetJavaEnv());
}
```

If your plug-in uses other Java classes that have native methods, call their initializers before you return to register their native methods with the JRI.

Make sure that you add the stub file (here, npCount.c) into your project so that it'll be compiled and linked into the plug-in.

 TIP You should always include an implementation of NPP_GetJavaClass() in your plug-in, even if you don't plan to connect to Java. Just write a stub implementation that returns NULL.

Implementing Native Methods

Follow the javah naming conventions (rather than C++ name mangling) when implementing the native methods. For example, you might write the following:

```
jbool native_npCount_post(
  JRIEnv* env,
  npCount* self,
  JRIMethodThunk* methodThunk,
  other parameters...);
```

You can use the `self` parameter to access any other class members. The other parameters in the last line are the parameters that you declared for this method in your Java class. The `env` parameter is supplied by the runtime in case you need to make calls back to Java. You can ignore the `methodThunk` parameter.

From the native method, you can access the plug-in instance by writing the following:

```
NPP npp = (NPP)self->getPeer(env);
```

From the plug-in, you can access the Java peer by calling `NPN_GetJavaPeer()`. The prototype of that function is:

```
jref NPN_GetJavaPeer(NPP instance);
```

If your plug-in is embedded on a page with JavaScript, the HTML author can activate the plug-in by calling it through the embeds interface. The first time JavaScript needs the Java peer object, Navigator makes an internal call to `NPN_GetJavaPeer()`, which instantiates the Java peer object. As part of `NPN_GetJavaPeer()`, Navigator calls the `init_` method.

JavaScript then actually communicates to the Java peer object, which does its work through the native methods.

Tying It All Together

Figure 9.2 shows the flow of control from JavaScript through npCount and back again.

FIG. 9.2
The npCount plug-in communicates both to and from JavaScript.

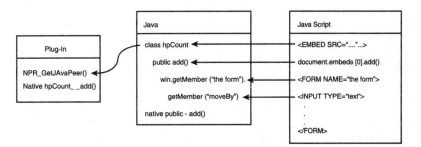

When the plug-in is loaded, it reads the current count from the Net—through NPP_Write()—and writes it to the window—through NPP_SetWindow(). When Navigator calls NPN_GetJavaPeer(), npCount returns its peer object, which is made available to JavaScript through embeds. When the user clicks a button, Navigator calls the method on the Java peer object pointed to by embeds[0]. If the method is add or decrease, the peer object talks to JavaScript to read the contents of the MoveBy field. All the remaining work of the Java class is done back in the plug-in. The plug-in runs the native method and calls InvalidateRect() to trigger an update of its window.

DisplayJavaMessage() Example

DisplayJavaMessage() is one of the larger and more interesting functions in Simple plug-in. Its parameters include a char pointer and an int (for length), as follows:

- This function is a utility routine that calls back into Java to print messages to the Java Console and to stdout (via the native method, native_Simple_printToStdout, defined below). Sure, it's not a very interesting use of Java, but it gets the point across.

```
*/
void DisplayJavaMessage(NPP instance, char* msg, int len)
{
  jref str, javaPeer;
  if (!env) {
    /* Java failed to initialize, so do nothing. */
    return;
  }
  if (len == -1)
    len = strlen(msg);
  /*
```

- Use the JRI (see jri.h) to create a Java string from the input message:

```
*/
str = JRI_NewStringUTF(env, msg, len);
/*
```

- Use the NPN_GetJavaPeer operation to get the Java instance that corresponds to our plug-in (an instance of the Simple class):

```
*/
javaPeer = NPN_GetJavaPeer(instance);

/*
```

■ Finally, call our plug-in's big "feature," the doit method, passing the execution environment, the object, and the java string:

```
   */
   Simple_doit(env, javaPeer, str);
}
```

The function calls the Java Runtime Interface (JRI) to allocate a string in Java:

```
jref str;
str = JRI_NewStringUTF(env, msg, len);
```

Part
III
Ch
9

Then the function calls NPN_GetJavaPeer() to get a Java reference (jref) to its own peer object. Because the peer is known to be an instance of Java class Simple, the plug-in calls the C stub of its peer class and runs Simple_doit(). Later in this chapter you'll read about Java class Simple and its doit() method.

Figure 9.3 traces the flow of control between the plug-in and the Java runtime.

FIG. 9.3
Netscape illustrates
how the plug-in
calls Java, with
DisplayJavaMessage().

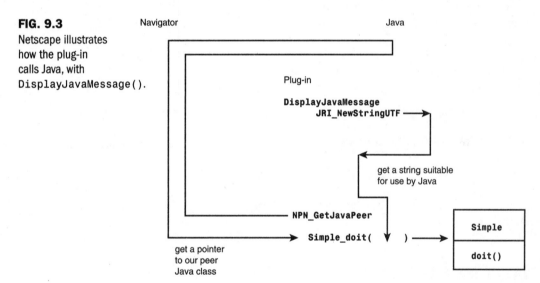

▶ **See** Chapter 5, "Programming Plug-ins."

LiveConnect Details

The real work of NPAvi example is done through the Java classes. Much of this work, in turn, is implemented back in the plug-in through native methods. Chapter 3, "Overview of Plug-In API," further details NPAvi. Figure 9.4 shows the interaction between JavaScript, Java, and the plug-in.

FIG. 9.4
Although the plug-in and JavaScript cannot talk directly, the Java peer object is quick and easy to set up.

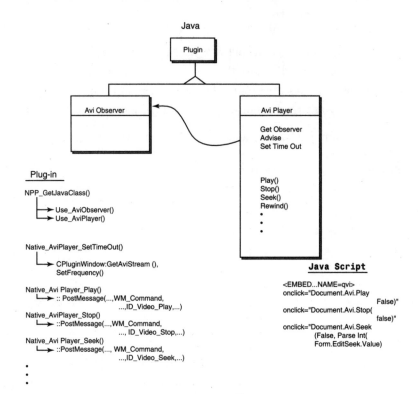

Java Class *AviPlayer*

Most of the methods in class AviPlayer are native. Follow the thread of control out of class AviPlayer and back to AviPlayer.c, in the _stubs directory. Pick one function, such as SetTimeOut(). SetTimeOut() is specified as native in AviPlayer.java, so it appears in the stub file AviPlayer.c. Here's the native declaration, in AviPlayer.java:

```
public class AviPlayer extends Plugin {
  .
  .
  .
  // set the timeout for the position checking timer
  public native void setTimeOut(int timeout);
  .
  .
  .
}
```

Note also that by specifying DEBUG, you get the typesafe C function AviPlayer_setTimeOut() rather than the macro. AviPlayer_setTimeOut() relies on use_AviPlayer_setTimeOut() being called as part of use_AviPlayer.

The programmer's implementations for native methods such as setTimeOut() are in the file avijava.cpp. There you learn that native_AviPlayer_setTimeOut() calls CAvi::SetFrequency(), which, in turn, calls the Window API ::SetTimer():

```
extern "C" JRI_PUBLIC_API(void)
native_AviPlayer_setTimeOut(JRIEnv* env, struct AviPlayer* self,
  ➡jint timeout)
{
  NPP instance = (NPP)self->getPeer(env);
  CPluginWindow* pPluginData = (CPluginWindow*)instance->pdata;
  pPluginData->GetAviStream().SetFrequency(timeout);
}
```

NOTE The timer in NPAvi is used in much the same way as the timer in CharFlipper is used—it sets the pace for the playback, so that each frame pauses on-screen long enough for the user to see it. The timer in an AVI movie, of course, runs on a much shorter interval than the timer in CharFlipper. ■

JavaScript Details

In order for a Java class to talk to JavaScript, you must import the Netscape javascript package in the Java file, as follows:

```
import netscape.javascript.*
```

The netscape.javascript package, described later in this chapter, includes two important classes—JSObject, which represents the JavaScript object, and JSException, which is raised to pass JavaScript errors back to your Java class.

For a Java class to call JavaScript, the HTML author must explicitly set the MAYSCRIPT attribute in the APPLET tag. For example:

```
<APPLET NAME="hello" CODE="hello.class" WIDTH=100 HEIGHT=100
MAYSCRIPT>
```

Note that in this example, a name was assigned to the applet. You will use the name when we begin talking to the applet from JavaScript.

> **CAUTION**
>
> If a Java applet attempts to run a page's JavaScript and the HTML author hasn't set MAYSCRIPT, Navigator raises an exception. You should catch this exception and put up an appropriate message to the user.
>
> One good way to put up an error message is to use the Java console defined by Netscape. From inside Java, write the following:
>
> ```
> System.out.println("Error: Applet unable to access JavaScript.
> Set the applet's MAYSCRIPT attribute and try again.");
> ```

To access JavaScript, your Java class must get a handle to the Navigator window, as shown in Figure 9.5. Your class's init() member is a good place to do this:

```
JSObject win;
public void init()
{
  win = JSObject.getWindow(this);
}
```

FIG. 9.5
Java gets a pointer to the JavaScript document in order to access its members.

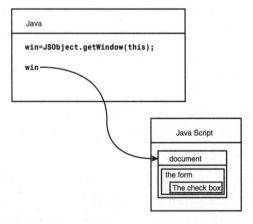

If the HTML page has a form named theForm which, in turn, has a checkbox named theCheckbox, you can access the status of this checkbox by following the membership hierarchy from the form to the checkbox, as follows:

```
JSObject win;
public void init()
{
  win = JSObject.getWindow(this);
  JSObject doc = (JSObject) win.getMember("document");
  JSObject theForm = (JSObject) doc.getMember("theForm");
  JSObject check = (JSObject) myForm.getMember("theCheckBox");
  Boolean isChecked = (Boolean) check.getMember("checked");
}
```

Part
III

Ch
9

Just as getMember() gives you access to the components of the JavaScript form, call() and eval() give you access to the JavaScript methods. You can write the following:

```
public void init()
{
  win = JSObject.getWindow(this);
}
public boolean mouseUp(Event e, int x, int y)
{
  win.eval("alert(\"Hello, world!\");");
  return true;
}
```

or, equivalently,

```
public void init()
{
  win = JSObject.getWindow(this);
}
public boolean mouseUp(Event e, int x, int y)
{
  win.call("alert(\"Hello, world!\");");
  return true;
}
```

▶ For more information about how Java and JavaScript work together, **see** Chapter 11, "Java to JavaScript Communication."

Java Details

Netscape intends the Java class `TimeMediaPlugin` to become a general-purpose tool for use with time-based content. A look at the Java code reveals that all of the real work is done in native methods:

```
class TimeMediaPlugin extends Plugin {
  public void SetSource(java.net.URL inSourceURL) {
    SetSourceNative( inSourceURL.toString() );
  }
  public void SetSource(java.lang.String inSourceString) {
    SetSourceNative( inSourceString );
  }
  public native void SetSourceNative( java.lang.String inSourceString
);
  public native void Start();
  public native void Stop();
  public native boolean IsRunning();
  public native void Loop( boolean inLoop );
  public native boolean IsLooping();
  // speed is in 60ths of a second
  public native void SetSpeed( int inSpeed );.
  public native int GetSpeed();
}
```

"Native" Java methods are the methods implemented outside of Java, usually in a language like C or C++. Netscape supplies a tool, javah, which reads Java files and writes function stubs. When javah reads the following line:

```
public native void Start();
```

in class `TimeMediaPlugin`, it writes a series of function definitions in _gen/ TimeMediaPlugin.h, including the following:

```
extern JRI_PUBLIC_API(void)
native_TimeMediaPlugin_Start(JRIEnv* env, struct TimeMediaPlugin*
self);
```

The plug-in programmer then writes an implementation of the native functions. The Netscape programmer has put these implementations in the file TimeMediaNatives.cpp. For example, `native_TimeMediaPlugin_Start()` is implemented as follows:

```
extern JRI_PUBLIC_API(void)
native_TimeMediaPlugin_Start(JRIEnv* env, struct TimeMediaPlugin*
self)
{
```

```
    NPP instance = (NPP) (self->getPeer(env));
    CCharFlipper* flipper = (CCharFlipper*) instance->pdata;
    flipper->StartAtFrame( 0 );
}
```

This function calls `CCharFlipper::StartAtFrame()` with `inFrame` set to zero. If that function passes its internal tests, `CCharFlipper::SetRunning()` is set to TRUE, and the flipper begins to flip.

 TIP

When tracing through large amounts of code, particularly in an object-oriented system where so many small functions call other small functions, it's good to be able to tell the system, "Show me where this function is used," or "Show me who defines this function." To get this kind of information from Microsoft, rebuild the project with "browse into" turned on.

▶ **See** Chapter 5, "Programming Plug-Ins."

Other Resources

 ON THE WEB

Sun maintains a complete set of documentation on Java at **http://www.javasoft.com**. At this site, you can find everything from language documentation to tutorials. Yahoo has a rather extensive index of pointers to Java resources. You can find this listing at **http://www.yahoo.com/Computers_and_Internet/Programming_Languages/Java**.

Again, for more information about plug-ins, take a look at the Plug-in Developer's Guide located at **http://home1.netscape.com/eng/mozilla/3.0/handbook/plugins/index.html**.

From this handbook, you can access documentation on calling Java methods from plug-ins at **http://home1.netscape.com/eng/mozilla/3.0/handbook/plugins/wr2.htm**, as well as documentation on calling plug-in native methods from Java at **http://home1.netscape.com/eng/mozilla/3.0/handbook/plugins/wr3.htm**.

From Here...

In this chapter, you learned that you can define *native methods* in Java that are implemented in C or C++. You follow the javah naming conventions (rather than C++ name mangling) when implementing the native methods. `DisplayJavaMessage()` is one of the larger and more interesting functions in Simple plug-in. You found that much of the work of NPAvi is implemented back in the plug-in through native methods.

The Java class `TimeMediaPlugin` is also a good example of what Java code reveals when implementing native methods.

- Chapter 5, "Programming Plug-Ins," looks at sample LiveConnect examples like Simple and CharFlipper.
- Chapter 7, "The Java Runtime Interface," looks at Java platform Support for native methods and Java classes.
- Chapter 10, "JavaScript to Java Communication," looks at accessing Java Directly, as well as controlling applets and plug-ins.
- Chapter 11, "Java to JavaScript Communication," looks at accessing JavaScript objects and properties, as well as call JavaScript methods.
- Chapter 12, "Netscape Packages," looks at using Netscape Packages, as well as a quick Netscape Package Reference.

LiveConnect Communication in JavaScript

CHAPTER 10

JavaScript to Java Communication

The LiveConnect environment is a merger of two other environments: Java and JavaScript. Java programmers would use a public identifier when defining a class. Now that LiveConnect enables JavaScript to be linked to a Java environment, all public classes can be controlled by the JavaScript script, which allows JavaScript scripts to access anything that a Java applet can access.

It's the Java Runtime Interface (JRI) that allows Netscape Navigator plug-ins to define Java classes and to call native C functions. The JRI, along with Netscape Navigator's application programming interface (API), is what allows plug-ins to be accessed in a Java environment. ■

Java Language Features

Java is really a bytecode-based interpreted language.

Controlling Java Applets

Develop Java applets and applications using the Java Development Kit (JDK).

How Java Works in Netscape

When you access a Web page that has an applet embedded in it, the browser fetches the code and takes care of running it.

Where to Find a Wealth of Online Java Resources

Everything from language documentation to tutorials.

How Much Java Do I Need to Know?

Recall that LiveConnect doesn't give a JavaScript programmer direct access to the plug-in, or vice versa. If you're comfortable with C++ and object technology, you can write a proxy class in Java that sits between your plug-in and JavaScript, giving a JavaScript programmer access to your plug-in.

To get started in Java, see the sidebar in this section titled "A Java Primer." To go further with Java, read on to the next section, "Accessing Java Directly," or check out *Special Edition Using Java* (Que, 1996). Then read on in this chapter to learn about the Netscape-specific packages that you need to connect Java to JavaScript and your plug-ins.

A Java Primer

To get started with Java, you need a Java development environment. The Java SDK from Sun is available at the following Web site:

www.quecorp.com/liveconnect/

To use LiveConnect with Java, you also need the java_30 file, which comes with Navigator 3.0.

Start by writing a Java "Hello, world!" program. The text file for this program is shown in Listing 10.1. This sidebar will describe how to put this applet into an HTML page. For now you can compile the applet from the command line with the following:

```
javac hello.java
```

The Java compiler, javac, produces a file with Java bytecodes that may be run in a browser like HotJava or Navigator. This output file is called hello.class. You can run it by typing this line:

```
appletviewer hello.html
```

The file hello.html need have only a single line:

```
<APPLET CODE="hello.class" WIDTH=120 HEIGHT=120></APPLET>
```

Let's go through hello.java, line by line.

Just as you do in C++, you usually can find some Java class to serve as a starting point for your program so that you don't have to write everything from scratch. Sun conveniently supplies class Applet, so we derive hello from Applet. (Note that Java, like C++, is case-sensitive.)

Java uses the following notation to access a specific method:

```
packageName.className.methodName
```

Therefore, to access the `drawString()` method of an instance of Java class Graphics, you import the class `java.awt.Graphics` and then call `drawString` on the instance. You can get all methods on all of the classes in a package by placing * in the className position.

Start by telling the Java compiler that Applet is defined in another file, in the classes\java\Applet subdirectory, which is what the following line does:

```
import java.applet.*;
```

All your applets will start with this line.

Many applets do some kind of drawing to the window, so you want to use class Graphics. Graphics is defined in the java\awt\Graphics subdirectory. For convenience, you bring in all of these useful built-in classes.

```
import java.awt.*;
```

By default, Java classes are not public. Because you want to be able to access class hello from the outside world, declare it to be public. You also declare that it is derived from class Applet. Note that when a class name is made public, the class must be defined in a file of the same name. Therefore, class hello must be saved to a file named hello.java, as follows:

```
public class hello extends Applet
```

Just like C++ classes in class libraries such as MFC, Java classes have methods that the outside world calls. When the class is constructed, its `init()` method is called. You define `init()` as a stub—anything that should be done by the class when it's constructed can go in here.

```
public void init()
{
}
```

Just as Windows sends the message `WM_PAINT` every time the windows need to be redrawn, and Navigator calls `NPP_SetWindow()`, so Java calls your class' method `paint()` when the window has to be displayed. `paint()` takes a Graphics object as its parameter, as follows:

```
public void paint(Graphics g)
{
  g.drawString("Hello, world!", 10, 50);
}
```

To access the applet from Navigator (rather than just from AppletViewer), copy the line from hello.html into the HTML file of your Web page. Now you have a (very simple) Java applet on your page.

Part

IV

Ch

10

Listing 10.1   hello.java—The Java "Hello, world!" Program

```
import java.applet.*;
import java.awt.*;
public class hello extends Applet
{
  public void init()
  {
  }
  public void paint (Graphics g)
  {
    g.drawString("Hello", 10, 50);
  }
}
```

ON THE WEB

You can download the latest version of Sun's Java Developers Kit (JDK), with Netscape modifications, as part of the Netscape Plug-ins SDK at **http://home.netscape.com/ eng/mozilla/3.0/handbook/plugins/index.html**.

You also can use commercial packages such as Symantec's Café or Natural Intelligence's Roaster, but you need the classes from Netscape's version of the kit. You also need Netscape's special version of javah (also part of the kit). Microsoft also offers a trial edition of Visual J++.

Accessing Java Directly

Java is a programming language created by Sun Microsystems that has created a lot more excitement than other programming languages usually generate. Programmers are excited about Java because the language supports many useful features, such as an object-oriented structure, intuitive multithreading (a program that can run two or more independent program portions at the same time), and built-in network support. The language also avoids many of the pitfalls of C++. Where C++ forces the programmer to keep track of the memory that he uses, a Java programmer doesn't need to worry about using memory reserved for the system or not freeing up memory appropriately.

Java programmers don't need to worry about how memory is utilized because of how a Java program is run. Java is a semi-compiled language. When you program in a compiled language like C++, the compiler takes your source code and creates a file that is ready for the system to execute. A Java compiler doesn't work this way. Instead, it creates a file that contains bytecodes. This file is then handed to an interpreter that sits on your computer. That interpreter executes the program. The interpreter keeps track of how memory is used, and can tell the programmer if something has gone wrong. This is different from an errant C++ program, which simply stops, sometimes after crashing the system. Because of this, it's much harder to debug C++ programs than programs written in Java.

But these advantages aren't the only reasons that Java is generating so much excitement. The language's semi-compiled nature allows it to be architecture-neutral, which means you can compile your Java program once and it's ready to run on many different platforms. But the real brilliance of Java is that it's designed with distributed systems in mind. Part of this is the built-in networking support. More importantly, a Java program can be transferred across the Internet to your computer, and the interpreter can make sure that it doesn't do anything bad to the system.

Part
IV
Ch
10

But you're probably asking, "Why should this interest me, a Netscape Navigator user?" The reason is that Netscape Navigator has a Java interpreter built in (as does Netscape 3.0), which means that instead of just downloading pictures, sound, and text, Netscape Navigator can download small programs called applets, which are then run on your computer. These applets, which are written in Java, can display animations, give you games to play, or get stock prices from a remote computer. Whatever these applets do, you don't have to worry about them crashing your system, spreading a virus, or wiping out your hard drive.

Java Language Features

Java was designed to be an object-oriented language, similar to C++, to make it familiar to a large number of programmers. As you'll see later in this chapter, the syntax of Java is very similar to C++. Because Java is an object-oriented language, this chapter assumes that you're familiar with basic object-oriented concepts, such as classes and inheritance.

N O T E   In Java, the basic object-oriented programming element is the *class*. A class is
a collection of related data members and functions, known as *methods*, that
operate on that data. Everything in Java exists within a class—there are no global
variables or global functions. ■

In developing Java, Sun chose to leave out several C++ language features. Specifically, Java does not support multiple inheritance, operator overloading, or extensive automatic coercion. Java also takes steps to make pointer operations much safer. Java's pointer model doesn't allow memory overwrites and data corruption. In fact, Java doesn't allow pointer arithmetic at all. It supports true arrays with bounds checking. You cannot change an integer to a pointer via a cast operator. In short, Java eliminates many of the confusing, often misused aspects of C++ and creates a smaller, easier to understand language.

Let's look at some of the new features that Java adds. The language has support for automatic garbage collection, so you no longer have to explicitly delete an object. Objects are automatically deleted whenever they're no longer needed. Java has extensive support for distributed applications. It has native support for the TCP/IP protocols, which allows programmers to easily work with objects as URLs.

Because Java was designed with native support for client/server applications, security is obviously an issue. Java has extensive security support to allow you to create tamper-free systems. Java uses a public-key encryption scheme to provide authentication, and its new pointer model makes it impossible to overwrite secure areas of memory.

If you look back to Sun's definition of Java, you're probably wondering about the architecture-neutral and portable part. Well, Java is really a bytecode-based interpreted language.

Bytecodes are essentially the components of a machine language. They're similar to the object files you get when you compile a C++ program with your favorite compiler. However, the "machine" that these bytecodes represent isn't a real machine at all. Bytecodes are really elements of a machine language for an imaginary machine.

By turning a Java program into bytecodes for an imaginary machine language, the bytecodes aren't tied to any one computer hardware platform. In fact, they need a special interpreter program to convert them into actual machine instructions for the destination computer.

Why do it this way? A couple of reasons. First, because the bytecodes don't represent an actual machine, the compiled Java file isn't restricted to any one type of computer. Second, the designers were able to avoid design problems that are specific to various types of computers. They were able to design their machine language in a very efficient way, so that even though Java files must be run through an interpreter, they're still very efficient.

When a Java program is compiled, it creates a bytecode image that is interpreted by a Java runtime system. Because this bytecode image has nothing to do with the architecture that the Java program was built on, it will run on any platform that has a Java runtime environment. This means that you only have to write a Java program once—one version is portable to any platform with the Java runtime environment!

In addition to being architecture-neutral, Java eliminates all platform-specific data types that have plagued C programmers for years. None of the primitive data types are architecture-dependent. All of them have specified sizes and arithmetic operations. For example, a float is always an IEEE 754 32-bit floating point number—on any platform.

A common problem with object-oriented development is that when a company releases a new version of a library, all client software that uses that library has to be recompiled and redistributed. Java was designed to allow classes to add new methods and instance variables with no effect on the client applications.

As you can see, Java is an object-oriented distributed language that solves a lot of problems with current object-oriented technology.

Hello World

We started our exploration of Java at the beginning of this chapter with an example that almost all good programming languages use—the Hello World program. In Java, there are two types of programs: applications and applets. An application is designed to run directly in the Java runtime environment. An applet is designed to run as a component of a network browser, such as Netscape Navigator. Of the two, applications are a bit simpler in structure.

The concept of the "Java runtime environment" gets fuzzy here. As you saw in the previous section, there's a stand-alone Java interpreter, Java, that executes a byte code-compiled file. This is how applications are executed. Applets, on the other hand, are designed to run within the context of a Web browser like Netscape. Applets require more complicated programming than applications because they're actually running within the context of another program. The other program, Netscape in this case, actually has a version of the Java interpreter embedded within it. This means that when Netscape executes a Java applet, it's actually acting as the Java runtime environment for the applet.

Here's the Java code for the Hello World application:

```
class HelloApp
{
public static void main(String args[])
{
System.out.println("Hello World!");
}
}
```

In Java, all functions and variables exist within a class object; there are no global functions or variables in a Java application. So the first line of this sample application defines a class named HelloApp.

Inside HelloApp's definition, there's a method called main. The main method is the one that's invoked when the application's execution is started in the Java runtime environment. Because you have to specify the class that you want to execute in the Java runtime environment, Java invokes the main method for that class.

The main method is declared to be public static void. The public keyword means that the main method is visible to all other classes outside this class. The static keyword indicates that main is a static method, which means that main is associated directly with the class HelloApp instead of with an instance of HelloApp. Without the static keyword, main would have been an instance method—a method that's associated with an instance of a class. We'll look at another example shortly.

The next line of code in the main method appears to print the "Hello World" string as output. So what exactly is System.out.println? System refers to Java's System class. The word out is an instance variable in the System class, and println is one of out's methods. Notice that we never declared an instance of the System class; we just called out.println directly. That is because out is a static variable of the System class. We can refer to it directly by just referring to the class itself.

Command Line Arguments

You'll notice that the arguments to main are different than they are in a regular C or C++ program. Instead of the traditional argv and argc arguments, Java gives you an array of strings that contain the command line arguments. This isn't an array of pointers, as it is under C and C++, but an array of real strings. You can get the length of the array with the .length function of the String class. For example, the length of the command line argument array is args.length.

Another major difference between Java and C++ is that the name of the application program isn't passed in the command line argument array. The name of the application program is always the same as the class name where the main method is defined. While under C++, for example:

```
foo arg1 arg2
```

Running the program foo with two arguments would make the first entry in the command line argument array "foo." While under Java:

```
java foo arg1 arg2
```

The word java invokes the runtime environment, and the word "foo" is the class that has main defined. Thus, the first argument in the command line arguments array, args[0], is "arg1."

Accessing JavaScript Code

It can be difficult to pick up a new programming language from scratch—even for experienced programmers. To make it easy for you to master JavaScript, this section presents some examples of JavaScript code and functions that you can use in your own pages. Each of them demonstrates a practical concept.

Dumping an Object's Properties

Let's look at DumpProperties( ), which gets all the property names and their values.

```
function DumpProperties (obj, obj_name) {
var result = ""      // set the result string to blank
for (i in obj)
result += obj_name + "." + i + " = " + obj[i] + "\n"
return result
}
```

As all JavaScript functions should, this one starts by defining its variables using the var keyword; it supplies an initial value, too, which is a good habit to start. The meat of the function is the for...in loop, which iterates over all the properties of the specified object. For each property, the loop body collects the object name, the property name (provided by the loop counter in the for...in loop), and the property's value. We access the properties as an indexed array instead of by name, so we can get them all.

Note that this function doesn't print anything out. If you want to see its output, put it in a page (remember to surround it with <SCRIPT>...</SCRIPT>!), then at the bottom of the page, use:

```
document.writeln(DumpProperties(obj, objName))
```

where obj is the object of interest and objName is its name.

Building a Link Table

You might want to automatically generate a list of all the links in a page, perhaps to display them in a separate section at the end of the page, as shown in Figure 10.1. DumpURL( ), shown in Listing 10.2, does just that; it prints out a nicely formatted numbered list showing the hostname of each link in the page.

FIG. 10.1
The DumpURL()
function adds a
numbered list of all
the links in a page at
the end of the page.

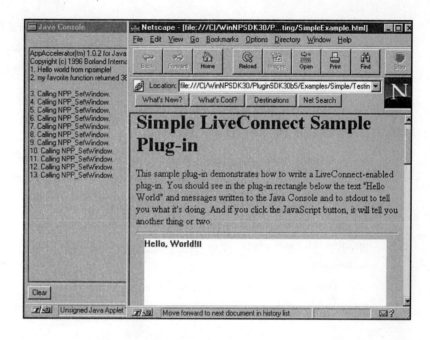

Listing 10.2 DumpURL( ) Displays a Numbered List of All the URLs on a Page

```
function DumpURL()
{
// declare the variables we'll use
var linkCount = document.links.length
var result = ""
// build our summary line
result = "<hr>\nLink summary: this page has links to <b>" + linkCount +
"</b> hosts<br>\n"
result += "<ol>\n"
// for each link in the document, print a list item with its hostname
for (i=0; i < linkCount ; i++)
result += "<li> " + document.links[i].hostname + "\n"
// add the closing HTML for our list
result += "</ol><hr>\n"
return result
    <LX>}
```

This function starts by declaring the variables used in the function. JavaScript requires that you declare most variables before using them, and good programming practice dictates doing so even when JavaScript doesn't require it. Next, you build the summary line for your table by assigning a string literal full of HTML to the result variable. You use a for loop to iterate through all the links in the current document and add a list item for each to the result variable. When you finish, add the closing HTML for your list to result and return it.

Updating Data in Form Fields

We've talked about the benefits of using JavaScript to check and modify data in HTML forms. Let's look at an example that dynamically updates the value of a text field based on the user's selection from one of several buttons.

To make this work, you need two pieces; the first is a simple bit of JavaScript that updates the value property of an object to whatever you pass in. Here's what it looks like:

```
function change(input, newValue)
{
input.value = newValue
}
```

Then, each button you want to include needs to have its onClick method changed so that it calls your change( ) function. Here's a sample button definition:

```
<input type="button" value="Mac"
onClick="change(this.form.display, 'Macintosh')">
```

When the button is clicked, JavaScript calls the onClick method, which happens to point to your function. The this.form.display object points to a text field named display; this refers to the active document, form refers to the form in the active document, and display refers to the form field named display.

Of course, this requires that you have a form input gadget named display!

Validating Data in Form Fields

When you create a form to get data from the user, you need to check that data to see if it's correct and complete before sending mail, or making a database entry, or whatever you collected the data for. Without JavaScript, you have to post the data and let a CGI script on the server decide if all the fields were correctly filled out.

You can do better, though, by writing JavaScript functions that check the data in your form on the client; by the time the data gets posted, you know it's correct.

For this example, let's require that the user fill out two fields on our form: ZIP code and area code. We'll also present some other fields that are optional. First, you need a function that will return True if there's something in a field and False if it's empty:

```
function isFilled(input)
{
return (input.value.length != 0)
}
```

That's simple enough! For each field you want to make the user complete, you'll override its onBlur( ) method. onBlur( ) is triggered when the user moves the focus out of the specified field. Here's what your buttons look like:

```
<input name="ZIP" value=""
onBlur="if (!isFilled(form.ZIP)) {
alert('You must put your ZIP code in this field.');
form.ZIP.focus() }">
```

When the user tries to move the focus out of the ZIP code button, the code attached to the onBlur( ) event is called. That code in turn checks to see if the field is complete; if not, it nags the user and puts the focus back into the ZIP field.

Of course, you could also implement a more gentle validation scheme by attaching a JavaScript to the form's submit button, like this:

```
<script language="LiveScript">
function areYouSure()
{
return confirm("Are you sure you want to submit these answers?")
}
</script>
<input type=button name="doIt" value="Submit form"
onClick="if (areYouSure()) this.form.submit();">
```

Figure 10.2 shows your finished page, including the politely worded dialog box that tells the user to go back and finish filling out the form.

FIG. 10.2
The fields on this page are tied to JavaScript functions that keep the user from moving the input focus until the user supplies a value.

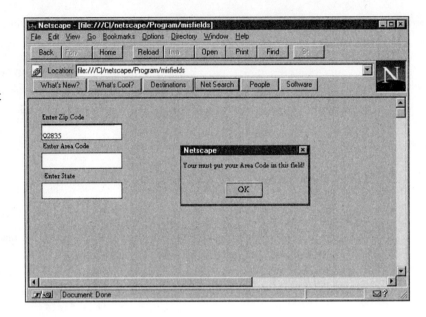

A Pseudo-Scientific Calculator

If you ask any engineer under a certain age what kind of calculator she used in college, the answer is likely to be "a Hewlett-Packard." HP calculators are somewhat different from ordinary calculators; you use reverse Polish notation, or RPN, to do calculations.

With a regular calculator, you put the operator between operands. To add 3 and 7, you push 3, then the + key, then 7, then = to print the answer. With an RPN calculator, you put the operator after both operands! To add 3 and 7 on my HP-15C, I have to push 3, then Enter (which puts the first operand on the internal stack), then 7, then +, at which time I'd see the correct answer. This oddity takes a bit of getting used to, but it makes complex calculations go much faster, since intermediate results get saved on the stack.

Here's a simple RPN example. To compute $((1024 * 768) / 3.14159)2$, you'd enter:

```
1024, Enter, 768, *, 3.14159, /, x2
```

to get the correct answer: 6.266475×1010, or about 6.3 billion.

Netscape provides an RPN calculator as an example of JavaScript's expressive power. Let's take a detailed look at how it works. Listing 10.3 shows the JavaScript itself (note that these are really in the same file; we've just split them for convenience). Figure 10.3 shows the calculator as it's displayed in Navigator.

FIG. 10.3

Navigator displays the RPN calculator as a table of buttons, with the accumulator (the answer) and the stack at the top.

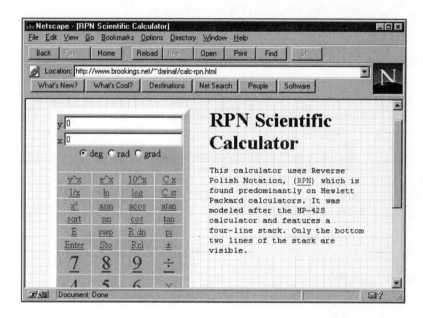

Part
IV
Ch
10

The HTML Page   Listing 10.3 shows the HTML for our calculator's page. For precise alignment, all the buttons are grouped into a table; the accumulator (where the answer's displayed) and the stack (where operands can be stored) are at the top.

Listing 10.3   The HTML Definition for the RPN Calculator Example

```
<table border="0">
<tr>
<td align=right>Stack:</td><td><input name="stack" value="0"></td>
</tr>
<tr>
<td align=right>Accumulator:</td><td><input name="display" value="0">
➥</td>
</tr>
</table>
</td>
```

continues

Listing 10.3   Continued

```
</tr>
<tr align=center>
<td>
<input type="button" value=" 7 "
onClick="addChar(this.form.display, '7')">
</td>
<td>
<input type="button" value=" 8 "
onClick="addChar(this.form.display, '8')">
</td>
<td>
<input type="button" value=" 9 "
onClick="addChar(this.form.display, '9')">
</td>
<td>
<input type="button" value=" / "
onClick="divide(this.form)">
</td>
</tr>
<tr align=center>
<td>
<input type="button" value=" 4 "
onClick="addChar(this.form.display, '4')">
</td>
<td>
<input type="button" value=" 5 "
onClick="addChar(this.form.display, '5')">
</td>
<td>
<input type="button" value=" 6 "
onClick="addChar(this.form.display, '6')">
</td>
<td>
<input type="button" value=" * "
onClick="multiply(this.form)">
</td>
</tr>
<tr align=center>
<td>
<input type="button" value=" 1 "
onClick="addChar(this.form.display, '1')">
</td>
<td>
<input type="button" value=" 2 "
onClick="addChar(this.form.display, '2')">
</td>
<td>
<input type="button" value=" 3 "
onClick="addChar(this.form.display, '3')">
```

```
</td>
<td>
<input type="button" value=" - "
onClick="subtract(this.form)">
</td>
</tr>
<tr align=center>
<td>
<input type="button" value=" 0 "
onClick="addChar(this.form.display, '0')">
</td>
<td>
<input type="button" value=" . "
onClick="addChar(this.form.display, '.')">
</td>
<td>
<input type="button" value="+/-"
onClick="changeSign(this.form.display)">
</td>
<td>
<input type="button" value=" + "
onClick="add(this.form)">
</td>
</tr>
<tr align=center>
<td colspan="2">
<input type="button" value=" Enter " name="enter"
onClick="pushStack(this.form)">
</td>
<td>
<input type="button" value=" C "
onClick="this.form.display.value = 0 ">
</td>
<td>
<input type="button" value=" <- "
onClick="deleteChar(this.form.display)">
</td>
</tr>
</table>
<LX>     <LX>   </form>
```

Part

IV

Ch

10

Notice that each button has an onClick() definition associated with it. The digits 0 through 9 all call the addChar() JavaScript function; the editing keys, C for clear and <- for backspace, call functions that change the value of the accumulator. The Enter key stores the current value on the stack, and the +/- button changes the accumulator's sign.

Of course, the operators themselves call JavaScript functions too; for example, the * button's definition calls the `Multiply( )` function. The definitions aren't functions themselves; they include function calls (as for the digits) or individual statements (as in the "clear" key).

The JavaScript   Of course, all these `onClick( )` triggers need to have JavaScript routines to call! Listing 10.4 shows the JavaScript functions that implement the actual calculator.

Listing 10.4 The JavaScript Code that Makes the RPN Calculator

```
<script language="LiveScript">
<! --hide this script tag's contents from old browsers
// keep track of whether we just computed display.value
var computed = false
function pushStack(form)
{
form.stack.value = form.display.value
form.display.value = 0
}
// Define a function to add a new character to the display
function addChar(input, character)
{
// auto-push the stack if the last value was computed
if(computed) {
pushStack(input.form)
computed = false
}
// make sure input.value is a string
if(input.value == null ¦¦ input.value == "0")
input.value = character
else
input.value += character
}
function deleteChar(input)
{
input.value = input.value.substring(0, input.value.length - 1)
}
function add(form)
{
form.display.value = (0 + form.stack.value) + form.display.value
computed = true
}
function subtract(form)
{
form.display.value = form.stack.value - form.display.value
computed = true
```

```
}
function multiply(form)
{
form.display.value = form.stack.value * form.display.value
computed = true
}
function divide(form)
{
var divisor = 0 + form.display.value
if(divisor == 0) {
alert("Don't divide by zero, pal...");
return
}
form.display.value = form.stack.value / divisor
computed = true
}
function changeSign(input)
{
// could use input.value = 0 - input.value, but let's show off substring
if(input.value.substring(0, 1) == "-")
input.value = input.value.substring(1, input.value.length)
else
input.value = "-" + input.value
    <LX>}
```

As you saw in the preceding HTML listing, every button is connected to some function. The addChar( ) and deleteChar( ) functions directly modify the contents of the form field named display—the accumulator—as do the operators (add( ), subtract( ), multiply( ), and divide( )).

This code shows off some subtle but cool benefits of JavaScript that would be difficult or impossible to do with CGI scripts. First, notice that the divide( ) function checks for division by zero and presents a warning dialog box to the user.

More importantly, in this example all the processing is done on the client—imagine an application like an interactive tax form, where all the calculations are done on the browser and only the completed, verified data gets posted to the server.

Controlling Applets

Sun Microsystems released a Web browser called HotJava, written in a new programming language called Java. This language was originally intended to handle such tasks as interactive television and coordination of household appliances. The explosion of the Web in 1994 revealed the real opportunity for Java, and work on the Web browser commenced.

Although this Web browser was rough around the edges, it could do some things no other Web browser could at that time. With this Web browser, a user could see animation, play games, and even view a ticker tape of their up-to-date stock prices. Almost immediately after its release, Netscape decided to license HotJava's technology and incorporate it into its browsers. Netscape's incorporation of this technology into Netscape Navigator makes this technology available to a much wider audience than before. This wider audience, along with the capabilities that Java provides, is revolutionizing the Web.

What Is a Java Applet?

Netscape Navigator can run Java applets, small programs that are downloaded from a Web server. There isn't anything special about how it does this; it downloads a Java applet in precisely the same manner as it downloads any other file. Just as any browser displays an image as it is received, a Java-capable browser runs the Java applet. When the Java applet runs, it is similar to (but not exactly like) any other program that can run on your computer. It can take input from your keyboard, mouse, or even a remote computer. The output is displayed on your screen.

But there are differences between a Java applet and the applications that sit on your desktop. You wouldn't want Netscape Navigator to download a virus. At the same time, you wouldn't want to have to check every program that came down, because most programmers have no interest in harming your computer. Because of the way the Java language is structured, you don't have to worry about a Java applet harming your computer.

But this does mean that there have been some restrictions placed on Java applets. In fact, a Java applet knows next to nothing about your computer. It can't look at or write to any file in your file system. It can use your computer's memory, but not directly. These restrictions keep your computer safe from harm, and also protect your privacy.

How a Java Applet Is Different from the CGI Program

Anyone who has been around the Web for a while knows that programs can be run on the Web without Java. One of the reasons the Web, without Java, has become so popular is that the Web allows simple interaction across the Internet. It does this through the Common Gateway Interface (CGI). The CGI underlies electronic forms, imagemaps, and search engines. Basically, it runs a program that resides on the server. The program, called a CGI program, outputs a Web page, and that Web page is sent back to the client. (See Figure 10.4.)

FIG. 10.4
How programs are transmitted over the Web.

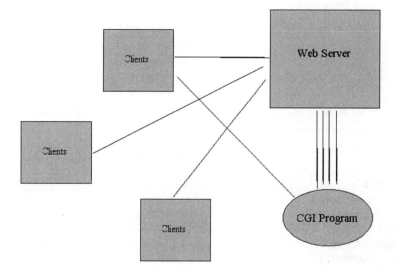

The Common Gateway Interface puts the Web a step above other information protocols such as FTP and Gopher because it allows you to tell a remote computer to do things for you. It's great for information providers because they can let you do very specific tasks without having to give you, and the rest of the world, the run of their machines.

CGI programs are great for a lot of things. For instance, let's say you're an officer of a club that's running a Web server. Through the use of a simple CGI program, you can give your members a way to keep their mailing addresses up-to-date. You can put an electronic form on your Web site, and if someone moves, she can just access that form and enter her new address. Then, the CGI program takes that information and updates the database.

However, there are many limitations of CGI programs that applets overcome. (See Table 10.1.)

Table 10.1   Differences Between CGI Programs and Java Applets

Property	Java Applet	CGI Program
Get information from remote computer	Yes	Yes
Computer that it runs on	Client	Server
How it handles input and output	Instantaneously across the Internet	Only after transmission

The limitations of CGI programs are outlined in Table 10.1, but let's also look at something that has been done with both a CGI program and a Java applet. Figure 10.5 shows a tic-tac-toe game that was done using a Java applet. Tic-tac-toe also has been done many times using CGI programs, and looks a lot like this.

FIG. 10.5
Tic-tac-toe with a Java applet is located at **http:// www.javasoft.com/ applets/applets/ TicTacToe/ example1.html**.

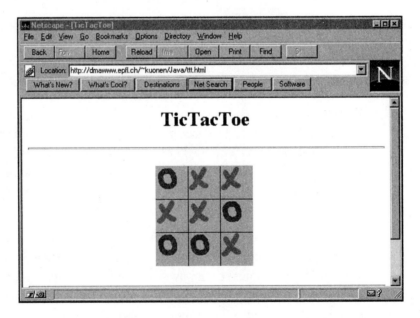

For both the CGI implementation and the applet implementation, you simply click where you want the X to go.

First, let's look at how the CGI implementation handles the input. Your Web browser takes that information and transmits it to the Web server. The Web server runs the CGI program. The CGI program figures out the best response and writes a Web page indicating this. That page is then transmitted back across the Internet.

When tic-tac-toe is implemented using a Java applet, the Java applet figures out the best move. Because no communication takes place across the Internet, it's much faster.

Of course, for something as simple as tic-tac-toe, one could argue that speed isn't very important. But for something like Tetris, speed *is* important. (See Figure 10.6.) It would be a boring game of Tetris if you had to wait several seconds between each move. Because a Java applet runs on your computer, it provides real-time animation. Also, when you interact with the applet by clicking the mouse or pressing a key, the applet knows about it immediately. A CGI program only knows after the data has been transmitted across the Internet.

Part

IV

Ch

10

FIG. 10.6
Tetris with a Java applet is located at **http:// www.mit.edu:8001/ people/nathanw/ java/Tetris.html**.

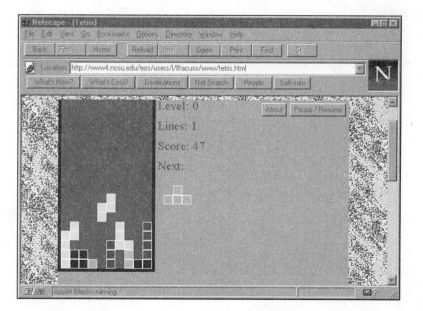

There are many other examples of Web applications that are best done by an applet. For instance, an applet can scroll the current prices of your stocks across your screen. A virtual world can be downloaded in the form of an applet, and if that virtual world is changed by someone else, your view of it is immediately updated.

Java applets are faster because they don't have to transmit input and output across the Internet. They are also better than CGI programs for many applications because the server doesn't have to process anything. This was a big problem with Netscape's first attempt at animation and interactivity, Server Push and Client Pull, based on the Common Gateway Interface. After the page was loaded, a CGI program would hold the connection open and update the page as necessary. This allowed a Web page designer to make a page dynamic and interactive.

But Tetris, for example, would have two distinct disadvantages as a CGI program. First, playing the game would be slower, because input and output would still have to be transmitted across the Internet. Second, the increased load resulting from such rapid-fire contact would slow down the server enough that other clients would experience the delay, as seen in Figure 10.7.

FIG 10.7
Interactivity through
the Common Gateway
Interface.

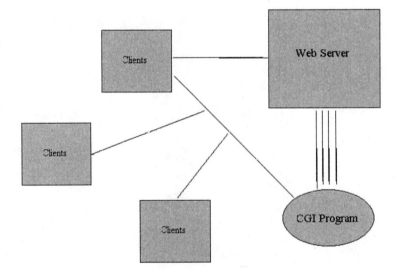

Because Server Push and Client Pull has such an ill effect on the server, many Web sites have banned their information providers from using it. This is a real shame, because any machine powerful enough to run a graphical Web browser could easily be a Web server. The processing power of the client machine sits idle while a busy server handles the computation.

The use of applets means that your machine can do processing that the server doesn't have to do, leaving the server to concentrate on its real purpose: serving information. Even in cases where speed might not be crucial, it's still better to use Java applets for interactivity. The processing is more evenly balanced, as shown in Figure 10.8.

FIG. 10.8
Processing responsibilities balanced with use of Java applets.

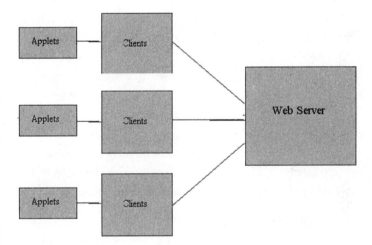

CGI Programs Versus Java Applets: When to Use What

If you're a Web page designer, you're probably wondering when a Java applet is appropriate and when a CGI program is. For two reasons, applets don't completely replace the Common Gateway Interface. First, not all Web browsers are able to run applets. Unless you're sure that the users of your particular service have a Java-enabled version of Netscape or some other browser, you should consider providing an alternative version of your service.

Second, if your program is using a central database, you should use a CGI program. For example, a search engine should function as a CGI program. Advanced search engines, such as WAIS, Lycos, and Harvest, maintain a database of keywords. Instead of directly searching Web pages for some keyword, a CGI program simply looks in the database. An applet couldn't act as a search engine nearly as well because it would have to traverse the network looking for some keyword.

In the search engine example, the database is only read. Because an applet isn't allowed to write to any file system, you can't use an applet to modify a database, either. If you want visitors to your Web site to fill out a survey, you probably want to use a CGI program.

Unless you're dealing with a central store of information, you should consider using Java applets. They reduce the load on the Web server and allow more interactivity. They also make more dynamic Web pages.

Remember, Java applets and CGI programs are not mutually exclusive. Let's look back at the search engine example. We definitely don't want an applet to search the entire Web when a CGI program can just do a quick lookup in its database. But by writing an applet that communicates with the CGI program, we can provide superior interactivity. The CGI program can generate the raw results of the search, while the applet provides an advanced interface. Instead of just providing a list of pages containing a keyword, an applet can display a map for each of those pages. That map can show the pages that are directly linked from a certain page containing that keyword. Then, you can focus your energies on those parts of the Web where the information you want is most centralized.

Also, an applet can easily keep track of what a user has done. Let's go back to the example of someone modifying a database that resides on your Web server. If you want people to be able to make a lot of modifications, you have to assume that they're going to make some mistakes. An applet can easily keep track of what they have done and correct any mistakes with the press of a button. However, a CGI program has a hard time providing this functionality because it's responsible for answering many users. It's quite difficult for a CGI program to keep track of who has done what, and even more difficult for it to provide an intuitive interface.

Let's expand this example a bit. Let's say that there are many databases on different machines that need to be manipulated by some user. An applet can make it appear that all of them are the same. When the user wants information from a certain one, the applet figures out which CGI program to connect to. This is much more intuitive and less time-consuming than forcing the user to link directly to the CGI program. Still, the applet can provide interactive features like an Undo key.

How Java Allows the Web to Evolve Itself

Java allows applet writers to build on the Web's current infrastructure. If there's some capability that a Web browser doesn't have, a Java applet can often be written to give the Web browser that capability. Such possible capabilities include interactive features that you expect from your normal desktop applications and the capability to understand new protocols. The applet writer doesn't have to write an entire Web browser. This is important, because it's unrealistic to expect the entire Internet to adapt to a new way of doing things, even if it is a great idea.

If a new way of compressing video data were to be invented, the inventors wouldn't have to convince everyone that it was great. Instead, they could just write an applet that utilizes their new method. They wouldn't have to distribute software that everyone would then have to install on their computers. They wouldn't have to wait for Web browser makers to adopt their technology. The applet could simply be downloaded at the same time the data is. If they decide to add a feature, they could just do it, and their improved software would be available instantly.

Java allows the Web to become a programming platform. Without Java, new network programs have to be developed from the ground up. Before, if you wanted to develop an Internet-wide conferencing system, you had to develop an application that would run on the user's desktop. Your users would have to acquire the software and install it themselves. With a Java-ized Web, you simply write an applet and put it on your Web site. Anyone with a Java-enabled browser, such as Netscape 3.0, has whatever level of access to the software that you allow. Your distribution costs drop to nothing. Also, the development is easier because the Java language was designed for distributed network computing.

This is what makes Java, in the words of Mark Andreessen, "as revolutionary as the Web itself." Given a Web server, anyone who can write a Web page can add information to the Web. With Java, any programmer can add to the Web's very infrastructure. The Web will grow, not only in terms of content. It now has the capability of evolving itself. In the future, instead of your bank or travel agent merely having information online, you'll be able to do all your banking and book an entire trip from your computer. The applets you'll use will have interfaces of equal or better quality than any other application on your desktop. Plus, you won't have to download them and install them on your computer; they'll be downloaded instantly when you access the Web site.

What Java Can Do Beyond the Web

Java is not just a part of the Web. It's a complete, object-oriented programming language designed to overcome some of the limitations of C++.

Right now, applets as we know them can only run in some Web browsers. But applets aren't limited to Web browsers. Any application that sits on your desktop can be upgraded to connect to the Web and make use of special applets.

Imagine that your spreadsheet program can deal with special applets. One of these special Java applets can talk to a server on Wall Street. When the price of one of your stocks changes, the server tells the Java applet and the Java applet updates your spreadsheet automatically.

Now your formulas that deal with stock prices always deal with live data, because when you open up your spreadsheet, it downloads this applet that puts the appropriate stock prices into the places they're supposed to be. No longer do you have to look up the prices and enter them into your spreadsheet. They're already there, and they're current. When you take your report to your meeting, the data is as current as when you printed it out.

Still, this isn't the end of what Java can do for the Internet and the programming world. You may or may not turn your computer off when you leave for home. Could you be persuaded to leave your computer on all night if it could help solve some massive problem, like global warming?

Consider the following scenario: A central computer checks with your computer at some appointed time, say, a few hours after you go home. If it isn't busy, it sends an applet across the Internet. Your computer runs that applet all night. When you come in the next morning and press a key, your computer sends the applet back across the Internet to the central "problem server." The problem server takes the data that has been crunched and incorporates it into a database. With the help of your computer and thousands of others, the problem is eventually solved. Better yet, the research institution working on this problem didn't have to go buy several supercomputers to solve it. And you were able to help solve a problem like global warming by simply leaving your computer on before you went home.

The thrust of these examples is based on a simple fact: There is a lot of information and a lot of processing power on the millions of computers all over the world. Java allows computers to access and deal with all of that information safely. There's no reason for you to manually insert data into a program when it's already available on the Internet. Your computer is capable of getting the data and inserting it. Along the same lines, there's no reason for your computer to sit idle when there are pressing problems to be solved. The use of Java in software not only makes the end user's life easier, but also brings all of the computers on the Internet together into a true working community.

How Java Works in Netscape Navigator

Netscape Navigator can run Java applets. Because of how a Java applet is set up, it knows next to nothing about your computer. This means you don't have to worry about a Java applet doing damage to your computer. But if you just want to see cool applets, you don't need to know anything about it. If this is all you want to do, just read the following section and start exploring.

How to Access Java Applets with Netscape

There's nothing complicated about accessing applets with Netscape Navigator. After your browser is set up correctly, you don't need to configure anything to enable Java. To the user, an applet is simply a part of a Web page, just like images and text. If a page contains an image, the browser takes care of getting that image and displaying it. With a Java-enabled browser, the same is true with applets. When you access a Web page that has an applet embedded in it, the browser fetches the code and takes care of running it.

Running an applet isn't hard. It takes no advanced planning or configuring. As long as your version of Netscape Navigator is Java-enabled, you can just point your Web browser at a page that contains the applet you want. There is a list of Web sites at the end of this chapter that have Java applet pages. As long as these Java pages don't tell you that your browser doesn't support Java, you're ready to start exploring the Java-ized Web.

> **CAUTION**
>
> Some Java applets cannot be accessed by earlier versions of Netscape Navigator, even if your version supports Java applet handling. This is because many Java applets were written while Java was still being developed. Those Java applets are not compatible with the current standard.

How Netscape Runs Java Applets

Now let's look at the technical issues involved in running an applet. When Netscape encounters an HTML page with an APPLET tag, it retrieves the compiled Java classes from the remote server in the same way that it retrieves any other object. After the applet has been downloaded across the network onto your machine, it's subjected to various security checks before it's actually loaded and run. These checks are performed by the Java verifier. After the code is checked, it's loaded into its own place in Netscape's applet runtime environment. This is done by the Java class loader in such a way that the applet is kept separate from system resources and other applets.

N O T E In object-oriented languages, classes are the definitions of objects. When a programmer is writing his program, he writes a class. When the program is run, the computer takes that definition and creates an object.

Because Java code is platform-independent, it must be interpreted, or translated, into instructions that your machine can understand. This translation is performed by the Java interpreter. The Java interpreter can be thought of as a special viewer application that allows Netscape version 3.0 and later to run applets inline.

This whole process prevents the applet from harming your computer in any way. This is explained further in the next section on Java and safety.

Why Java Applets Won't Harm Your Computer

The idea that your machine executes code fragments downloaded from a public network probably makes your stomach a bit uneasy. People often ask if a Java applet could erase their files or propagate a virus into their computer. Luckily, safe execution was a major consideration from the very start of creating Java.

The Java language, and the technology Netscape uses to run applets, provides many defenses against malicious applets. These strict language security mechanisms, coupled with Netscape's watchful eye, create an environment in which code can be run on your machine with virtually no chance of it accessing your private data or starting a virus.

The Java Console Window

Many programmers write their applets so that they print out messages while they're executing. Usually, this information helps the programmer see whether or not an applet is encountering problems. In Netscape Navigator, the Java Console window allows you to view the direct output of an applet as it's running. Just select Show Java Console Window from the Options menu. The Java Console window pops up, as shown in Figure 10.9.

Part
IV

Ch

10

FIG. 10.9
The Java Console window.

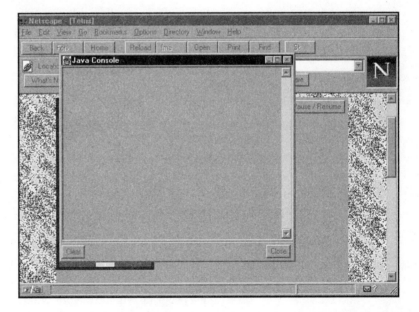

Later, if you write your own applets, this window is your way of keeping tabs on your applet during the development process. If you need to, you can copy from this window and paste in another document.

The Four Layers of Defense

Java contains multiple layers of security, each serving to filter out harmful code. This section will show you how Java's security layers protect your machine, and will give you the background necessary to program your own applets.

The four layers of security built into Java and Netscape are as follows:

- The Java language and compiler
- Java bytecode verification and strong type information
- Java's class loader
- Restrictions on local file system and network access

Safety Layer One—The Java Language's Defenses   The first layer of safety in the Java language comes from the absence of the harmful language and compiler features that C and C++ both possess. Java doesn't allow the programmer to directly manipulate memory. C and C++ *do* allow direct manipulation of memory, which means that a careless programmer can manipulate memory that the system has reversed for its use. This is the usual cause for a system crash. A malicious programmer can also use this weakness to propagate a virus.

Let's focus on how the Java applet interacts with Netscape Navigator after it's downloaded. The fundamental line of defense is that Netscape Navigator keeps the Java applet from dealing with a specific memory address on your computer. Of course, a Java applet does use your computer's memory. It's just that Navigator won't let an applet look at or write to a specific memory address. If the applet needs to change something in that data, it hands its changes back to Netscape Navigator. (See Fig. 10.10.) Netscape actually changes the data in memory.

Unlike C and C++, the structure of the Java language requires this interpreter. With a C or C++ program, the programmer might not be malicious or careless, and maybe he used an advanced compiler that doesn't produce evil programs. You don't have to worry that a Java program will harm your computer; the interpreter simply won't allow it. Because a Java program must access memory through the interpreter, that interpreter is in complete control. Navigator acts as a firewall between a Java applet and your computer. It does this by isolating the program from the rest of the system and acting as its guardian. By forcing a Java program to obey its guardian, the Java language itself keeps the program from misbehaving and harming your system.

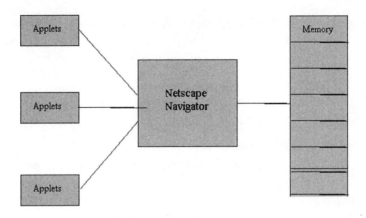

FIG. 10.10
How a Java applet accesses memory.

Besides direct memory manipulation, the Java language also deals very carefully with casting. Casting allows a programmer to change one data type to another, even if this shouldn't be done. In C++, a programmer can cast a complex object to a much simpler type, like an array of bytes. Generally, this is an error and causes the program to crash. However, a malicious programmer can use this to change the object itself. He can overwrite the individual bytes that make up the object so that it does something the language doesn't allow. The Java language only allows the programmer to cast between types when it makes sense to cast. It checks all attempts to cast very carefully, while C and C++ allow the programmer to cast between literally any two data types. Java's strong checking of casting closes the back door on the type of memory manipulation described earlier.

These are the ways that the Java language itself assures a certain degree of safety for all Java programs. But these features aren't enough to prevent an applet from harming your computer. This layer is just the foundation for the other layers of safety in the Java environment. You will now see why this layer means very little without the support of the following layers.

Safety Layer Two—Making Sure the Applet Isn't Faking It   After a Java, C, or C++ program is written, the author compiles it. For C and C++, the compilation process produces an executable file. This file can be loaded into your computer's memory and run. Most programs on your desktop have been created through this process.

Java is a semi-compiled language, and its compilation process is different. When Java is compiled, the compiler produces platform-independent machine instructions called bytecodes. These bytecodes are what Netscape retrieves from a remote server and then executes on your machine. Because a compiler can easily be altered to bypass the first level of security, these bytecodes must be subjected to strong tests before being executed on your machine.

The second layer of safety accomplishes this. When Navigator downloads an applet, the bytecode of that applet is examined by your browser's verifier. The verifier subjects each code fragment to a sequence of tests before it's allowed to execute. It first looks to see that the bytecode has all the information about the different data types that are going to be used. There's actually more of this type of information than strictly necessary. This excess information helps the verifier analyze the rest of the bytecode.

It's possible for a malicious programmer to write a Java compiler that doesn't follow all the rules of the Java language. He could write it to produce code that tricks the compiler into harming your computer. The verifier ensures that no such code ever reaches the interpreter. It makes sure the bytecode plays by the rules of the Java language and protects the integrity of the interpreter.

N O T E   An example of an alternate Java compiler is Borland's C++ Development Suite, version 5.0. It will compile Java bytecode all by itself, but it's still checked by the verifier for security. ▧

Safety Layer Three—Keeping an Applet Separate   The class loader offers Java's third line of defense. As independent pieces of code are loaded and executed, the class loader makes sure that different applets can't interfere with each other, and that each and every applet is completely separate from the Java objects already resident that it needs to actually run. This means that an applet can't replace parts of Navigator needed to run applets.

If it could replace these parts, all layers of safety could be undermined. All applets depend on the interpreter to provide them with some of the basic constructs of the Java language. If the applets aren't kept strictly separate, an applet can override some of these basic constructs. By overriding these basic constructs, the applet can violate the integrity of the Java language itself and trick the interpreter into hurting your system.

Safety Layer Four—Protecting Your File System   The fourth level of defense against harmful applets comes in the form of file system access protection. Applets are restricted from any access to the local file system, so they can't read your files, overwrite your existing files, or generate new ones. This not only protects your privacy, but also prevents your files from being corrupted or infected by viruses.

The interpreter protects your computer's safety by simply disallowing all Java language calls that deal with files. The Java language itself, being equivalent to C++, does have the capability to deal with a file system. But the interpreter in Netscape 4.0 (and Netscape 3.0 as well) doesn't give applets that capability. If an applet tries to open a file, the interpreter just tells the applet that the file system doesn't exist.

N O T E The Java language ensures that a Java program can only affect your system in safe ways. Even if someone went to the trouble of writing a fake Java compiler, the verifier in Navigator would figure it out and refuse to run the applet. The class loader makes sure that applets are kept separate from your system and other applets. To top it all off, the interpreter doesn't even allow an applet to access the file system. This means that an applet only knows about the Netscape Navigator applet runtime environment and can't access any part of your computer beyond that.

Part

IV

Ch

10

Java Development Tools

In order to develop Java applets and applications, you need a copy of the Java Development Kit (JDK). At the time this book went to press, the JDK version 1.0.1 had been released and was available on Windows 95 and NT and Sun Solaris 2.x platforms. A Macintosh port of the JDK is under development.

ON THE WEB

You can get the JDK from the Sun Microsystems Java Web site at **http://java.sun.com/**.

The process of turning Java source code into compiled Java bytecodes is performed by the Java compiler, javac. To compile a Java program, write your code using your favorite text editor and save it in ASCII text format. The name of the file must have a .JAVA extension. Then, compile the file by typing:

```
javac filename.java
```

where filename.java is the name of your Java source code file. For each class that's defined in your Java source file, the javac compiler generates a file named classname.class where classname is the name of the particular class. For complete details of the Java compilation process, see the online documentation for Java programmers at **http://java.sun.com/doc/programmer.html**.

N O T E Java places exactly one class in each bytecode compiled .class file. ▪

After you've compiled your Java application into a .class file, you can run the file with the Java bytecode interpreter, which is coincidentally named java. To do this, you run the java command followed by the name of the .class file that has the `main( )` method for your Java application. For example:

```
java myclass.class
```

This command starts the Java runtime environment and causes it to execute the file myclass.class.

Much of Java's functionality is encapsulated in prewritten collections of classes known as *packages*. These packages are provided with the Java development environment. Each of these packages contains several different classes that are related to a particular topic.

Table 10.2 lists the packages in the Java development library at the time this book was written. Packages prefixed with java are actual Java language classes. The other classes are HotJava classes, used in the development of Sun's HotJava browser.

Table 10.2. Java Packages in the Development Library

Package Name	Description
java.lang	Basic language support classes
java.util	Utility classes such as encoders and decoders
java.io	Different types of I/O streams
java.awt	A platform-independent windowing system
java.awt.image	Class for handling images in the AWT windowing system

Package Name	Description
`java.applet`	Class for building applets to run within Web browsers
`java.net`	Support for TCP/IP networking

Using the *APPLET* Tag

Including an applet in a Web document is accomplished via an extension to HTML called the APPLET tag. This tag, along with the PARAM tag, allows the Web page designer to include and configure executable content in documents. The general syntax for including an applet in a Web page is as follows:

```
<APPLET CODEBASE=codebaseURL   CODE=appletFile.class WIDTH=pixels
➡HEIGHT=pixels>
<PARAM NAME=someAttributeName VALUE=1st_attributeValue>
<PARAM NAME=someOtherAttributeName VALUE=Nth_attributeValue>
{Alternate HTML displayed by non-java enabled browsers}
</APPLET>
```

The following are the definitions of the various tags:

- APPLET—Signifies that an applet is to be included in the document.
- CODEBASE—The path to the classes directory containing the Java code. If this field is omitted, the CODEBASE is assumed to be the same as the document's URL.
- CODE—The name of the applet to be included in your page. This file always ends in .class, which indicates that it's a compiled Java class. It should be noted that this variable is relative to the applet's base URL and should not be given as absolute.
- HEIGHT and WIDTH—The dimensions in units of pixels that the applet takes up on your Web page.
- PARAM—Used to pass a parameter to an applet.
- NAME—The name of the parameter. This name must be understood by the applet.
- VALUE—The value that corresponds to a given name. This is where you may enter your configurations.

Part
IV

Ch
10

As shown previously, alternate HTML can be included between the open and close APPLET tags. This code is intended to be displayed if the person who accesses your page isn't using a Java-enabled browser, such as Netscape 2.0. If Netscape Navigator can't download the Java applet, it shows the alternate HTML.

If the browser can run the Java applet, the alternate text is not shown. This feature comes in very handy when you're designing pages for an audience of both Java-enabled and non-Java-enabled browsers.

 TIP   When including applets in your Web pages, use alternate HTML inside the APPLET tag as a courtesy to people whose browsers aren't Java-enabled.

The PARAM tag makes it possible for Web page designers to configure an applet to their special needs. This feature allows applets to be written as generalized tools that can be configured to work in many different situations. Someone who doesn't want to learn all of the details of programming applets can customize other people's Java applets to fit his own needs. For example, a simple animation applet can be told which sequence of images it should load and display. Because such an applet can be configured, many people can run different animations using the same code. You can imagine that without the PARAM tag, using Java would become much more difficult for designers. If applets weren't configurable, in the case of the animation applet, individual designers would each have to customize their own copy of the program.

Let's look at a simple example that shows how to include a configurable applet on a Web page. For simplicity, we will use the Blinking Text example from the Java Product Development Team. This applet displays a text string in multiple colors and then blinks each word at random. It takes two parameters; lbl is the text string that's displayed and speed is the rate at which the text blinks.

To include this applet in one of your Web pages, add this code:

```
<HR>
<APPLET
CODEBASE="http://www.javasoft.com/JDK-prebeta1/applets/Blink/"
CODE="Blink.class" WIDTH=300 HEIGHT=130>
<PARAM NAME=lbl VALUE="Configuring Applets is easy and very useful.
```

```
with Netscape 3.0, we can make an applet do what WE WANT!">
<PARAM NAME=speed VALUE="4">
Sorry, you should be using Netscape 3.0. <BR>
Your browser is not Java enabled!!!!
</APPLET>
<HR>
```

Figure 10.11 shows what you should see when you load your page if you're using Netscape Navigator version 3.0 or later.

FIG. 10.11
Results of configuration.

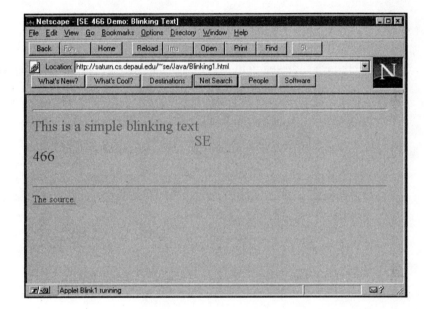

In this example, the Blinking Text applet is loaded from a remote site (**http://www.javasoft.com**, in this case). This shows that you're not obligated to download the applet onto your own machine just to include it on a Web page. As always, when including someone else's work in your pages, you should make sure you have the permission of the author first.

N O T E It's impossible to describe how Java applets should be configured. It's totally up to the author of a Java applet to decide how it may be configured and to provide documentation for the applet user. ▪

Java Classes

Classes form the basic program component in Java. Every function and variable must be contained in a class. There are no global functions or variables supported by Java. Here's an example of a Java class declaration:

```
/** latitude and longitude of a location **/
public class Location
{
int lat, long;    //latitude and longitude
...
}
```

This Java code segment declares a class named Location, which contains two instance variables that hold the latitude and longitude of some location.

> **NOTE** In this example, the ellipsis (...) just means that there could be additional members or variables—we just didn't write them in the example. ■

You might have noticed that this class doesn't appear to have any parent class. In Java, all classes are subclasses of the class Object. So the preceding code sample is identical to:

```
/** latitude and longitude of a location **/
public class Location extends Object
{
int lat, long;    //latitude and longitude
...
}
```

In this example, the extends keyword is used to indicate that the new class, Location, is a subclass of the class Object. In effect, it extends the Object class by adding new features. We'll look at this further in the next section.

LiveConnect with Java Applets and Plug-Ins

The LiveConnect environment is a merger of two other environments: Java and JavaScript. Java programmers would use a public identifier when defining a class. Now that LiveConnect enables JavaScript to be linked to a Java environment, all public classes can be controlled by the JavaScript script, which allows JavaScript scripts to access anything that an Java applet can access.

It's the Java Runtime Interface (JRI) that allows Netscape Navigator plug-ins to define Java classes and to call native C functions. The JRI, along with Netscape Navigator application programming interface (API), is what allows plug-ins to be accessed in a Java environment.

Part

IV

Ch

10

Netscape Communicator, as well as Version 3.0, Includes Borland's Java JIT Compiler

Netscape enhanced its Java support when they struck a deal with Borland International Inc. to include the Borland JIT compiler, AppAccelerator, for Windows 95.

Although the Java programming language produces dynamic live Web pages, users and developers have complained of its slow compile time. AppAccelerator translates Java bytecodes into machine code (Intel in this case), allowing programs to execute 5-10 times faster. The JIT compiler will entice more developers to create Java programs and, given its fast compile time, will enable users to quickly use Java applets without further time delays.

You don't need to know about how a Java applet is constructed to use JavaScript to control it, since all applets' public variables, methods, and properties can be accessed by JavaScript.

Each applet in a document is accessed in JavaScript by document.appletName, where appletName is the value of the NAME attribute of the APPLET tag. Here's an example of how HTML starts an applet called "myApplet":

```
<APPLET CODE=Mytest.class NAME=MyApplet WIDTH=80 HEIGHT=50>
<PARAM NAME=label VALUE=Mytest>
<PARAM NAME=debug VALUE=86>
</APPLET>
```

There are two ways that you can access this applet in JavaScript:

```
document.MyApplet
document.applets["MyApplet"]
```

To access this applet through an applets array, notice the following example of an applet that's the fourth applet in an HTML document:

```
document.applets[3]
```

It's just as simple to control a plug-in in a document accessed in JavaScript as an element in the embeds array. For instance, the following HTML includes an AVI plug-in:

```
<EMBED SRC=plugavi.avi WIDTH=280 HEIGHT=150>
```

This HTML defines the first plug-in in a document, while the following code starts it:

```
document.embeds[0]
```

ON THE WEB

Again, for more information about plug-ins, take a look at the Plug-in Developer's Guide at **http://home.netscape.com/eng/mozilla/3.0/handbook/plugins/index.html**.

From this handbook, you can access documentation on calling Java methods from plug-ins at **http://home.netscape.com/eng/mozilla/3.0/handbook/plugins/wr2.htm**, as well as documentation on calling plug-in native methods from Java at **http://home.netscape.com/eng/mozilla/3.0/handbook/plugins/wr3.htm**.

Using LiveConnect to Talk to JavaScript

The first step in connecting a script in JavaScript to your plug-in is to connect JavaScript to Java. After that, you'll build a Java class that does its work by calling your plug-in. From the point of view of JavaScript, this Java class serves as a proxy for your plug-in.

Calling JavaScript from Java Methods   In order for a Java class to talk to JavaScript, you must import the Netscape javascript package in the Java file, as follows:

```
import netscape.javascript.*
```

The netscape.javascript package, described later in this chapter, includes two important classes—JSObject, which represents the JavaScript object, and JSException, which is raised to pass JavaScript errors back to your Java class.

For a Java class to call JavaScript, the HTML author must explicitly set the MAYSCRIPT attribute in the APPLET tag. For example:

```
<APPLET NAME="hello" CODE="hello.class" WIDTH=100 HEIGHT=100
➥MAYSCRIPT>
```

Note that in this example, a name was assigned to the applet. You will use the name when we begin talking to the applet from JavaScript.

CAUTION

If a Java applet attempts to run a page's JavaScript and the HTML author hasn't set `MAYSCRIPT`, Navigator raises an exception. You should catch this exception and put up an appropriate message to the user.

One good way to put up an error message is to use the Java console defined by Netscape. From inside Java, write the following:

```
System.out.println("Error: Applet unable to access JavaScript.
    Set the applet's MAYSCRIPT attribute and try again.");
```

To access JavaScript, your Java class must get a handle to the Navigator window, as shown in Figure 10.12. Your class's `init()` member is a good place to do this:

```
JSObject win;
public void init()
{
  win = JSObject.getWindow(this);
}
```

FIG. 10.12

Java gets a pointer to the JavaScript document in order to access its members.

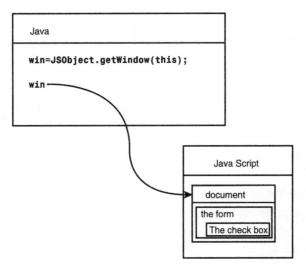

If the HTML page has a form named theForm which, in turn, has a checkbox named theCheckbox, you can access the status of this checkbox by following the membership hierarchy from the form to the checkbox, as follows:

```
JSObject win;
public void init()
{
  win = JSObject.getWindow(this);
  JSObject doc = (JSObject) win.getMember("document");
  JSObject theForm = (JSObject) doc.getMember("theForm");
  JSObject check = (JSObject) myForm.getMember("theCheckBox");
  Boolean isChecked = (Boolean) check.getMember("checked");
}
```

Just as getMember( ) gives you access to the components of the JavaScript form, call( ) and eval( ) give you access to the JavaScript methods. You can write the following:

```
public void init()
{
  win = JSObject.getWindow(this);
}
public boolean mouseUp(Event e, int x, int y)
{
  win.eval("alert(\"Hello, world!\");");
  return true;
}
```

or, equivalently,

```
public void init()
{
  win = JSObject.getWindow(this);
}
public boolean mouseUp(Event e, int x, int y)
{
  win.call("alert(\"Hello, world!\");");
  return true;
}
```

Calling Java Methods from JavaScript   You can communicate in the opposite direction, from JavaScript to the applet, by making sure that the applet has a name. As a further example, suppose that you had a Java class like count, shown in Listing 10.5.

Listing 10.5   count.java—A Simple Java Class that Accepts Two Commands

```java
import java.applet.*;
import java.awt.*;
public class count extends Applet
{
  int i;
  public void init()
  {
    I = 0;
  }
  public void paint (Graphics g)
  {
    g.drawString("The count is" + i, 10, 50);
  }
  public void increment()
  {
    I++;
    repaint();
  }
  public void decrement()
  {
    I--;
    repaint();
  }
}
```

You can install count on your Web page, as shown in Listing 10.6.

Listing 10.6   count.html—A Web Page with a Controllable Applet

```html
<HTML>
<HEAD>
<TITLE>Test count/TITLE>
</HEAD>
<BODY>
<H1>Test the Count Applet</H1>
<APPLET NAME="count" CODE="count.class" WIDTH=100, HEIGHT=100></APPLET>
<FORM>
<INPUT TYPE="Button" VALUE="Increment" NAME="IncrementButton"
➥onClick="document.count.increment()">
<INPUT TYPE="Button" VALUE="Decrement" NAME="DecrementButton"
➥onClick="document.count.decrement()">
</FORM>
</BODY>
</HTML>
```

Now that you know how Java and JavaScript can talk, you just have to get the plug-in to talk to Java.

Talking to the Plug-In

When you add plug-ins to an HTML page, JavaScript puts them into an array named embeds. For example, if the following is the first <EMBED> tag on your page, JavaScript shows the associated plug-in in document.embeds[0]:

```
<EMBED SRC="http://www.somemachine.com/myFile.tst HEIGHT=100
➥WIDTH=100>
```

From JavaScript, you can access document.embeds.length to find out how many plug-ins are on the page.

> **N O T E** Because full-page plug-ins are, by definition, on a page with no JavaScript
> (and no HTML!), it only makes sense to talk about controlling embedded
> plug-ins. ▪

To make a plug-in visible from inside Java, your Java class must use netscape.plugin.Plugin. Netscape provides a file, java_30, with Netscape version 3.0 and later. This file contains three Java packages, java, sun, and netscape:

- java
- sun
- netscape.applet
- netscape.net
- netscape.javascript
- netscape.plugin

The java and sun packages are replacements for packages of the same name in the Sun 1.0.2 Java Development Kit (JDK). They include security enhancements necessary for LiveConnect. Netscape and Sun are working together to ensure that these new packages are included in a future release of the Sun JDK.

- `netscape.applet` is Netscape's replacement for `sun.applet`. Similarly, `netscape.net` replaces `sun.net`.

- `netscape.javascript` implements `JSObject` and `JSException`, described previously in this chapter.

- `netscape.plugin` implements the `Plugin` class. As a Java programmer, you use methods on the `Plugin` class to communicate with the plug-in.

NOTE To use the Netscape-supplied packages with the JDK compiler, add the path of the java_30 and classes.zip to the compiler's classpath. You can either specify a CLASSPATH environment variable or use the `-classpath` command line option when you run javac. ▦

TIP As a plug-in programmer, you have a C++ development environment such as Microsoft Visual C++ handy. Don't waste time running javac from the command line. Put your plug-in's Java proxy class in the makefile, and automatically call javac each time your plug-in is rebuilt. If you use Visual C++, just add the javac command line (with the `-classpath` option) to the Custom Build settings.

While setting up the makefile, add the call to javah described in the following section. It will save you time later.

Part **IV**

Ch **10**

Where to Find More Info on Java

Sun maintains a complete set of documentation on Java at **http://www.javasoft.com**. At this site, you can find everything from language documentation to tutorials. Yahoo! has a rather extensive index of pointers to Java resources. You can find this listing at **http://www.yahoo.com/Computers_and_Internet/Languages/Java**.

Finding Java Applets

If it's Java applets you seek, check out the Gamelan site at **http://www.gamelan.com/**. This site acts as a registry of applets. It contains links to hundreds of applets, all categorized by subject.

The Java Development Team also maintains their own listing of applets, which can be found at **http://www.javasoft.com/Applets**.

Language References

The definitive overview of the Java language is the Java Language White Paper, written by the Java Development Team. It's at **http://www.javasoft.com/whitePaper/javawhitepaper_1.html**.

The Java Development Team also has an online overview of the security features inherent to applets at **http://www.javasoft.com/1.0alpha3/doc/security/security.html**.

Newsgroups and Mailing Lists

For information specific about Java, you should regularly read the Usenet newsgroup comp.lang.java at news:comp.lang.java.

Sun Microsystems, the inventor of Java and applets, also maintains a mailing list concerning Java. To subscribe, send mail to majordomo@www.javasoft.com, and enter "subscribe java-interest@www.javasoft.com <your email address>" in the body of the message. Replace "<your email address>" with your full Internet e-mail address.

Other Resources

Digital Espresso, produced by Mentor Software Solutions, is a well-formatted, easy-to-read summary of the newsgroups and mailing lists pertaining to Java and Java applets. Information is updated weekly and broken down into categories. You can find Digital Espresso at **http://www.io.org/~mentor/JavaNotes.html**.

From Here...

In this chapter, you learned about Java language features, and discovered that Java is really a bytecode-based interpreted language. You learned about JavaScript, controlling Java applets, applications, and about the Java Development Kit (JDK). You now know how Java works in Netscape. When you access a Web page that has an applet embedded in it, the browser fetches the code and takes care of running it. LiveConnect connects Java with JavaScript, HTML elements, and plug-ins so that they can interact with one another.

- The next chapter, "Java to JavaScript Communication," looks at accessing JavaScript objects and properties and calling JavaScript methods.
- Chapter 7, "The Java Runtime Interface," looks at Java platform support for native methods and Java classes.
- Chapter 8, "Calling Java Methods from Plug-Ins," shows how fields are accessed, Java names and parameters, and security issues.
- Chapter 9, "Calling the Plug-In from Java Methods," shows how to define a plug-in class and has more about native methods and globals.
- Chapter 12, "Netscape Packages," shows how to use Netscape packages with LiveConnect communication.

Java to JavaScript Communication

Java Language Features

Java is really a bytecode-based interpreted language.

Controlling Java Applets

Develop Java applets and applications using the Java Development Kit (JDK).

How Java Works in Netscape

When you access a Web page that has an applet embedded in it, the browser fetches the code and takes care of running it.

In this chapter, we will fully examine the synergy that exists between Java and the JavaScript environment under LiveConnect. We'll start with an overview of the Netscape packages supporting Java to JavaScript interaction and how users can use these with Java applets. We'll then delve into the *netscape.javascript* package in detail and fully examine its workings with the help of an in-depth example.

The benefits of using the LiveConnect environment for enabling Java to JavaScript communication is finally highlighted by two important examples. The first case study explores how Java data can be preserved and accessed using client-side cookies. The second case study tackles the challenge of enabling inter-applet communication between applets that reside in different frames using LiveConnect. ∎

This chapter assumes that you have a working familiarity with JavaScript and Java programming.

The Netscape Packages

The *java_30* file distributed as part of Navigator 3.0 contains Netscape's reimplementation of the Sun JDK, along with some extra packages supporting the LiveConnect environment. It's interesting to note that Netscape has reimplemented the Sun JDK, which includes the *java* and *sun* packages, with additional security enhancements for the LiveConnect environment. The *netscape.javascript* package implements the functionality responsible for the Java to JavaScript interaction.

Using the Netscape Packages

Before you can use the packages within java_30, you have to make sure that they lie within the classpath of the Java compiler. A foolproof way of ensuring this is to:

- Create a subdirectory, say, NCLASSES.
- Unzip the java_30 file into NCLASSES.
- Set the CLASSPATH environment variable to include the path of the Netscape classes.

For example, on Windows NT, your CLASSPATH environment variable may resemble:

```
CLASSPATH=C:\JDK\java\lib\classes.zip;C:\NCLASSES
```

where classes.zip contains the Sun JDK implementation packages.

N O T E Instead of setting the CLASSPATH environment variable with the path of the Netscape classes, you can elect to specify it with the Java compiler's `-classpath` option as an alternative. ▓

The *MAYSCRIPT* Attribute

By default, Java applets included within an HTML page don't have access to the JavaScript methods and properties. Applets have to be explicitly given permission to be able to invoke JavaScript functionality. This is done via the MAYSCRIPT attribute. For example:

```
<APPLET NAME=MyApplet CODE=MyApplet.class MAYSCRIPT>
```

indicates that the java applet MyApplet.class has access to JavaScript.

If the Java applet tries to access JavaScript functionality without the MAYSCRIPT attribute denoted in the APPLET tag, an exception is thrown.

The *javascript* Package

The *javascript* package consists of two classes—JSObject and JSException. The JSObject class, which extends java.lang.Object, gives Java applets access to JavaScript methods and properties (see Figure 11.1).

Part
IV

Ch
11

FIG. 11.1
The *netscape.javascript* package.

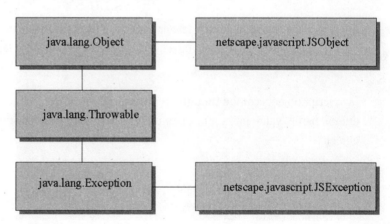

The *JSObject* Class

The methods available within the JSObject class are the primary LiveConnect interface for Java applets to communicate with JavaScript.

Before we start interacting with the JavaScript environment, we need to obtain a JSObject for the window that contains the applet. It is usually done by calling the static method:

```
public Object getWindow(Applet thisapplet)
```

during applet initialization.

JavaScript functions can be accessed from within Java applets using either:

```
public Object call(String methodname, Object[] args)
```

or:

```
public Object eval(String s)
```

The call method is used if any arguments need to be passed over to the target JavaScript function, defined as, say, function myScript(arg1, arg2, args,...). The function arguments are always passed as part of an Object array when using the call method. The eval method can be used to evaluate any JavaScript expression passed as the String argument, including function calls. However, when you're using eval to invoke JavaScript functions that accept parameters, the data for the function must appear as part of the eval expression.

N O T E If the JavaScript function returns any data, it has to be cast to the appropriate subclass of java.lang.Object before being used within the Java environment. ▪

JavaScript objects can be thought of as associative arrays, made up of a number of unique name/value pairs. For example, the following is a user-defined "person" object:

```
person.name="Joey";
person.age =33;
person.addr = "250 Ocean Blvd.";
person.city = "San Francisco";
person.state ="CA";
```

The JSObject class offers three convenient methods through which we can easily manipulate JavaScript objects.

```
    public Object getMember(String name)
```

retrieves the value of a named member of a JavaScript object.

```
    public void removeMember(String name)
```

deletes a named member of a JavaScript object, and

```
    public void setMember(String name, Object val)
```

changes the value of a named member of a JavaScript object.

JavaScript also allows us to have object arrays that can be referred to by a numerical index, rather than by a name. The "person" object, if defined with a numerical index, will now be:

```
    person[0] = "Joey";
    person[1] = 33;
    person[2] = "250 Ocean Blvd."
    person[3] = "San Francisco";
    person[4] = "CA";
```

To manipulate JavaScript objects of this type, we make use of:

```
    public Object getSlot(int index)
```

which retrieves an indexed member of a JavaScript object, and:

```
    public void setSlot(int index, Object val)
```

which changes the value of an indexed member of a JavaScript object.

Finally:

```
    public String toString()
```

is used to give a String equivalent of the JSObject class.

The *JSException* Class

The JSException is used to throw an exception when JavaScript execution fails for any reason. The JSException class comes with three constructors, and you can call any one of them depending on the level of detail you need for your exception message.

```
public JSException()
```

is the default constructor without a detail message.

```
public JSException(String s)
```

can be used to show the detail messages, when the exception gets thrown:

```
public JSException(String s,String myfile, int line, String jscode,
int jsindex)
```

Here, along with the detail messages, you can choose to give all the relevant information that's available with a JavaScript error condition. Here, `myfile` is the URL containing the JavaScript code; `line` is the line number within this URL where the error occurred; `jscode` is the JavaScript code that was being evaluated; and `jsindex` is the index within `jscode` where the error occurred.

In Detail—The *JSObject* Methods in Action

Let's take a look at the following example (see Listing 11.1), which demonstrates the use of most of the `JSObject` methods.

The HTML file objects.html defines a user-defined JavaScript object of type person, and includes the Java applet ModifyObj.class. The HTML file also contains a form that defines a pushbutton to display the contents of the person object.

Listing 11.1   Source for objects.html

```
<html>
<head>
<script language="JavaScript">
// used to print the person object from within HTML
function dumpObject() {
    displayPerson(aPerson,"aPerson");
}
//constructor function for the person object
function person(name, age, addr, city, state) {
    this.name=name;
    this.age=age;
    this.address=addr;
    this.city=city;
    this.state=state;
    return this;
}
```

```
//create a new person
aPerson = new person("Joey",33,"250 Ocean Blvd.","San
Francisco","CA");
//walk through the person object and gather the member fields
//and values. Display the results through a JavaScript alert dialog.
function displayPerson(obj, name) {
    var myObject ="";
    for (var i in obj)
        myObject += name + "." + i + " = "+ obj[i] + "\n";
    alert(myObject);
}
</script>
</head>
<body bgcolor=white>
<center>
<applet code=Obj.class width=200 height=40 MAYSCRIPT>
</applet>
<form name=myform>
<input type=button name=mybutton value="Dump Original JS Object"
onClick="dumpObject()">
</form>
</center>
</body>
</html>
```

The JavaScript person object previously defined can be accessed and modified from within the Java applet ModifyObj.class, which is obtained by compiling the source, `ModifyObj.java`. We make use of a variety of JSObject methods for this purpose. (See Listing 11.2 and Figures 11.2 and 11.3.)

Listing 11.2 Source Code for *ModifyObj.java*

```
import java.awt.*;
import java.applet.*;
import netscape.javascript.*;
/**
* ModifyObj.java
* This applet demonstrates the usage of the various
* JSObject methods for JavaScript object access and
* manipulation from within Java.
* The applet also shows how to call JavaScript functions while
passing
* Java objects as parameters to it.
*/
public class ModifyObj extends Applet {
    void changeButton_Clicked(Event event) {
        try {
```

continues

Listing 11.2   Continued

```
        //access the user-defined JavaScript object
        //Since JavaScript objects are passed as JSObjects to Java
        //it is important to have the relevant cast.
    JSObject myObj = (JSObject) win.eval("this.aPerson");
        //the getMember() method allows us to query the object by
name
    String myPerson =(String) myObj.getMember("name");
        //since the original value was a JavaScript number, it is
passed back
        //to Java as a Double
    Double age = (Double) myObj.getMember("age");
    int newage = age.intValue() +10;
    age = new Double(newage);
        //update the person object with a new age and city
        myObj.setMember("age",age);
    myObj.setMember("city","Los Angeles");
        //delete the state attribute from the person object
    myObj.removeMember("state");
        //change the value of the form button
    win.eval("document.myform.mybutton.value=\"Dump Modified JS
Object\"");

        //Note that you always need to pass JavaScript function
arguments
        //in the form of an Object array
    Object args[] = new Object[2];
    args[0]=myObj;
    args[1]="aPerson";
    //dump the modified person object via a JavaScript alert
    win.call("displayPerson",args);
  }
  catch(Exception e) { System.out.println(e); }
  }
    public void init() {
        super.init();
        //You should always first obtain a JSObject handle to your
applet
        win = JSObject.getWindow(this);
        addNotify();
    changeButton = new Button("Modify JavaScript Object");
    add(changeButton);
  }
  public boolean handleEvent(Event event) {
  if (event.target == changeButton && event.id ==
Event.ACTION_EVENT) {
        changeButton_Clicked(event);
            return true;
        }
```

```
        return super.handleEvent(event);
    }
    Button changeButton;
    JSObject win;
}
```

FIG. 11.2
The person JavaScript
object before
modifying it from
within Java.

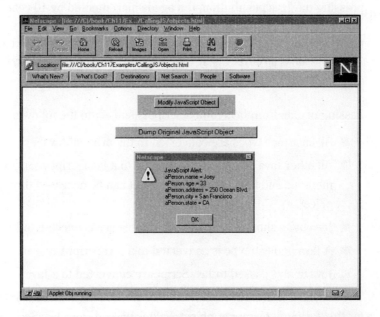

FIG. 11.3
The person JavaScript
object after modifying
it from within Java.

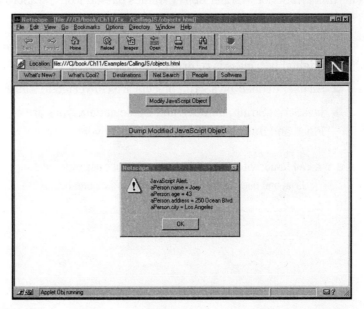

Part
IV

Ch
11

The program Modify Obj.java shows how we can modify JavaScript objects from within Java applets. We not only change the city attribute's value from "San Francisco" to "Los Angeles", but we also increment the age and delete the state attribute from the person object. Notice that each time you dump the object by pressing the Java pushbutton, the age is incremented by 10 years!

N O T E Note that arguments to a JavaScript function should always be passed in the form of an Object array from within Java. Applets can pass any valid Java object as a parameter to a JavaScript function. ■

Passing of data from Java to JavaScript is subject to the following conversions:

- All JSObject types are converted to the original JavaScript objects.
- All other Java objects are converted to a JavaScript wrapper. All public Java methods and fields of the Java object can be accessed through this wrapper object.
- Java byte, short, int, long, float, double are converted to JavaScript numbers.
- A Java boolean type is converted to a JavaScript Boolean.
- Java arrays passed to JavaScript are converted to a JavaScript wrapper object.

The standard Java array properties like array.length and array[index] hold good for this JavaScript wrapper object. Values passed from JavaScript to the Java environment also undergo some conversions:

- JavaScript object wrappers around Java objects are unwrapped, and the original Java class is returned.
- All user-defined JavaScript objects are converted to a JSObject type.
- JavaScript String, number, and Boolean data types are converted to String, Float, and Boolean Java objects, respectively.

N O T E All JavaScript values end up as some subclass of java.lang.Object within Java, and need to be cast to the appropriate one before use. ■

Case Study 1: Java Data Persistency Using Cookies

No doubt, Java applets are a quantum leap beyond what HTML by itself has to offer, but data persistency is still a problem. Currently there are no easy solutions for this, most of them involving highly complex mechanisms geared toward persisting data at the server end. Browser technology provides us with client-side cookies, and JavaScript allows us to easily manage the process of setting, deleting, and modifying the cookies. What if we could take advantage of this powerful feature of JavaScript and simply invoke the functions from within Java applets? The following case study examines just that and demonstrates the ease with which applets can preserve and access data stored as client-side cookies (see Listings 11.3 and 11.4 and Figures 11.4 and 11.5).

Part

IV

Ch

11

Listing 11.3   Source for cookie.html

```
<html>
<head>
<script language="javascript">
// return cookie value by name
function sendCookie (cookiename) {
 var index=0;
 var pattern=cookiename + "=";
 var psize=pattern.length;
 while (index < document.cookie.length) {
    var i = index + psize;
    if (document.cookie.substring(index, i) == pattern) {
        var tmps = document.cookie.indexOf (";", i);
        if (tmps == -1)
            tmps = document.cookie.length;
        return unescape(document.cookie.substring(i, tmps));
    }
    index = document.cookie.indexOf(" ", index) + 1;
    if (index == 0) break;
 }
 //cookie name not found
 return null;
}
// set cookie value by name
function setCookie (name,value) {
 var expiry = new Date ();
 expiry.setTime (expiry.getTime() + (100 * 24 * 60 * 60 * 1000)); //
```

continues

Listing 11.3   Continued

```
cookie valid for 100 days!
 document.cookie = name + "=" + escape (value) + "; expires=" +
expiry.toGMTString()
}
</script>
</head>
<body bgcolor=white>
<center>
<applet code=Cookie.class width=650 height=150 MAYSCRIPT>
</applet>
<p>
Use SHIFT Reload to see cookies in action!
</center>
</body>
</html>
```

We see that cookie.html offers us a couple of JavaScript functions to set and retrieve named cookies. For an excellent explanation of how to set and manipulate
cookies from within JavaScript, refer to the book *Special Edition Using JavaScript*.

Listing 11.4   Source for Cookie.java

```
import java.awt.*;
import java.applet.*;
import netscape.javascript.*;
/**
 *    Cookie.java
 *    This applet shows how we can have Java data persistency by
 *    making use of client-side cookies. JavaScript functions to
 *    set and retrieve cookie values are called from within the Java
 *    applets via the JSObject methods.
 */
public class Cookie extends Applet {
    void register_Clicked(Event event) {
        //set the user name as a cookie
        //observe that arguments to JavaScript
        //functions need to be passed as an Object array
        Object params[] = new Object[2];
        params[0] = "name";
        params[1] = name.getText();
        win.call("setCookie",params);
        //set the number of times user visits the URL as
        //a cookie
        params[0] = "visit";
```

```
        params[1] = "2";
        win.call("setCookie",params);
        visit="1";
        aName=name.getText();
        //hide the register pushbutton and the textbox since
        //user is done
        greet1.setText("Thanks for registering, "+aName);
        greet2.setText("Reload this page to see cookies in action!");
        name.hide();
        register.hide();
    }
    public void init() {
        super.init();

        setLayout(null);
        setFont(new Font("TimesRoman", Font.BOLD, 18));
    register = new Button("Register!");
    //Note: All the positional values for the GUI components
    //were obtained through a GUI painter.
        register.reshape(273,72,54,25);
        register.setFont(new Font("Dialog", Font.BOLD, 12));
        add(register);
    name = new TextField();
        name.reshape(90,71,163,26);
        add(name);
    greet2 = new Label("");
        greet2.reshape(8,37,515,21);
        greet2.setForeground(new Color(16711680));
        add(greet2);
    greet1 = new Label("");
        greet1.reshape(8,5,515,21);
        greet1.setForeground(new Color(16711680));
        add(greet1);
    //get a handle for the JSObject for this applet
    win = JSObject.getWindow(this);
    //check for existence of the visit cookie. If it exists
    //user has been here before. Else display the register
    //message
    visit = (String) win.eval("sendCookie(\"visit\")");
    if (visit == null) {
        greet1.setText("Hello stranger...I see that this is your
first time here.");
        greet2.setText("Please register yourself.");
    }
    else {
        aName = (String) win.eval("sendCookie(\"name\")");
        greet1.setText("Hello "+aName+ "...I see that this is your
visit #"+visit);
        greet2.setText("Welcome back!");
        name.hide();
        register.hide();
```

continues

Part
IV

Ch
11

Listing 11.4   Continued

```
          Integer count = new Integer(visit.trim());
          int c = count.intValue() +1;
          visit = new Integer(c).toString();
          //increment the visit count and reset the cookie
          Object params[] = new Object[2];
          params[0] = "visit";
          params[1] = visit;
          win.call("setCookie",params);
      }
    }
    public boolean handleEvent(Event event) {
          if (event.target == register && event.id ==
    Event.ACTION_EVENT) {
                register_Clicked(event);
                return true;
          }
          return super.handleEvent(event);
    }
  Button register;
  TextField name;
  Label greet2;
  Label greet1;
    JSObject win;
    String visit;
    String aName;
}
```

FIG. 11.4

Before setting
cookies from Java.

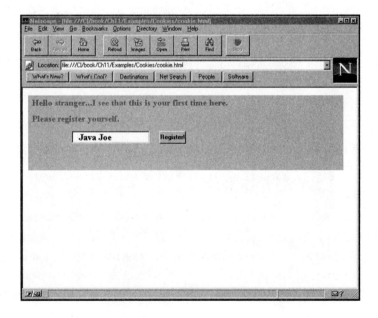

FIG. 11.5
After setting cookies
from within Java.

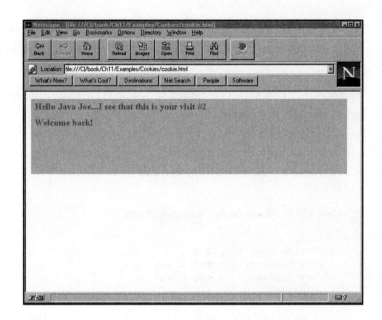

Cookie.java simply invokes the appropriate JavaScript function to set and retrieve applet data, which is stored as client-side cookies. We see that each time the user reloads the page, the visit count is incremented and displayed. The data persistency can be observed by exiting the browser after having "registered" and then reloaded the page. The applet recognizes the fact that the user is "registered" and displays the name and count.

N O T E   It may be necessary to hold down Shift when you reload the applet for it to be accessed again from disk. ■

Case Study 2: Inter-Applet Communication Using LiveConnect

Although inter-applet communication is possible using methods made available by the Applet class, it's highly restrictive. By default, inter-applet communication can take place only between applets on the same page. But what if two applets in separate frames wanted to communicate with each other? A typical situation would be to dynamically synchronize the behavior of the second applet based on user input

Part
IV

Ch
11

to the first, and vice versa. For instance, you may want to start an animation applet in a different frame while the user is waiting for the first applet to finish processing.

We know that Java applets included within an HTML page are nothing but a level included within the JavaScript object hierarchy. Since we can access any level of the JavaScript object hierarchy from within Java by using the JSObject object methods, referencing other applets is as easy as referencing any other valid HTML property (see Listings 11.5, 11.6, and 11.7).

Listing 11.5   Source for interapp.html

```
<html>
<frameset rows=50%,50%>
<frame name=one src=one.html>
<frame name=two src=two.html>
</frameset>
</html>
```
The HTML file interapp.html straightforward, and creates a couple of frames, and names them "one" and "two".

Listing 11.6   Source for one.html

```
<html>
<body bgcolor=white>
<center>
<applet code=Applet1.class name=myApp width=400 height=100 MAYSCRIPT>
</applet>
</center>
</body>
</html>
```

Listing 11.7   Source for two.html

```
<html>
<body bgcolor=white>
<center>
<applet code=Applet2.class name=myApp width=400 height=100 MAYSCRIPT>
</applet>
</center>
</body>
</html>
```

Notice that the files one.html and two.html include the applet. More importantly, they give it a name, "myApp", so that the applets are now accessible within the JavaScript object hierarchy. As usual, the MAYSCRIPT tag is mandatory for enabling Java to JavaScript communication (see Listings 11.8 and 11.9 and Figure 11.6.).

Listing 11.8   Source for Applet1.java

```
import java.awt.*;
import java.applet.*;
import netscape.javascript.*;
/**
*      Applet1.java
* This applet recognizes user mouse clicks within
* the applet, and calls the showMsg() method of the
* second applet which is in a different frame. We can make
* use of JSObject's eval() method to invoke showMsg() since
* we are here passing the * argument by value as part of the
* statement itself.
*/

public class Applet1 extends Applet {
    void Applet1_MouseDown(Event event) {
        //update the count and create a new message
        count++;
        String clickMsg ="Applet1: click #"+count;
        try {
            //it is important to fully qualify the target method
            //within the
            //JavaScript object hierarchy
            win.eval("parent.two.document.myApp.showMsg(\""+clickMsg+"\")");
        }
        catch (Exception e) {
         System.out.println(e);
        }
    }
     // It is mandatory that the method has public
    // scope so that it can be invoked by
    // another applet via LiveConnect
    public void showMsg(String aMsg) {
        msg.setText(aMsg);
        repaint();
    }
     public void init() {
        super.init();
          //get a handle to the JSObject by passing the current
```

continues

Part
IV

Ch
11

Listing 11.8   Continued

```
applet to the static            //method getWindow().
        try {
         win = JSObject.getWindow(this);
        }
        catch (JSException e) {
             System.out.println(e);
        }
    msg = new Label("              ");
        msg.setFont(new Font("TimesRoman", Font.BOLD, 14));
        add(msg);
    }
    public boolean handleEvent(Event event) {
       if (event.target == this && event.id == Event.MOUSE_DOWN) {
          Applet1_MouseDown(event);
              return true;
       }
       return super.handleEvent(event);
    }
    Label msg;
    JSObject win;
    int count=0;
}
```

Listing 11.9   Source for Applet2.java

```
import java.awt.*;
import java.applet.*;
import netscape.javascript.*;
/**
*      Applet2.java
* This applet recognizes user mouse clicks
* within the applet, and calls the showMsg() method
* of the first applet which is in a different frame.
* We can make use of JSObject's eval() method to invoke
* showMsg() since we are here passing the argument by
* value as part of the statement itself.
*/

public class Applet2 extends Applet {
    void Applet2_MouseDown(Event event) {
        //update the count and create a new message
        count++;
```

```
        String clickMsg ="Applet2: click #"+count;
        try {
            //it is important to fully qualify the target method
            //within the
            //JavaScript object hierarchy
        win.eval("parent.one.document.myApp.showMsg(\""+clickMsg+"\")");
        }
        catch (Exception e) {
         System.out.println(e);
        }
    }
    // It is mandatory that the method has
//public scope so that it can be invoked by
    // another applet via LiveConnect
    public void showMsg(String aMsg) {
        msg.setText(aMsg);
        repaint();
    }
     public void init() {
         super.init();
         //get a handle to the JSObject by passing
// the current applet to the static
//method getWindow().
         try {
          win = JSObject.getWindow(this);
         }
         catch (JSException e) {
             System.out.println(e);
         }
     msg = new Label("              ");
         msg.setFont(new Font("TimesRoman", Font.BOLD, 14));
         add(msg);
    }
    public boolean handleEvent(Event event) {
        if (event.target == this && event.id == Event.MOUSE_DOWN) {
            Applet2_MouseDown(event);
                return true;
        }
        return super.handleEvent(event);
    }
    Label msg;
    JSObject win;
    int count=0;
}
```

FIG. 11.6
Inter-applet
communication using
LiveConnect in
action.

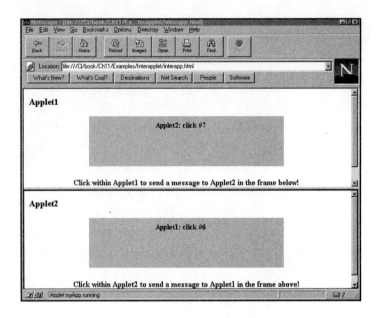

In the preceding example, we see how events triggered within an applet on one
frame can cause an action to occur within an applet on a different frame! Specifically, mouse clicks for Applet1 in frame1 update a counter within Applet2 in
frame2, and vice versa.

Other Resources

A comprehensive reference of Java to JavaScript communication can be found
within Netscape Navigator's JavaScript Reference at **http://
home.netscape.com/eng/mozilla/3.0/handbook/javascript/index.html**.

Gamelan, the Java repository on the Web, maintains an extensive collection of
LiveConnect examples at **http://www.gamelan.com/pages/
Gamelan.programming.examples.liveconnect.html**.

Finally, the comp.lang.java.programmer and the comp.lang.javascript newsgroups
are good places to resolve LiveConnect issues and keep up with evolving issues.

From Here...

In this chapter, you learned that LiveConnect can provide seamless Java to JavaScript integration. You now know how to set up the Java environment such that you can use the netscape.javascript classes within your applets. You also can call any JavaScript function from within Java. The case studies walked you through Java data persistency using client-side cookies, as well as inter-applet communication using LiveConnect. For more relevant information:

- Chapter 8, "Calling Java Methods from Plug-Ins," shows you how fields are accessed, Java names and parameters, and security issues.

- Chapter 9, "Calling the Plug-In from Java Methods," shows you how to define a plug-in class, as well as more about native methods and globals.

- Chapter 12, "Netscape Packages," shows you how to use Netscape packages with LiveConnect communication.

Part
IV

Ch
11

Netscape Packages

LiveConnect has two applet API packages: `netscape.javascript` and `netscape.plugin`. The `netscape.javascript` applet API package has the following classes: `netscape.javascript.JSObject` and `netscape.javascript.JSException`. The `netscape.plugin` applet API package has the following class: `netscape.plugin.Plugin`. ■

Interfaces

A collection of method definitions without providing the method implementation.

Packages

A collection of classes and interfaces. Every class is contained in a package.

LiveConnect and Netscape Packages

Navigator contains a java_30 file that includes the two important Java packages.

Importing the JavaScript Package

You can call JavaScript methods, properties, and data structures from your Java applet by importing the Netscape javascript package.

Introduction to Interfaces and Packages

Java includes two mechanisms for logically grouping and working with classes: the interface and the package. While a class can implement an interface, a package is a collection of classes and interfaces.

Interfaces

An interface is a collection of method definitions without the method implementation. A class can implement an interface by providing method bodies for all the methods in the interface definition. Interfaces can be defined as either public or private. All methods in an interface are public. Java uses interfaces to provide some of the features of multiple inheritance in C++.

The following code segment defines two interfaces:

```
public interface Test1
{
Method1();
Method2(int x);
}
public interface Test2
{
Foo1(float myFloat);
}
```

A class can then choose to implement either or both of these interfaces. For example:

```
public class IntfExample implements Test1, Test2
{
Method1()
{
... // method body
}
Method2(int x)
{
... // method body
}
Foo1(float myFloat)
{
... // method body
}
}
```

In this example, the class IntfExample implements both the Test1 and Test2 interfaces by providing method bodies for each method defined in the interface.

By using interfaces, you can specify an interface as a data type in a parameter list. This allows you to pass an object in the parameter list, as long as the object implements the specified interface. You don't have to know the exact class details of the object—only that it implements the interface. For example:

```
public class Blah
{
void TestMethod(Test1 x)
{
...
}
}
```

In this example, the name of an interface, Test1, is used as a parameter type in the method TestMethod. This means that any object that implements the Test1 interface can be passed as a parameter.

Using Netscape Packages

A package is a Java construct that's used to manage the program namespace. It's a collection of classes and interfaces. Every class is contained in a package. If no package name is explicitly given, the class is contained in the default package. You may remember from the earlier section on classes that if a class doesn't give an access specifier to a method, it's considered public for its enclosing package.

To define a package for a compilation unit, you use the package statement. This statement must be the first statement in the file.

N O T E The compilation unit is the basic compiled unit in Java. It's a file that contains one or more classes. ▪

Sun's convention for Java packages is that they be given period-separated names. The name of the organization that developed the package should be the leftmost item in the package name.

The easiest way to use a class that's in another package is through the import statement. With the import statement, you can import a specific class from a package or you can import every public class at once.

Assume you have a package called test.package that contains the classes Location and Mapper. If you want to use all the public classes from test.package in our current compilation unit, put the line:

```
import test.package.*
```

at the top of your code, right after the statement defining your current package. The * character tells Java to import all the public classes in test.package. To import just one specific class, such as Location, use the following line instead:

```
import test.package.Location
```

You're now able to create and use objects of the Location class as if it were a local class.

To make a plug-in visible from inside Java, your Java class must use netscape.plugin.Plugin. Netscape provides a file, java_30, with Netscape 3.0. This file contains three Java packages: java, sun, and netscape, which also include the Netscape classes below:

- java
- sun
- netscape.applet
- netscape.net
- netscape.javascript
- netscape.plugin

LiveConnect and Netscape Packages

Navigator contains a java_30 file that includes the two important Java packages. The first is made up of the Netscape packages to enable JavaScript and Java communication, and the second and third are the Java and Sun packages to provide security enhancements for LiveConnect.

NOTE The new Java and Sun packages replace packages in the Sun 1.0.2 Java Development Kit (JDK) classes.zip. Sun has tested these packages. Use these packages until the security enhancements are implemented in future releases of the Sun JDK.

The Netscape packages contain the following:

- `netscape.javascript` implements the `JSObject` class, which allows a Java applet access to JavaScript methods and properties. It also implements the `JSException` to throw an exception when an error is returned in JavaScript code.

- `netscape.plugin` implements the `Plugin` class to allow communication between JavaScript and plug-ins. You can compile your plug-in with this class to allow applets and JavaScript code to control the plug-in.

The file java_30 also contains other important Netscape packages. The `netscape.applet` replaces the Sun JDK package `sun.applet`, and the `netscape.net` replaces the Sun JDK package `sun.net`. These packages are implemented in the same way as the original Sun packages.

The java_30 file can be found in the \Program\java\classes directory in your Netscape Navigator directory. To access the packages in java_30, place this file in the classpath of the JDK compiler in one of the following ways:

- Create a `CLASSPATH` environment variable to specify the paths and names of java_30 and classes.zip.

- Specify the location of java_30 and classes.zip when you compile by using the `-classpath` command line parameter.

To identify an environment variable in Windows NT, double-click the System icon in the Control Panel and create a user environment variable called `CLASSPATH` with the value shown below:

```
E:\JDK\java\lib\classes.zip;E:\Navigator\Program\java\classesjava_30
```

Importing the JavaScript Package   You can call JavaScript methods, properties, and data structures from your Java applet by importing the Netscape javascript package. (See Table 12.1 for a list of class methods and descriptions.) See the following example:

```
import netscape.javascript.*
```

The netscape.javascript package defines the `JSObject` class, as well as the `JSException` exception object.

The author of an HTML document can only allow an applet to access JavaScript if he or she designates the MAYSCRIPT attribute of the APPLET tag. The example below shows an applet that has access to JavaScript on a document:

```
<APPLET CODE = "applet.class" WIDTH=300 HEIGHT=45 NAME="imageApp"
➥MAYSCRIPT>
```

If a user tries to access JavaScript when there is no MAYSCRIPT attribute designated, it results in an exception.

Before you can access JavaScript, you must get a handle for the Navigator window. To do this, use the getWindow method in the class netscape.javascript.JSObject to get a window handle. The example below shows type JSObject assigning a window handle to variable win:

```
public void init() {
    win = JSObject.getWindow();
}
```

To access JavaScript objects and properties, use the getMember method in the class netscape.javascript.JSObject. Call getWindow to get a handle first, then call getMember to access each JavaScript object. The Java code example below shows a variable MyForm that has access to theJavaScript object document.MyForm.

```
public void init() {
    win = JSObject.getWindow(this);
    JSObject doc = (JSObject) win.getMember("document");
    JSObject MyForm = (JSObject) doc.getMember("MyForm");
}
```

The eval method in the class netscape.javascript.JSObject allows you to call JavaScript methods. Again, first use getWindow to get a JavaScript window handle, then use eval to call a JavaScript method. The example below shows how to call JavaScript methods from Java. Note that expression is a JavaScript expression that evaluates to a JavaScript method:

```
JSObject.getWindow().eval("expression")
```

The example code below uses eval to call the JavaScript alert method when a mouseUp event occurs:

```
public void init() {
    JSObject win = JSObject.getWindow();
}
public boolean mouseUp(Event e, int x, int y) {
    win.eval("alert(\"Welcome to the World of LiveConnect!\");");
    return true;
}
```

Table 12.1   netscape.javascript.JSObject Class Methods

Method	Description
call	Calls a JavaScript method
eval	Evaluates a JavaScript expression
getMember	Retrieves a named member of a JavaScript object
getSlot	Retrieves an indexed member of a JavaScript object
removeMember	Removes a named member of a JavaScript object
setMember	Sets a named member of a JavaScript object
setSlot	Sets an indexed member of a JavaScript object
toString	Converts a JSObject to a string
getWindow	Static method gets a JSObject for the window containing the given applet

Java Development Tools

In order to develop Java applets and applications, you need a copy of the Java Development Kit (JDK). At the time this book went to press, the JDK version 1.0.1 has been released and is available on Windows 95, Windows NT, and Sun Solaris 2.x platforms. A Macintosh port of the JDK is under development. You can get the JDK directly from this CD.

ON THE WEB

You can also obtain the JDK from the Sun Microsystems Java Web site at **http://java.sun.com/**.

The process of turning Java source code into compiled Java bytecodes is performed by the Java compiler, javac. To compile a Java program, write your code using your favorite text editor and save it in ASCII text format. The name of the file must have a .JAVA extension. Then, compile the file by typing:

```
javac filename.java
```

Part IV
Ch 12

where filename.java is the name of your Java source code file. For each class that's defined in your Java source file, the javac compiler generates a file named classname.class, where classname is the name of the particular class. For complete details of the Java compilation process, see the online documentation for Java programmers at **http://java.sun.com/doc/programmer.html**.

N O T E   Java places exactly one class in each bytecode-compiled .class file. ■

After you've compiled your Java application into a .class file, you can run the file with the Java bytecode interpreter, which is coincidentally named java. To do this, you run the java command followed by the name of the .class file that has the `main()` method for your Java application. For example:

```
java myclass.class
```

This command would start the Java runtime environment and cause it to execute the file myclass.class.

Much of Java's functionality is encapsulated in prewritten collections of classes known as *packages*. These packages are provided with the Java development environment. Each of these packages contains several different classes that are related to a particular topic.

Table 12.2 lists the packages in the Java development library at the time this book was written. Packages prefixed with java are actual Java language classes. The other classes are HotJava classes, used in the development of Sun's HotJava browser.

Table 12.2   Java Packages in the Development Library

Package Name	Description
java.lang	Basic language support classes
java.util	Utility classes such as encoders and decoders
java.io	Different types of I/O streams
java.awt	A platform-independent windowing system
java.awt.image	Class for handling images in the AWT windowing system
java.applet	Class for building applets to run within Web browsers
java.net	Support for TCP/IP networking

Netscape Packages Reference

The *netscape.javascript.JSObject* Class Methods

This section includes the `netscape.javascript.JSObject` class methods and descriptions, as well as example code.

call Method

Calls a JavaScript method. Equivalent to "this.methodName(args[0], args[1],...)" in JavaScript.

Declaration

```
public Object call(String methodName,
        Object args[])
```

eval Method

Evaluates a JavaScript expression. The expression is a string of JavaScript source code that's evaluated.

Declaration

```
        public Object eval(String s)
getMember Method.
```

Retrieves a named member of a JavaScript object.

Declaration

```
        public Object getMember(String name)
getSlot Method.
```

Retrieves an indexed member of a JavaScript object.

Declaration

```
        public Object getSlot(int index)
getWindow Static method.
```

Returns a JSObject for the window containing the given applet.

Declaration

```
        public static JSObject getWindow(Applet applet)
removeMember Method.
```

Part
IV

Ch
12

Removes a named member of a JavaScript object.

Declaration

```
        public void removeMember(String name)
setMember Method.
```

Sets a named member of a JavaScript object.

Declaration

```
public void setMember(String name,
        Object value)
```

setSlot Method

Sets an indexed member of a JavaScript object.

Declaration

```
public void setSlot(int index,
        Object value)
```

toString Method

Converts a JSObject to a String. (Overrides: toString in class Object.)

Declaration

```
public String toString()
```

The *netscape.javascript.JSException* Constructor

JSException Constructor

Constructs a JSException. You specify whether the JSException has a detail message and other information.

Declaration

```
1. public JSException()
2. public JSException(String s)
3. public JSException(String s,
        String filename,
        int lineno,
        String source,
        int tokenIndex)
```

Arguments

- s is the detail message.
- filename is the URL of the file where the error occurred.
- lineno is the line number if the file, if possible.
- source is the string containing the JavaScript code being evaluated.
- tokenIndex is the index into the source string where the error occurred.

Description

A detail message is a string that describes this particular exception.

Each form constructs a JSException with different information:

- Form 1 of the declaration constructs a JSException without a detail message.
- Form 2 of the declaration constructs a JSException with a detail message.
- Form 3 of the declaration constructs a JSException with a detail message and all the other information that usually comes with a JavaScript error.

The *netscape.plugin.Plugin* Class Constructor and Methods

Constructor

```
Plugin
```

Constructs a Plugin.

Declaration

```
public Plugin()
```

Methods

destroy Method

Called when the plug-in is destroyed. You never need to call this method directly; it's called when the plug-in is destroyed.

Declaration

```
public void destroy()
```

getPeer Method

Returns the native NPP object—the plug-in instance that's the native part of a Java Plugin object.

Declaration

```
public int getPeer()
```

getWindow Method

Returns the JavaScript window on which the plug-in is embedded.

Declaration

```
public JSObject getWindow()
```

init Method

Called when the plug-in is initialized.

Declaration

```
public void init()
```

isActive Method

Determines whether the Java reflection of a plug-in still refers to an active plug-in.

Declaration

```
public boolean isActive()
```

From Here...

In this chapter you learned that a package is a Java construct that's used to manage the program namespace. It's a collection of classes and interfaces. Every class is contained in a package. If no package name is explicitly given, the class is contained in the default package. You may remember from the section on classes that if a class doesn't give an access specifier to a method, it's considered public for its enclosing package.

- The previous chapter, "Java to JavaScript Communication," looks at accessing JavaScript objects and properties and calling JavaScript methods.
- Chapter 10, "JavaScript to Java Communication," looks at accessing Java directly, as well as controlling plug-ins and applets.

Glossary

abstract class   A class that cannot be instantiated because it has one or more *pure virtual* functions. See also *pure virtual*.

access method   A *method* that encapsulates data members.

AIFF   Audio Interchange File Format. Developed by Apple Computer for storing high-quality sampled sound.

allocate   To grant a resource, such as memory, to a requesting program.

ANSI   American National Standards Institute. A major U.S. standards-setting organization.

API   Application Program Interface. A specification for functions, routines, and data available from a library or program shared or integrated with another program.

applet   A small Java program, designed to run in connection with a Web browser such as Netscape Navigator.

applications   Software designed and written to solve a problem or create a Web-based environment through dynamic page generation or system tasks.

associative class   A container class in which the position of each instance depends upon the contents of the instance. See *container class*. Contrast *sequence container*.

asynchronous   Used to describe the multitude of individual events that occur simultaneously and without relation to other events except within a larger closed system.

back end   The system-level support that is unseen by the client user, but that provides the Web server, database, and external services to help create the interfaces available to the client user.

browser   A software application that allows a user to look up information on the Internet, primarily on the World Wide Web.

buffer   A temporary storage area for information, usually for a short period and in the order in which the information is received.

cache   To store a copy of something, usually for fast local access; also, the storage space used for caching.

CCITT   The international standards-setting organization for telephony and data communications.

CGI   Common Gateway Interface. A mechanism that allows Web users to access non-Web programs.

CGM   Computer Graphics Metafile. A file format that accommodates both vector and raster images in a single file.

class variables   Variables that are associated with the class as a whole, rather than any specific instance of the class.

client pull   Technology developed for the Web environment that allows a page to reload automatically when the client requests new pages. The client software must be capable of recognizing the special tags, which are added to HTML for this purpose.

CMM   Capability Maturity Model. A multiple-layer description of software engineering process maturity developed at the Software Engineering Institute.

concrete class   A class with no *pure virtual* functions, so it may be *instantiated*.

container class   A class, such as a vector or set, that holds instances of other classes.

copy constructor   In C++ and in Java, a constructor that takes an instance of the class as its parameter and sets the data members to match the value of that instance.

daemon   A program that's left running in the background, waiting for a particular set of circumstances (such as a request) to trigger it into action.

database   A system of applications and data that stores information (retrievable by way of a query interface) in a persistent, stable, and organized fashion.

DBMS   Database Management System. A mechanism for storing data in files and accessing it with a high-level language. See also *SQL* and *RDBMS*.

deallocate   To release control of memory that was previously allocated.

default constructor   In object-oriented programming languages, the class constructor that takes no parameters (and consequently, sets all data members to their default values).

DNS   Domain Name Service. A system that translates between human-readable domain names and machine-usable IP addresses.

document root   The directory in the Web server's file system that is the beginning of the file tree of documents available from the Web server. In the URL **http:/ /some.where.com/**, for example, the trailing slash (/) signifies the document root.

dynamic library   A code resource designed to be linked into an application on the end user's computer, at load time or run-time. See also *static library*.

dynamically generated   Made at run-time by the invocation of scripts or programs that are ultimately requested by a user, or the programmed/scheduled events supported by the Web server. A feedback-acknowledgment page is dynamically generated. A sports-score page that updates after every new score, independently of the user, also is dynamically generated.

environment variables   The shell data components of a process in the UNIX environment.

environments   Places within a Web site where the associations between pages lead to the belief that the pages have a common theme to explore or use for a specific purpose. A Web chat environment, for example, is a set of pages that supports the chat model.

EPS   Encapsulated PostScript. A self-contained PostScript program that draws an image; also known as EPSF.

EPSF   See *EPS*.

file system   The hardware and software component of an operating system that manages the access and management needs of electronic files.

filter   A hardware or software component that processes an input data stream into an output data stream in some well-defined way.

flat   Lacking any internal structure.

flat file   A flattened representation of some database or tree or network structure as a single file from which the structure implicitly can be rebuilt. Esp. one in flat-ASCII form.

flat-ASCII   Said of a text file that contains only 7-bit ASCII characters and uses only ASCII-standard control characters. Also known as plain-ASCII or plain-text.

flatten   To remove structural information, esp. to filter something with an implicit hierarchical structure into a simple sequence; also tends to imply mapping to flat-ASCII.

flush   To discard all remaining data in an input or output device. But in C and UNIX, the `fflush(3)` call forces buffered disk I/O to complete. These two meanings are logically opposite.

FTP   File Transfer Protocol. Part of the TCP/IP family of protocols. *Anonymous FTP* is a common way of offering files to the public.

GET   An access method in HTTP.

handle   A pointer to a pointer to data.

helper application   An application invoked by a Web browser for MIME types that the browser cannot handle internally. See also *plug-in*.

HTML form   An HTML construction that includes the <FORM> tag declaration with one or many <INPUT> tags, with the purpose of collecting data to be passed as input to a CGI program.

HTTP   Hypertext Transport Protocol. The protocol of the World Wide Web.

httpd   The HTTP daemon, the UNIX name for the Web server.

IEEE   Institute of Electrical and Electronics Engineers. An international professional group and standards-setting organization.

IESG   Internet Engineering Steering Group. This committee was formed to help the IETF chair.

IETF   Internet Engineering Task Force. This group develops the specifications that become Internet standards.

imagemap   A graphic set up to allow a user's click to select different pages or programs, depending on where the click is on the graphic. It's customary to associate hot spots on the graphic with specific files or programs. Imagemaps can be implemented on the client or on the server.

instance variables   Data members that appear in every object (instance) made from the class.

instantiate   To make an object from a class.

Internet   The world-wide interconnection of networks to form the network of networks. The Internet originally was a research project for the U.S. Department of Defense called the ARPANET; now it's mostly organized for commercial and educational purposes.

IP   Internet Protocol. One of the communications protocols of the Internet. IP usually is specified as part of a family known as TCP/IP.

IP address   Four 8-bit numbers used to uniquely identify every machine on the Internet. An IP address usually is written with dots between the numbers, such as `127.0.0.1`.

IPC   Inter-Process Communication. The mechanisms by which software processes talk with one another. Typical UNIX IPC mechanisms include shared memory, pipes, semaphores, and message queues.

ISO   International Standards Organization. An international standards-setting organization.

ISOC   Internet Society. A professional society to facilitate, support, and promote the evolution and growth of the Internet as a global research communications infrastructure.

ISP   Internet Service Provider. An organization that provides access (usually dial-up) to the Internet.

JFIF   JPEG File Interchange Format (commonly referred to as *JPEG*), a popular image format for Web pages.

JPEG   Joint Photographic Experts Group; also, the common name for the JFIF image standard.

LAN   Local Area Network. A collection of computers at one physical location or campus that share resources, and their internetworking hardware and software. See also *WAN*.

local guide   The manual or documentation, assembled for users, that describes the custom software and tools installed.

make   A utility used to generate an output file based on changes in a set of component files.

markup language   A syntax and procedure for embedding in-text documents tags that control formatting when the documents are viewed by a special application. A Web browser interprets HTML (Hypertext Markup Language).

method   A function that is a member of a class.

MIME   Multimedia Internet Media Extensions. A mechanism used by e-mail and Web servers to tell a client what type of content is being sent so that the client can interpret the data correctly.

mix-in classes   Classes that typically cannot be instantiated themselves, but that are added to an *abstract class* by multiple inheritance to add features to a new *concrete class*.

Mozilla   The internal name of the Netscape browser.

MPEG   Moving Pictures Experts Group. Also, the audio and video compression standards developed by that group.

multitasking   Performing more than one task at the same time. Multitasking is a feature of some operating systems, such as UNIX.

navigation   The act of traversing a chain of hypertext links from a starting point to a final result.

NCSA   National Center for Supercomputer Applications. Developed the NCSA Server, a popular UNIX-based Web server. Visit NCSA's Web site at **http://hoohoo.ncsa.uiuc.edu/**.

Netscape Communications Corporation   Developer of a popular browser (Netscape Navigator) and several commercial servers.

Netscape Navigator   A popular Web browser by Netscape Communications Corporation.

NIST   U.S. National Institute of Standards and Technology. Formerly known as the National Bureau of Standards.

operating system   A collection of software written to provide the fundamental instructions that a computer needs to manage resources such as memory, the file system, and processes.

overloading   In a programming language, the ability to have more than one function of the same name that differ only in the number and type of parameters. See *signature*.

PATH   An environment variable used to list directories that should be searched for a given file.

PCL   Hewlett-Packard Printer Control Language. An HP-proprietary language used to render pages on Hewlett-Packard printers. See also *PDL*.

PDL   Page Description Language. A generic term, encompassing PostScript and Hewlett-Packard's PDL.

Perl   Practical Extraction and Report Language (also Pathologically Eclectic Rubbish Lister). A rich language developed by Larry Wall. Perl is often used to implement CGI scripts.

PERL   The interpreter for Perl, typically located on a UNIX system at `/usr/bin/perl`.

plug-in   A technology developed by Netscape and now adopted by some other Web browser vendors to handle certain *MIME* media types inside the browser environment, instead of with a helper application.

PNG   Portable Network Graphic. An alternative to GIF for Web graphics.

polymorphism   The ability in a programming language to use instances of a subclass as though they were instances of the parent class.

POST   An access method in HTTP.

PostScript   A sophisticated *page description language* (PDL) that's used for high-quality printing on laser printers and other high-resolution printing devices.

process ID   A number associated with a process, which can be used to uniquely identify the process.

proof of concept   A prototype that's built to show that the technique, system design, or marketability of a proposed application or system is likely to be as good as expected.

pure virtual   As of a function, a virtual function that must be overridden by a derived class. See *virtual*.

PUT   An access method in HTTP.

QUERY_STRING   The environment variable that contains the information passed to a CGI script by means of GET.

QuickTime   Apple Computer's standard for time-based material, such as video, sound, and multimedia sequences. Available for Windows and UNIX computers, as well as for Macintoshes.

RDBMS   Relational Database Management System. A database mechanism in which the user's logical view of the data is based on tables (also known as *relations*).

real-time   Describes an application that requires a program to respond to stimuli within some small upper limit of time (typically, milli- or microseconds).

reloading   The act of requesting a page from a Web server that is already visible in the Web browser. The main purpose of reloading is to verify changes in documents or to reinvoke certain actions (such as CGI scripts) on the Web server.

RFC   Request for Comment, the place where all of the official standards in the Internet community are published.

RIFF WAVE   An audio format, commonly known as WAV.

script   A program that runs on the Web server, written in an interpreted language such as Perl or Tcl.

SEI   Software Engineering Institute. A research center at Carnegie-Mellon University.

semaphore   A mechanism for restricting access to critical sections of code to a single user or process at a time.

sequence container   Container classes in which the order of the stored instances depends upon how and when the instance was added to the container, rather than the contents of the instance. See also *container class*. Contrast with *associative class*.

server push   Technology developed for the Web environment that allows a page to reload automatically when the server generates new content. The MIME type used for server push is `multipart/x-mixed`.

SIGHUP   The hang-up signal. In UNIX, SIGHUP is commonly used to tell a daemon to reread its configuration files. Signals are sent in UNIX with the `kill` command.

signature   Of a function, the number and type of parameters.

skeleton   A program that contains the proper header and footer declarations but lacks actual code to perform a task; also, a file stub that provides the framework for the details of the program to be inserted.

SLOC   Source Line of Code. One line in a computer program. In many languages, each SLOC ends with a semicolon. SLOC is used in COCOMO and PROBE as the basis for estimating software-development time.

SQL   (Pronounced "*sequel*.") Structured Query Language. An ANSI-standard language for accessing databases.

SSI   Server-Side Include. A method by which Web pages can include small pieces of information that isn't directly stored in their file.

static HTML file   An HTML document that's represented and stored as a file under the Web server's document root. A static HTML file can be changed or updated only by editing the file.

static library   A code resource designed to be linked into an application on the developer's machine when the application is linked. See also *dynamic library*.

STDERR   Standard Error. A file handle open for output by default in many operating systems and languages; typically used for program error messages.

STDIN   Standard Input. A file handle open for input by default in many operating systems and languages; typically used for program input.

STDOUT   Standard Output. A file handle open for output by default in many operating systems and languages; typically used for program output.

tag   In HTML (Hypertext Markup Language), a code (enclosed with < >) that indentifies an element of a Web document so that the Web browser will know how to display it.

TCP   Transmission Control Protocol. One of the communications protocols of the Internet. TCP usually is specified as part of a family known as TCP/IP. TCP connections are set up by using a three-way handshake to ensure the delivery of every packet.

text box   An area of a Web page, usually created with <INPUT> tags, that accepts a single line of input.

thread   A "lightweight process" that allows asynchronous work to be done within another process's address space.

TIFF   Tag Image File Format. A popular high-end file format for images.

time stamp   Time of day, encapsulated in an alphanumeric quantity for registering an event. When files are modified, their "last modified" time stamp is updated with a new time.

toolbar   A compact textual or graphical region of a page that contains hypertext links to other parts of the site or the Web.

URL   Uniform Resource Locator. The address of an Internet resource, such as a Web page.

virtual   As of a function. May be overridden by derived classes. See also *pure virtual*.

WAN   Wide Area Network. A collection of computers that are geographically distributed but that share resources, and their internetworking hardware and software. See also *LAN*.

Web server   A machine (or a set of machines) connected to the network that runs software supporting the HTTP requests for documents from client machines.

Webmaster   The person who usually maintains the content and operational status of a Web server. Most Webmasters are involved with design and development issues for new content, and also with business and marketing issues, network topology design, and any other issues related to the development and maintenance of the Web server.

World Wide Web   A network of hosts on the Internet that share data and information with the public (or with private groups) through the transfer of documents via the HTTP protocol.

XBM   X Bit Maps. A simple graphics standard used in the X Window system.

Index

Database Management System *see* **DBMS (Database Management System)**

databases, defined, 327

DBMS (Database Management System), defined, 327

deallocating, defined, 327

DEBUG flag, 70, 73

Debugger Module, JRI (Java Runtime Interface), 205-207

debuggin plug-ins, 68-71

declaring JSException class (constructors), 322

def file (plug-ins), 74-75

default constructors, defined, 327

defects, flagging compilers, 69

defining plug-ins, 226-228

demos, Web sites, 43

DES (Data Encryption Standard), 175

designing
  applets, JDK (Java Developer's Kit), 319-320
  CD-ROM (Compact Disk-Read Only Memory), 162-172
  documents
    compound, 98-100
    zero, 49-50
  plug-ins, 21, 121
    Macintosh, 114-115
    processes, 121-122
    for Windows, 110-113
  product protections, 172-178
  table links, 250-252
  tools, cross-platform, 165-166
  Web pages, 28
  will, 73

destroy() method, 228, 323

developers, plug-ins, 226-227

developing, *see* designing

dialog boxes
  File Open, 57
  Project Settings, 76

Digital Espresso Web site, 288

dir targets, 73

directories
  AVI (Audio Video Interleaved), 112-113
  files (source codes), 112-113

disk files, 61

DisplayJavaMessage() method, 131-132, 230-231

DLL (Dynamic Link Library), 100, 121, 327
  targets, 74-75

DNS (Domain Name Service), defined, 327

documents
  compound, 98
    designing, 98-100
    Microsoft Word, 100
    UNIX, 98-99
    WWW (World Wide Web), 98
  root, defined, 327
  HTML (Hypertext Markup Language), *see* Web pages
  zero, designing, 49-50

doit() method, 136-138

Domain Name Service, *see* DNS (Domain Name Service)

downloading
  applets, 260
  JDK (Java Developer's Kit), 18, 72, 244
  JRI (Java Runtime Interface) from Netscape Web site, 211
  plug-ins
    Communicator, 116
    SDK (Software Development Kit), 29
  scripts, installing, 106-107
  Web pages, 103-104

drawString() method, 243

drives, CD-RW (Compact Disk-Rewritable), 172

DumpURL() method, 250

dynamic
  content, CD-ROM (Compact Disk-Read Only Memory), 20-25
  methods, calling, 192-193

Dynamic Link Library, *see* DLL (Dynamic Link Library)

dynamically generated, defined, 327

E

editing JAVA_CLASSES, 73

elements, LiveAudio, 37-42

ellipsis (...), 280

<EMBED> tag, 34, 52, 66, 79, 101, 109, 120, 125, 144, 219

embedded plug-ins, 66
  arrays, 109-110
  printing, 67

Embedding Module, JRI (Java Runtime Interface), 199-204

embeds array, 109-110

EmeraldNet Web site (LiveAudio), 40

enabling LiveConnect, 10-11

Encapsulated PostScript, *see* EPS (Encapsulated PostScript)

environments
  defined, 328
  JRI (Java Runtime Interface), executions, 202-203
  LiveConnect, 36
  merging, 21
  variables
    CLASSPATH, 20, 317
    defined, 328

EPS (Encapsulated PostScript), defined, 328

eval() method, 235, 321

examples, plug-ins, 29

ScriptX, 166

scroll bars, 66

SCSI (Small Computer System Interface), 176

SDK (Software Development Kit), 121, 242
applications (Windows), 30-31
organizing, 29
plug-ins, 29-34
downloading, 29
files, 123
Macintosh, 114
overview, 122-124
Simple, 122-140

SDK_ROOT, undefining, 73

security
applets, 270-271
IVES (Information Vending Encryption System), services, 174-175
Java, 221
layers, 221
Java, 272-282
Netscape, 272
packages, 286-289

seekable streams, 61-64

segment codes (interfaces), 314

SEI (Software Engineering Institute), defined, 333

semaphore, defined, 333

sequence containers, defined, 333

Server Push, 265, 333

Server-Side, see SSI (Server-Side)

servers (Web), HTTP (Hypertext Transport Protocol), 61

services (security), IVES (Information Vending Encryption System), 174-175

setMember() method, 322

SetProp() method, 133

setSlot() method, 322

SetTimeOut() method, 92, 232

SetTimer() method, 155

setting LiveCache, 161-162

Show Java Console command (Options menu), Navigator, 123

Show Java Console Window command (Options menu), 11

SIGHUP, defined, 333

signatures, defined, 333

Simple plug-ins, 30-31, 122-140
codes, 135-137
DisplayJavaMessage() method, 230-231
exiting, 138-140
flow of control, 124-134
interfaces, 124
streams, 135
see also plug-ins

simple.class file, 135

Simple_doit() method, 132

SimpleExample.html file, 124

sites (Web)
Adobe, 102, 105
Allegiant Technologies, Inc, 171
CD-MAX, Inc., 176
Digital Espresso, 288
EmeraldNet, 40
Gamelan, 37, 288, 310
HP (Hewlett-Packard), 171
Infosafe Systems, Inc., 177
JavaSoft, 222, 237, 287-288
Netscape, 11, 207, 310
Oracle, 164
Phillips, 171
QuickTime, 166
RadMedia, 169
Ricoh, 171
Sony, 171
Sun Microsystems, 319
Teleshuttle, 167
Wave Systems Corporation, 178
Yahoo!, 222
see also Web sites

skeletons, defined, 333

SLOC (Source Line of Code), defined, 333

Small Computer System Interface, see SCSI (Small Computer System Interface)

software
platforms (internationalized), 106
PowerMedia, 168-169
SuperCard (Macintosh), 170-171
Teleshutte, 167

Software Development Kit, see SDK (Software Development Kit)

Software Engineering Institute, see SEI (Software Engineering Institute)

Sony Web site, 171

source codes, directory files, 112-113

Source Line of Code, see SLOC (Source Line of Code)

SQL (Structured Query Language), defined, 334

SSI (Server-Side), defined, 334

stack frames, inspecting, 205-206

Standard
Error, see STDERR (Standard Error)
Input, see STDIN (Standard Input)
Output, see STDOUT (Standard Output)

Start() method, 154

StartAtFrame() method, 154, 237

starting
Java, 242-243
plug-ins, 66

statements, packages, 315-321

static
fields, activating, 193-194
from class objects, 213-214

use_Simple() method, 127
users (plug-ins)
  installing, 100-110
  interacting, 66-67

V

validating data in form fields, 252-253
variables, environments (CLASSPATH), 20, 317
versions of JRI (Java Runtime Interface), 186
video files (LiveConnect), 28-43
View/Controller model, 148
virtual, defined, 335
Visual C++, *see* **C++**

W

WAN (Wide Area Network), defined, 335
warnings, 70
  ASSERT, 71
Wave System Corporation Web site, 178-179
WaveMeter (metering device), 177
Web browsers
  applets, 267
  HotJava, 259
Web pages
  applets, 278-279
  counts, installing, 219
  designing, 28
  downloading, 103-104
  MAYSCRIPT attribute, 293
  plug-ins, 48, 104
    inserting, 286-287
Web, *see* **WWW (World Wide Web)**
Web servers
  defined, 335
  HTTP (Hypertext Transport Protocol), 61

Web sites
  Adobe, 105
    Amber (Portable Document Format reader), 102
    Allegiant Technologies, Inc, downloading SuperCard, 171
  CD-MAX, Inc., 176
  Digital Espresso, 288
  EmeraldNet, LiveAudio, 40
  Gamelan, 37, 288, 310
  HP (Hewlett-Packard), 171
  Infosafe Systems, Inc., 177
  JavaSoft, 222, 287-288
    Java, 237
  LiveConnect demos, 43
  Netscape
    inter-applet communication, 310
    JRI (Java Runtime Interface), 43, 207
    LiveAudio, 42
    LiveConnect Developer Info. Web page, 11
    Plug-in Developer's Guide, 43-44, 237
  Oracle, 164
  Phillips, 171
  QuickTime (Apple Media Tool), 166
  RadMedia, 169
  Ricoh, 171
  Sony, 171
  Sun Microsystems, JDK (Java Developer's Kit), 319
  Teleshuttle, 167
  Wave Systems Corporation, 178
  Yahoo!, 222
  see also sites (Web)
Webmaster, defined, 335
WebMotion, 43
Wide Area Network, *see* **WAN (Wide Area Network)**
Windows
  plug-ins, 122-124
    CharFlipper, 140-142
    designing for, 110-113
    installing, 101
    overview, 122-124
    SDK (Software Development Kit) applications, 30-31

windows (Java Console), 11, 271
WM_PAINT handler, 134
World Wide Web, *see* **WWW (World Wide Web)**
writing
  applets, 11
  plug-ins (Macintosh), 127
WWW (World Wide Web)
  applications, navigating, 58
  CD-ROM (Compact Disk-Read Only Memory), designing, 162-172
  compound documents, 98
  defined, 335
  hybrid technology, future of, 163-164
  Java, writing applets, 267
  see also sites (Web); Web sites

X-Y-Z

X-Window system, 49
XBM X Bit Maps, defined, 335
Yahoo! Web site, 222
zero
  calling, 50-51
  documents, designing, 49-50
  plug-ins, 13
    NPP() methods, 49-52
zero file, 49
ZIP targets, 74

Complete and Return this Card
for a *FREE* Computer Book Catalog

Thank you for purchasing this book! You have purchased a superior computer book written expressly for your needs. To continue to provide the kind of up-to-date, pertinent coverage you've come to expect from us, we need to hear from you. Please take a minute to complete and return this self-addressed, postage-paid form. In return, we'll send you a free catalog of all our computer books on topics ranging from word processing to programming and the internet.

Mr. ☐ Mrs. ☐ Ms. ☐ Dr. ☐

Name (first) ☐☐☐☐☐☐☐☐☐☐☐☐ (M.I.) ☐ (last) ☐☐☐☐☐☐☐☐☐☐☐☐☐☐☐☐☐

Address ☐☐☐☐☐☐☐☐☐☐☐☐☐☐☐☐☐☐☐☐☐☐☐☐☐☐☐☐☐☐☐☐☐☐

☐☐☐☐☐☐☐☐☐☐☐☐☐☐☐☐☐☐☐☐☐☐☐☐☐☐☐☐☐☐☐☐☐☐

City ☐☐☐☐☐☐☐☐☐☐☐☐☐☐☐☐☐ State ☐☐ Zip ☐☐☐☐☐ ☐☐☐☐

Phone ☐☐☐ ☐☐☐ ☐☐☐☐ Fax ☐☐☐ ☐☐☐ ☐☐☐☐

Company Name ☐☐☐☐☐☐☐☐☐☐☐☐☐☐☐☐☐☐☐☐☐☐☐☐☐☐☐

E-mail address ☐☐☐☐☐☐☐☐☐☐☐☐☐☐☐☐☐☐☐☐☐☐☐☐☐☐☐

1. Please check at least (3) influencing factors for purchasing this book.

Front or back cover information on book .... ☐
Special approach to the content .... ☐
Completeness of content .... ☐
Author's reputation .... ☐
Publisher's reputation .... ☐
Book cover design or layout .... ☐
Index or table of contents of book .... ☐
Price of book .... ☐
Special effects, graphics, illustrations .... ☐
Other (Please specify): _____ ☐

2. How did you first learn about this book?

Saw in Macmillan Computer Publishing catalog .... ☐
Recommended by store personnel .... ☐
Saw the book on bookshelf at store .... ☐
Recommended by a friend .... ☐
Received advertisement in the mail .... ☐
Saw an advertisement in: _____ ☐
Read book review in: _____ ☐
Other (Please specify): _____ ☐

3. How many computer books have you purchased in the last six months?

This book only .... ☐   3 to 5 books .... ☐
2 books .... ☐   More than 5 .... ☐

4. Where did you purchase this book?

Bookstore .... ☐
Computer Store .... ☐
Consumer Electronics Store .... ☐
Department Store .... ☐
Office Club .... ☐
Warehouse Club .... ☐
Mail Order .... ☐
Direct from Publisher .... ☐
Internet site .... ☐
Other (Please specify): _____ ☐

5. How long have you been using a computer?

☐ Less than 6 months   ☐ 6 months to a year
☐ 1 to 3 years   ☐ More than 3 years

6. What is your level of experience with personal computers and with the subject of this book?

	With PCs	With subject of book
New	☐	☐
Casual	☐	☐
Accomplished	☐	☐
Expert	☐	☐

Source Code ISBN: 0-7897-1171-0

7. Which of the following best describes your job title?

- Administrative Assistant ☐
- Coordinator ☐
- Manager/Supervisor ☐
- Director ☐
- Vice President ☐
- President/CEO/COO ☐
- Lawyer/Doctor/Medical Professional ☐
- Teacher/Educator/Trainer ☐
- Engineer/Technician ☐
- Consultant ☐
- Not employed/Student/Retired ☐
- Other (Please specify): _____ ☐

8. Which of the following best describes the area of the company your job title falls under?

- Accounting ☐
- Engineering ☐
- Manufacturing ☐
- Operations ☐
- Marketing ☐
- Sales ☐
- Other (Please specify): _____ ☐

9. What is your age?

- Under 20 ☐
- 21-29 ☐
- 30-39 ☐
- 40-49 ☐
- 50-59 ☐
- 60-over ☐

10. Are you:

- Male ☐
- Female ☐

11. Which computer publications do you read regularly? (Please list)

_____
_____
_____
_____
_____
_____
_____
_____
_____

Comments: _____
_____
_____

Fold here and scotch-tape to mail.

Check out Que® Books
on the World Wide Web
http://www.quecorp.com

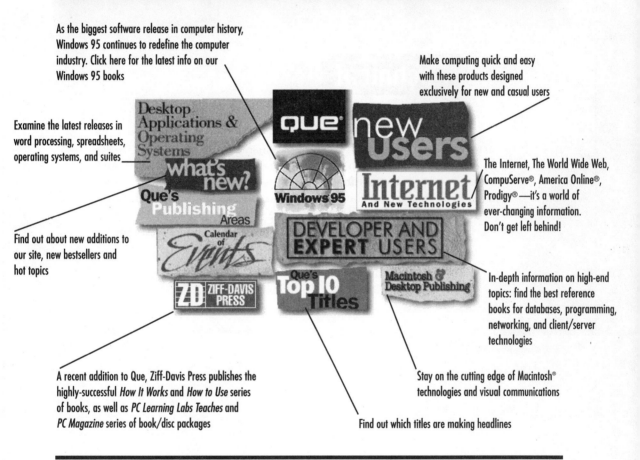

As the biggest software release in computer history, Windows 95 continues to redefine the computer industry. Click here for the latest info on our Windows 95 books

Make computing quick and easy with these products designed exclusively for new and casual users

Examine the latest releases in word processing, spreadsheets, operating systems, and suites

The Internet, The World Wide Web, CompuServe®, America Online®, Prodigy®—it's a world of ever-changing information. Don't get left behind!

Find out about new additions to our site, new bestsellers and hot topics

In-depth information on high-end topics: find the best reference books for databases, programming, networking, and client/server technologies

A recent addition to Que, Ziff-Davis Press publishes the highly-successful *How It Works* and *How to Use* series of books, as well as *PC Learning Labs Teaches* and *PC Magazine* series of book/disc packages

Stay on the cutting edge of Macintosh® technologies and visual communications

Find out which titles are making headlines

With 6 separate publishing groups, Que develops products for many specific market segments and areas of computer technology. Explore our Web Site and you'll find information on best-selling titles, newly published titles, upcoming products, authors, and much more.

- Stay informed on the latest industry trends and products available
- Visit our online bookstore for the latest information and editions
- Download software from Que's library of the best shareware and freeware

MACMILLAN COMPUTER PUBLISHING USA

A VIACOM COMPANY

Technical
Support:

If you need assistance with the information in this book or with a CD/Disk accompanying the book, please access the Knowledge Base on our Web site at **http://www.superlibrary.com/general/support**. Our most Frequently Asked Questions are answered there. If you do not find the answer to your questions on our Web site, you may contact Macmillan Technical Support **(317) 581-3833** or e-mail us at **support@mcp.com**.